D1756495

90 0911008 2

The Sciences Po Series in International Relations and Political Economy

Series Editor, Christian Lequesne

This series consists of works emanating from the foremost French researchers from Sciences Po, Paris. Sciences Po was founded in 1872 and is today one of the most prestigious universities for teaching and research in social sciences in France, recognized worldwide.

This series focuses on the transformations of the international arena, in a world where the state, though its sovereignty is questioned, reinvents itself. The series explores the effects on international relations and the world economy of regionalization, globalization (not only of trade and finance but also of culture), and transnational flows at large. This evolution in world affairs sustains a variety of networks from the ideological to the criminal or terrorist. Besides the geopolitical transformations of the globalized planet, the new political economy of the world has a decided impact on its destiny as well, and this series hopes to uncover what that is.

Published by Palgrave Macmillan:

Politics In China: Moving Frontiers
  edited by Françoise Mengin and Jean-Louis Rocca
Tropical Forests, International Jungle: The Underside of Global Ecopolitics
  by Marie-Claude Smouts, translated by Cynthia Schoch
The Political Economy of Emerging Markets: Actors, Institutions and Financial Crises in Latin America
  by Javier Santiso
Cyber China: Reshaping National Identities in the Age of Information
  edited by Françoise Mengin
With Us or Against Us: Studies in Global Anti-Americanism
  edited by Denis Lacorne and Tony Judt
Vietnam's New Order: International Perspectives on the State and Reform in Vietnam
  edited by Stéphanie Balme and Mark Sidel
Equality and Transparency: A Strategic Perspective on Affirmative Action in American Law
  by Daniel Sabbagh, translation by Cynthia Schoch and John Atherton
Moralizing International Relations: Called to Account
  by Ariel Colonomos, translated by Chris Turner
Norms over Force: The Enigma of European Power
  by Zaki Laidi, translated from the French by Cynthia Schoch
Democracies at War against Terrorism: A Comparative Perspective
  edited by Samy Cohen, translated by John Atherton, Roger Leverdier, Leslie Piquemal, and Cynthia Schoch

Justifying War? From Humanitarian Intervention to Counterterrorism
    edited by Gilles Andréani and Pierre Hassner, translated by John Hulsey,
    Leslie Piquemal, Ros Schwartz, and Chris Turner
An Identity for Europe: The Relevance of Multiculturalism in EU Construction
    edited by Riva Kastoryano, translated by Susan Emmanuel

An Identity for Europe

The Relevance of Multiculturalism in EU Construction

Edited by
Riva Kastoryano

Translated by
Susan Emmanuel[*]

First published in 2009 by
PALGRAVE MACMILLAN®
in the United States—a division of St. Martin's Press LLC,
175 Fifth Avenue, New York, NY 10010.

Where this book is distributed in the UK, Europe and the rest of the world,
this is by Palgrave Macmillan, a division of Macmillan Publishers Limited,
registered in England, company number 785998, of Houndmills,
Basingstoke, Hampshire RG21 6XS.

Palgrave Macmillan is the global academic imprint of the above companies
and has companies and representatives throughout the world.

Palgrave® and Macmillan® are registered trademarks in the United States,
the United Kingdom, Europe and other countries.

ISBN-13: 978–1–4039–7540–9
ISBN-10: 1–4039–7540–X

Library of Congress Cataloging-in-Publication Data is available from the
Library of Congress.

A catalogue record of the book is available from the British Library.

Design by Newgen Imaging Systems (P) Ltd., Chennai, India.

First edition: May 2009

10 9 8 7 6 5 4 3 2 1

Printed in the United States of America.

CONTENTS

FOREWORD

RIVA KASTORYANO

This book is the product of a workshop with the same title that took place in 1996 at the CERI (Centre d'Etudes et de Recherches Internationales), Sciences Po, in Paris. The purpose was to reflect on multiculturalism in a European context: its definition(s); the actions through which it is realized; the interactions that reinforce it; and its implications for the identity of a new political space under construction.

From its very inception, united Europe is a de facto multicultural due to its linguistic and cultural diversity due to the coexistence and representation of several cultures—both national (those of the European Union member states and the "others") and regional—and its institutional diversity stemming from differences between national traditions. The European political project cannot disregard this diversity as political markers. But European multiculturalism is also being shaped by supranational institutions to give cultural, national, and linguistic diversity legal status. Is it thus possible that multiculturalism, a fact, might become an explicit theory for a European political identity?

Today, in 2008, the question of European identity remains just as open, and the responses are as normative as ever. Yet the Union has gone from twelve to twenty-seven member states. It has therefore expanded its borders, included new territories, integrated new political traditions, and taken on a new geographic shape. Its indeterminate boundaries have shifted, turning territory into an open, abstract space. These changes have not altered the nature of the questions and doubts about its identity, particularly its political identity, or the existence of a European society and the emergence of a European public space and the civic participation of peoples inhabiting it. The question remains as to how to combine the universal and the particular, more specifically the universalist ideology of the nation-states and the cultural and historic particularism that characterizes each of them. How can so many and complex belongings and allegiances of individuals, groups, and peoples be articulated so as to build European unity or rather inspire its "peoples" to identify with Europe?

In 2005, the Constitutional Treaty intended to render explicit an identitarian concern that until then seemed masked by the universality of the European project. Indeed, the first line of the preamble of the constitution states that "Europe is a continent that has brought forth civilisation." It then affirms the "inspiration from the cultural, religious and humanist inheritance of Europe." The idea is taken up again in the preamble of the Reform Treaty of Lisbon which reiterates the "inspiration from the cultural, religious and humanist inheritance of Europe, from which are developed the universal values of the inviolable and inalienable rights of the human person, freedom, democracy, equality and the rule of law." Furthermore, the Charter of Fundamental Rights of the European Union states that "conscious of its spiritual and moral heritage, the Union is founded on the indivisible, universal values of human dignity, freedom, equality and solidarity; it is based on the principles of democracy and the rule of law." Such are the common values that the peoples of Europe have allegedly decided to share, thus asserting a unity inspired by the political history of states, civilization, and the moral, spiritual, and religious spirit on one hand, and democratic values based on human rights that have made the history of Europe on the other.

In the course of the debate surrounding the signing of Maastricht Treaty (1993), historians sought a common past for Europe, justified by the Enlightenment, in the process of political modernization and economic development. The constitution seemed to mark the end of a quest for unity since it was now formalized into law and legitimated by "common heritage," the national histories "united in diversity." This brings to the surface two contradictory rationales that are a source of tension: a rationale of *Europe* as heritage and a rationale of the *Union* as a project, or as J-L. Bourlanges suggests, as a "political adventure yet to be written."[1]

The constitution on the one hand, the opening of negotiations with Turkey in November 2005 on the other—a coincidence of the calendar—, place the rhetorical and judicial aspect of the European project in competition: a rhetoric based on universal values, the respect for human rights and the diversity of its peoples, while legal instruments seek to unify this diversity and forge for it a common destiny while *retrospectively* ascribing to it a cultural, religious, and spiritual heritage. This is the paradox of European integration. Despite Europe's lack of unity, Turkey's otherness has managed to create an image of a Europe unified not around a civic political culture but around a European "us" on the basis of criteria that the European project itself rejected as it was conceived and developed, for example, in terms of religious heritage or again of civilization.

In light of these recent debates, the challenge of European multiculturalism analyzed in this volume is all the more relevant. The question remains as to whether multiculturalism can take shape as a new form of political organization and give cultural and national diversity a legal status on an equal footing. In his most recent work, W. Kymlcika discusses again the definition of multiculturalism, stating "I am using multiculturalism as an umbrella term to cover a wide range of policies designed to provide some level of public recognition, support or accommodation to non-dominant ethno-cultural groups whether those groups are 'new' minorities (e.g. immigrants or refugees), or 'old' minorities (e.g. historically settled national minorities and indigenous peoples)."[2]

As it is stated in the general introduction to this volume, nation-states each have their own definition of minority and a specific relation between state and minorities. In the context of the European Union, multiculturalism refers to relations among member states. Even though important recommendations regarding minority rights and minority protection have been established—mainly in the area of education, language, and culture, and even though minority rights are an accession criteria for candidate states, the term "minority" remains ambiguous.

Progress in the judicial sphere now involves questions regarding minority cultural and religious rights in the fight against all forms of discrimination. That does not resolve the issue of how to define a minority: territorial or nonterritorial. In fact, the definitions continue to remain ambiguous and differ according to national experiences. However, Emmanuel Decaux reminds us that since 1996, new legal documents consider education, linguistic rights, political participation, and the use of the minority language in national media. These apply to territorialized minorities that appeared with events in the Balkans. As for nonterritorialized minorities, such as foreigners or immigrants, Virginie Guiraudon take stock of European Court of Human Rights and European Union jurisprudence with regard to religious and cultural rights and shows that the legal provisions made at the European level still have little effect on a national level. On the other hand, the fight against discrimination—the criteria being easier to define and being unanimously agreed by the states—is part of the Charter of Human Rights and reaffirmed in the constitution.

In developing the issue of multiculturalism in the European Union, the authors of this edited volume aim to reach beyond the ambiguities of the term "minority" as well as the relations between minority and majority, and try to see in the principle of multiculturalism the establishment of a common political space for exchanges and interactions guided by the principle of universality beyond national minority and majority particularities—a multiculturalism in which the various territorial and cultural identities appear as political markers, an identity produced by legal bodies that would emphasize cultural and political exchanges through formal and informal communication networks among various national and nonnational groups. If not, by what other process could a European political culture be shaped that can serve as a foundation for European citizenship and identity?

Deterritorialized protection of minorities is related to the exercise of European citizenship, deterritorialized as well. Will it enable the member states' "desire to live together" to be transferred to citizens and residents of the Union, those seeking to build their common destiny on this vague new geographic entity and produce a unified political community sharing the same political culture and a public space for democratic debate?

Europe has sought to formalize its integration via the Constitutional Treaty. This updated and augmented edition shows that despite the legal, geographic, discursive, and symbolic advances of the European Union, it remains difficult to combine the singular and plural, or national particularities and a collective quest for European unity. On the contrary, as the famous article by Jürgen Habermas and Jacques Derrida points out "Europe is composed of nation-states that delimit one another polemically. National consciousness formed by national languages, national literatures, national histories has long operated as an explosive force."[3] It indeed remains difficult to get beyond rivalries between member states that want to project their political vision on the European level, to the extent that, to reuse an argument developed in a recent article on European identity "some states, France in particular, see in their investment in European identity and extension of themselves."[4] Such remarks and assertions go against the cosmopolitan perspective that according to Ulrich Beck corresponds to the second age of modernity—that is beyond nation-states—, a perspective developed within the framework of globalization characterized by increasing interdependence of states[5]; and he suggests that "the crucial first insight is that without Europe there can be no response to globalization."[6]

The constitution could serve to encapsulate "a reflection of our collective identity as a people, as a nation, as a state, as a Community, as a Union," Joseph Weiler claims. But constitutional integrity is not independent of states and national constitutions. By the same token, if human rights are a universal ideal and the foundation for Europe's common values, Weiler emphasizes that "significantly, when national courts, in acts of *national judicial empowerment*, claiming to protect *nationally defined human rights*, strike out at the European Court of Justice, they are celebrated as protecting national values and identity sovereignty," that the definition of human rights always differs from one country to another and that this difference is often a function of societal choices. Thus he asserts that "in essence, the exercise of European judicial protection of human rights inevitably manifest in the inbuilt dilemma of a multi-nation and multi-cultural polity—that of reconciling the vindication of universal fundamental rights with the vindication of national autonomy guarded by fundamental boundaries."[7]

In 2003, the reactions toward the war in Iraq pointed up a gulf between state decisions and general mobilization. Thus European civil society asserted itself in opposition to the union of states that was incapable of projecting a unified vision and defining itself as a political community consolidated around the general interest. Furthermore, the mobilization of opinions and emotions over Turkey has shown a diversity of representations of Europe in terms of both states and its peoples.[8] This makes it difficult to speak of a unified public space as a source of solidarity and European integration. There is instead a diversified space of public opinion at variance over the same object of identification and the same project. These evolutions arouse questions today about the need for a single European space or instead several interacting public spaces, a public space "with multiple voices."[9] In this perspective, European integration is no longer an issue posed in terms of unified public space but of communication. A public space based on communication does not rule out mutual recognition of the differences between peoples and states.[10]

Reflection on the concept of European multiculturalism pertains precisely to such recognition as the basis for constituting the identity of a new legal, social, cultural, and political space. Christian Joppke, in his critique of multiculturalism, emphasizes the importance of reciprocity in the recognition of cultures.[11] In the European Union context, such reciprocity comes to national cultures. This amounts to examining the emergence of a European political community, the quest for a political culture shared by all communities that make up this new entity and all the member states that impose themselves with their history, their traditions, and their values. In this perspective, Turkey's accession can only add another element to Europe's internal diversity, rather than sustain the belief in a consolidated and unified European identity stemming from a de facto diversity that seeks to assert itself in opposition to a diversity perceived as external.

To reduce Turkey to a culture defined in religious and civilizational terms would result in provoking a resurrection of fears, a tendency that, as Rémy Leveau pointed out, has been heightened since 2001. Turkey as a member state defies the multiculturalism discussed in this book not because of Islam as such—the religion of a nonterritorial minority in Europe—but in that it represents a territorialized Islam, as do other territorialized religions of other member states, all with, however, having secularization as a common denominator. Excluding Turkey from European multiculturalism would boils down to a Euronationalism that is likely to be as dangerous as nationalisms within

Europe.[12] On a pessimistic note, Philippe Reynaud believes that "if immigrants become Europeans, it is because without having to renounce their origins they integrate into a historic community that has been constituted through tensions between Christianity and modernity," and he adds, "today it is hard to see how a political community with no identity other than human rights can be a factor of stability in a world where the decline of classical wars has in no way erased tensions."[13]

Europe, despite its constitution, remains an indeterminate political project: the cultural and legal output of Europe continue to be confined to states. The lack of communication among identities and the absence of mutual recognition of national cultures still remain weaknesses of the European project. Is relying on the *symbolic capacity* of a constitution then the best way to achieve a common European political culture and try to see it as a way of combining the multitude of national cultures and the political unity necessary to define a European identity?

The question posed by European multiculturalism in this volume constantly calls up the question of European democracy, the mutual recognition of differences and the combination of multiple belongings on the basis of a representation of the European citizen socialized in the context of a common political culture. To reiterate the question posed by Guy Hermet, could multiculturalism constitute a challenge to "the hypothetical European democracy of the future?"

Notes

* Except for the foreword, translated by Cynthia Schoch and the two chapters by Joseph H. H. Weiler.

1. Jean Louis Bourlanges. "De l'identité de l'Europe aux frontières de l'Union." *Etudes* 4006, June 2004: 729–743; see also Christian Vandermooten and Bernard Dézert. *L'identité de l'Europe. Histoire et géographie d'une quête d'unité.* Paris: Armand Colin, 2008. See especially Chapter 8: 263–287.
2. Will Kymlicka. *Multicultural Odysseys. Navigating the New International Politics of Diversity.* Oxford: Oxford University Press, 2007: 16.
3. Jürgen Habermas and Jacques Derrida. "February 15, or, What Binds Europeans Together: Plea for a Common Foreign Policy, Beginning in Core Europe." *FAZ* and *Libération*, May 31, 2003, and *Constellations* 10, 2003: 291–297, and in Daniel Levy, Max Pensky, and John Torpey. *Old Europe, New Europe, Core Europe.* New York: Verso, 2005: 3–14.
4. Guillaume Klossa and Stéphane Rozès. "L'identité à l'épreuve de l'Europe." *Commentaire* 121, Spring 2008: 235–243.
5. Ulrich Beck. "The Cosmopolitan Perspective: Sociology of the Second Age of Modernity." *British Journal of Sociology* 51(1), January/March 2000: 79–105.
6. Ulrich Beck. *What Is Globalization?* Cambridge: Polity Press, 2000: 158.
7. In this volume.
8. A *Figaro* exclusive survey from December 13, 2003, tapping the French and German reactions against Turkey's accession shows the various country differences. See also the

report by Katinka Barysch. "What Europeans Think about Turkey and Why." *Centre for European Reform*, September 2007. Available online at: www.cer.org.uk/pdf/briefing_kb_turkey_24aug07.pdf (last accessed on July 4, 2008).

9. Jürgen Habermas and Jacques Derrida, "February 15, or, What Binds Europeans Together: Plea for a Common Foreign Policy, Beginning in Core Europe."

10. Craig Calhoun. "The Democratic Integration of Europe: Interests, Identity and the Public Sphere," in Mabel Berezin and Martin Schain (eds.). Europe without Borders: Remapping Territory, Citizenship and Identity in a Transnational Age. Johns Hopkins University Press, 2003: 243–275.

11. Christian Joppke. "L'effacement du multiculturalisme dans l'Etat libéral," in Riva Kastoryano (ed.). Les codes de la différence. Race-Origine-Religion. France-Allemagne-Etats-Unis. Paris: Presses de Sciences Po, 2005: 297–321.

12. Jean-Marc Ferry. "Quelle Europe chrétienne?" Esprit, December 2004: 45–49.

13. Philippe Reynaud. "L'Europe peut-elle avoir des frontières?" in Jean-Paul Burdy. La Turquie est-elle européenne ? Paris: Turquoise, 2004: 97–102.

INTRODUCTION

"Multiculturalism": An Identity for Europe?

RIVA KASTORYANO

What is Europe—a geographical space or a model of civilization? An economic machine or a political vision? A new historical reality or a philosophical concept? These questions come along the making of Europe and its implication for the diverse and multiple identities consolidated within the framework of the nation-state, defined by Max Weber as the only political organization born of modernity.

Europe as a political project unquestionably challenges the history of nation-states, their political traditions and their sovereignty, and raises debates about the formation of a new entity. The member states engaged in this project deploy various efforts to prove their "will to live together." Similarly, historians search for a common past, as validated by the history of civilizations and by the processes of political modernization and economic development. Reflecting on educational curricula in Europe, for example, they explore how to transmit to younger generations a European identity, considering the role of history and how it is taught in defining nations and their futures, and in the case of Europe, the future of a new identity that remains to be defined.[1] As Edgar Morin stressed, "Europe [which he called our 'community of faith'] certainly does not emerge from a past that belies it. It emerges timidly from our present because it is our future that requires it."[2]

Uncertainty turns the past into a refuge, into identities constructed and elaborated during the process of forming nation-states. Hence the innumerable debates and questions around the implications of a new political space for identities that are national, regional, linguistic, religious—and of a European identity that might encompass the whole. But at what price? How to combine a universalist ideology of the nation-state with the cultural and historical particularisms that characterize each of them? How to choose between economic interests and a common political will on the one hand and the sovereignty of states and political traditions on the other? How to conjugate the pluralistic and complex sense of belonging of individuals, groups, and peoples to construct a political identity that is purportedly European, or rather, to arouse identification with Europe as a new political space for action and demands? Drawing upon Rawls's distinction between the individual's public and institutional identity as opposed to a noninstitutional or moral identity, how to construct a European public identity accompanied by an identification with a "European political culture" in which other identities—ethnic, religious, regional, even national—would be considered as private identities?[3]

Should we look for an answer in the concept of multiculturalism? A multiculturalism that might be discerned as a new form of political organization and turn cultural and national diversity into a right based on egalitarianism? A multiculturalism in which different territorial and cultural identities appear as political markers? In fact, taking into account the multitude of cultures that want to be territorialized but often do not conform to state boundaries, can one imagine a territorial multiculturalism combined with a cultural multiculturalism that is often analyzed within the nation-state framework to construct a political Europe? One might suppose that a multiculturalism born from an initial diversity might in fact become an explicit theory of European identity.

The term "multiculturalism" lends itself to confusion. It can be defined as a situation born from cultural diversity, from a pluralism pertaining to any industrial society. At the national level, this statement of fact gives way to ideology when diversity leads to particularist identity expressions that spill into the public sphere, thus challenging the unifying forces and integrity of nations. Evidently, from the start, a united Europe arises from de facto pluralism: linguistic diversity and cultural diversity (national and regional, majoritarian and minoritarian) as well as institutional diversity in which each carries strong cultural and political traditions. The European political project cannot ignore this plurality within which various national cultures are necessarily expressed.

Asking about a new political space amounts to asking about the constitution of a new model of society—a model of pluralist society, of course, founded on the principles redefined by input from different national and/or minority cultures that claim nationhood to form a common European political culture. This leads to questions about modes of participation and representation of individuals and groups and about the means of expression of all collective identities, as complex and heterogeneous as they may be. In addition, there are the "non-European" foreigners who are resident in Europe. Although policies of immigration and integration pertain to national domains, the populations resulting from immigration who proclaim other kinds of belongings than to the nation-states of their residence find support in the new political space being constructed, although its identity is uncertain, promoting collective identities often labeled "ethnic" (*d'origine*), whether religious or national. The weakening—if not retreat—of national identities, combined with the implementation of common political projects entails mobilizing the representation of "minority" identities within a European space searching for new references.

If it is true that "multiculturalism" generates divisions among the nation-states, could it not also be the basis for European identity—an identity produced by juridical institutions that will implement cultural and political exchanges; an identity organized around both formal and informal networks of communication between various national and nonnational groups? How, then, can "European citizenship" be defined? How do supranational institutions participate in the definition and elaboration of the concepts of citizenship and identity in Europe? But most especially, by what other process could the "European citizen's culture" (to use Jean-Marc Ferry's phrase) be formed, to achieve, beyond any legal definition, the actual formation of a European political culture?

These are the questions that guide the chapters in this book. Whether anthropologists, sociologists, jurists, philosophers, or political scientists, the authors examine the permanence of nations, the formation of a political Europe from the cultural and juridical norms produced by supranational European institutions, and the new plan for a civilization that might be located at the heart of European political culture. Coming from different approaches, they reflect on the very concept of "multiculturalism" within the European context: its definition(s); the activities that make it concrete; the interactions that strengthen it; its implications for the current building of a new juridical, social, cultural, and political space that includes nonnationals (foreign residents, immigrants) as well as nationals.

The Question of Multiculturalism

The concept of multiculturalism refers to the nation-state, which in principle tends toward territorial, linguistic, and cultural unification. It appears as a response to the management of cultural diversity within the nation-state, as means of equal inclusion of minorities in the political community. A defense of the principle of the recognition of cultural particularities by public institutions, it has become since the 1980s one of the most controversial debates in all the social sciences.[4] For some, multiculturalism corresponds to cultural identities, to equal rights and the equality of chances, and it constitutes the foundation of democracy; for others, on the contrary, it is related to "tribalism" and in fact challenges the national integrity and unity heretofore guaranteed by the state. For some, it serves to thwart nationalism and for others, inversely, it serves as the basis of national sentiments and expressions.

The debates pit those who defend a liberal vision—respect for individual freedom in the face of a communitarian approach—against a republican vision of "pluralist" society on the terrain of social justice.[5] Reflection on multiculturalism thus bears on the relation between pluralism and democracy.[6] As a whole, the analysis of multiculturalism fundamentally questions both universalist ideology (opposed to the particular) and the idea of a common civic space in which everyone participates. This has transformed a simple anthropological analysis of cultural diversity into an ideological vision of pluralism, in which society is presented as a terrain of confrontation for cultural values that are transformed into particular interests in the political domain; society is no longer the quest for the common interest but turns political life into a space where identities perceived as majority or minority[7] compete with each other in search of representativity. Multiculturalism is thus systematically associated with questioning national unity and its defined identity. In reality, the debates point to the link (or absence of one) between social reality and the ideology of the nation-state's construction: hence the importance of "contextuality" in its application.[8]

The term has circulated in North America since the 1960s in response to a "demand for recognition" by populations who are situated as national minorities (territorial and linguistic) or by ethnic minorities due to migration. The concept is accompanied by a policy Charles Taylor called "the politics of recognition" and relates to the "democratic defense of cultural diversity within a universalist perspective."[9] In Canada, the confrontation between the French and English languages and the debates around a bilingual and bicultural society, defined as such by the Royal Commission on Multiculturalism, gave political legitimacy to the concept thanks to the constitutional multiculturalism used in the Charter of Rights and Freedoms, which was thus officially accepted as the fundamental characteristic of the Canadian State.[10]

Much ink has also been spilled over multiculturalism in the United States. Founded in the civil rights movement of the 1960s, it took shape with the establishment of measures for *affirmative action* starting in 1965. Translated into French as "positive discrimination" on the basis of sociologist Nathan Glazer's interpretation, these measures seek to reduce racial or other inequalities by trying to repair the bad effect of past policies, notably slavery and racial segregation. The multiculturalist program is often associated with education programs and with politically correct language and has become a source of polemics in universities, political life, and the media. A multiculturalist fever is translated into tensions between the defenders of a "politics of difference" and those who are most concerned about the social link. Everyone disputes the consequences of multiculturalism for U.S. national unity. For some it divides society into microsocieties, the one nation into many; it is the source of ethnic conflicts, of "American disunion," to use Arthur Schlesinger Jr.'s words, and therefore in contradiction with the founding principle expressed in the motto *E Pluribus Unum,* unity based on diversity.[11] Others see in multiculturalism and its application an opening of American society toward those excluded from assimilation and perceive the perverse effects of multiculturalism instead as a failure of assimilation, notably for African Americans.[12]

In Europe, multiculturalism corresponds to various situations according to the structure of the state and its recognition of regional and linguistic particularities[13] and of its minorities. In effect, some countries of the old continent have institutionalized pluralism through the creation of regions granted limited power, as in Italy and Spain; others have built the state upon linguistic pluralism, as in Belgium and Switzerland,[14] where the linguistic and territorial communities each have their own institutions. But in France, Germany, Great Britain, and the Netherlands, the term multiculturalism refers, as in the United States, to the supposedly communitarian form of organization of immigrant populations around a common nationality or religion (or both) and the accompanying demand for their specific voices in the public sphere, as with ethnic minorities or African Americans.

To some extent, similar situations entail recourse to concepts that, used in different national contexts, require new definitions because they do not travel well. These concepts are charged with ideology;

they carry the weight of political and cultural traditions. In Western Europe, the term "multiculturalism" marks the shift from temporary economic immigration to the permanent presence of immigrant populations and their political participations that move in this direction. This implies the extension of the welfare state to a new realm—that of identity—with the establishment of social policies aimed to "guarantee integration" of these minorities in the larger society. Thus, as Frank-Olaf Radtke points out concerning Germany, it is not the composition of the foreign population that has changed since the 1980s but the terminology, the codes of describing society, and institutional practices with respect to immigrant populations.[15]

In Germany, the term multiculturalism has spread since the 1980s. The city of Frankfurt even created a sector of "Multicultural Affairs" whose head, also the deputy mayor, Daniel Cohn-Bendit, was advocating a "multicultural democracy" inspired by Rousseau's social contract.[16] In France, too, during the same period, the media as a political class described French society as "multiracial," "multicultural," "plural," "pluricultural." This terminology found legitimacy in a political discourse that privileged "the right to difference," accompanied after 1981 by liberalization of the law on foreign associations, which gave legal status to organizations that privileged identities, whether defined as principally social, cultural, secular, or religious. In Great Britain, the Commission for Racial Equality promulgated in 1976 the Race Relations Act. The main objectives were to fight against racism, to eliminate discrimination, and to assure an equality of opportunity and thus establish good relations among different "racial groups."[17] For Harry Goulbourne, this heralded British society as a multicultural society as opposed to a monocultural one. It is this conception of society that led, according to him, to redefining the curriculum (the Swann Report called *Education for All*) to stress common values and assist social cohesion.[18] In the Netherlands in the 1980s, a minority policy took the objective of "promoting multiculturalism and the emancipation of ethnic communities."[19]

Gradually the European countries are approaching each other in their discourses and in a sort of "applied multiculturalism" although not all of them define it the same way. In Germany, militants and opposition party spokespeople use multiculturalism as a way of making public opinion and politicians aware that "foreigners are here to stay"; that Germany is de facto a country of immigration and de facto a multicultural society. In France, too, concerned with a democratic society governed by equal rights, these discourses aim to create acceptance in public opinion for diversity as a fact inherent in any modern society.

The reactions to multiculturalism underline the paradoxes of policies that privilege culture and identities while valorizing differences in the search for equality. The accent is then put on the controversial consequences of such "openness": the fragmentation of society into communities turned in on themselves, identifications differentiated from the political community that defy a civic sense of the nation, and finally a politics of difference that, applied by the state, leads to a "clientism" of political actors and so undermines individual free choice.[20]

Similar reactions lead to an increasingly pronounced differentiation of nationally oriented discourses. In Germany, the "auto-ethnicization of minorities" as the result of multiculturalism is denounced.[21] In France, strong reactions lead to banal reminders of republican political traditions that object to any communitarian representation of populations; the French state recognizes only the individual as interlocutor. Thus there appear specific national "models" that search for justification in each nation-state's history of formation.

Reference to national models is all the more apparent in political visions of Europe. The search for resemblances to realize a united Europe makes differences come to the fore, notably an equation "people = nation = state" that does not have the same meaning in each country. Each country projects its "model" onto the European level: a model of integration, a model of citizenship, a model of nationality, a model of sovereignty, even economic and social models. These disparate references arise from the paradoxes and ambiguities of political projects for European construction. They not only underline the predominance of national particularities but also the need to redefine them in a supranational political space where interactions grow.

The European Political Project

Thus a united Europe as a political space implies a new model of society. For Ferry, "it is important to reflect on the conditions of the emergence of a civil society that does not amount to a large market, therefore of a political society, that is to say, of a milieu in which political interests and passions are summoned to confront each other and thereby to mutually recognize each other." The philosopher adds that the political unity that is needed "should be able to be reconciled with the plurality of national cultures." Posing the question of multiculturalism within the framework of the Union means, precisely, asking about the emergence of a European political community, about the quest for a political culture common to all the nations that make up this new entity and to all its member states, each with its own history, traditions, and values—in short, about the definition of a public identity, to employ John Rawls's expression, about the unity of a "European people," that would, to return to Ferry, "aim not at the suppression of national differences but at the formation of a common spirit." This spirit, thanks to a "pedagogic program for universal culture, might in turn shape the European citizen" (Ferry). Hence, the principal task of Europe might be defined as the management of the diversity of political cultures within the framework of universal democracy, a democracy that, as Jacques Lenoble hopes, *"might underwrite both the universalist goal and the actual rootedness of our identity."*[22]

Different approaches—both functionalist and liberal—have tried to define a political vision moving in this direction. However, theoretical considerations give rise to normative discourses about a model of society as European construction advances, as its objectives become concrete. In fact, from treaty to treaty, the transformation of an economic *Community* of six countries into a *Union* that includes fifteen member states, posed the national question from the start. That change in terminology carries a message about the very meaning of the European project. In this context, the concept of community, according to Dominique Wolton, "refers more to an intention than a reality"; Marc Abélès says this implies "a vision of the world, the adherence to values, and even the implementation of an overall project (...) and 'union'—although it carries a voluntarist and implicitly more political connotation."[23]

Ernest Renan relied on the idea of voluntarism to define the nation as a political unit. The feeling of belonging attached to it is incarnated by a citizenship that transcends the anthropological diversity of national societies, its political unity being guaranteed by the state and its institutions. The scenario that leads to the nation-state, Daniel Fabre reminds us, is accompanied by the production of knowledge and the installation of a new space of society, and especially of a "civilizing project," as Ferry puts it.[24]

Can the construction of political Europe reproduce the model of formation of the nation-state? Of course, the reality of Europe does not correspond to a nation-state. This political structure emanating from modernity in the eighteenth century relies on a necessary coincidence between territory, language, and culture, with the ensemble under the control of a central administration,[25] whereas it is impossible to speak of territorial and national unity in European construction. Evidently

Europe cannot ignore the multiplicity of languages, the diversity of traditions, and the plurality of cultures that together challenge the political integration of Europe and its identity. But, like any nation-state, European Union (EU) is presented, at least in its member states, as the expression of a "will to live together" or rather a will on the part of states to make Europe together. Above all, it responds to the will to renounce violence to resolve conflicts. Europe is integrated by the establishment of a common jurisdiction guaranteed by the European Court of Justice (ECJ) and a community-wide jurisprudence independent of any international law. From its beginnings, the supranational institutions acted upon the states like national institutions do upon the nation. Foremost as site of socialization, these institutions are the source of the political formation of the "masons of Europe," in Yves Hersant's words, or the "practitioners of Europe," in Abélès's, people who find themselves despite their different nationalities united by a European interest now redefined as the general interest. Moreover, the installation of European bureaucracy figures forth a "*Identikit portrait of* homo communautarius" (Abélès), the goal being "to make the Union a State that is totally sovereign, inside and out" (Ferry).

In effect, European integration seems to occur through its juridical construction. The establishment of "a space without internal frontiers in which the free circulation of merchandise, goods and capitals is guaranteed" introduces a de facto legislative procedure that influences the decision making resulting from cooperation among states.[26] Networks of bilateral and multilateral treaties as well as collateral conventions lead to the elaboration of a framework agreement by which all states agree to respect the principles that assure the protection of national minorities (Emmanuel Decaux). Similarly, the convergence of legislation on immigration and the right of political asylum (Virginie Guiraudon), and on questions of security and police services (Rémy Leveau), all contribute to the construction of a common juridical space.

Supranational institutions, guided by the principles of regulating state's traditions and of political and juridical harmonization, are imposed on states in the name of the "general interest" protected by the ECJ. In effect, the latter has erected, under pressure from national courts, the legislative architecture of legal protection of human rights and has also exerted the "direct effect" of its founding clauses and treaties so as to guarantee the respect of fundamental rights at the community level (Joseph Weiler). Is this sufficient for us to foresee a European legal system that would evolve along the lines of the U.S. Supreme

Court, thus approaching the model of a federal institution that unifies a nation?

But Europe is neither a nation nor a supernation. Moreover, "Europe cannot be constituted into nations; its political integration cannot be achieved in the conventional form of a state," affirms Ferry. It lacks various things: the "weight of history," a "profound reflection on the constitution," and, most decisively, "the institution of an educational medium for cultural reproduction and social integration" (Ferry). But Europe does not pretend to compete with states and nations. The political and administrative system to which Ferry refers, "even in its constitutional appearance, is not bound to be married to the classical form of a legal state."

The making of Europe introduces a "normative supranationalism"[27] that exceeds the framework of the nation-state while reproducing at the European level the same principles as nation-states'. In return, these norms are imposed on member states. But while issues of human rights, immigration, and minority rights remain within the exclusive domain of states, the latter find themselves constrained to accept new legal norms produced by European institutions. The European Convention of Human Rights (ECHR), for example, authorizes a European citizen (in this case, one who has the nationality of one of the states that has accepted individual recourse) to appeal directly to the Council of Europe, and a foreigner (who does not have the nationality of a country in the EU) to have recourse to the European Court of Human Rights. In short, the juridical construction of a united Europe leads to a reinterpretation of the concept of universality as well as of human rights and citizenship.

A European Public Space

Is the institutional construction of Europe sufficient to create a unified public space, a space of production of European political power and a space of citizenship? "Since it took centuries to form national public spaces, acculturated to the principles of democracy and the rule of law, how can we imagine that we can in a few years put in place—by decree—a European public space?" asks Ferry. Evidently, governmental cooperation is marked by the concern of European institutions to harmonize cultural, political, and legal differences among states and that in fact results in a convergence, at least in certain domains.[28] Supranationalism in itself offers the notion of the formation of a unified (or rather standardized) political space. But to what extent can supranational institutions activate a popular will, guarantee the "people's" participation, arouse a common identification, and assure loyalty—in short, produce a citizenship that would turn European construction into a democratic project?

Clifford Geertz would respond to this series of questions by recalling that "political processes are more vast and more profound than the formal institutions entrusted with regulating them." "Some of the most critical decisions concerning the direction of public life," he adds, "are not made in parliaments and presidiums; they are made in the unformalized realisms of what Durkheim called 'the collective consciousness' (. . .)"[29] In the framework of a EU, this would amount to seeking new affective anchors beyond the instrumental link with an economic space, to going beyond competition for power among the member states, to defining new solidarities among nations and among citizens, to imagining a citizenship that would be the motor of a European identity.

According to Didier Lapeyronnie, it is precisely this "national consciousness" that is lacking in the making of Europe. This is due to the insufficient capacity of Europe to "offer a language of reference alternative to the nation's, which is alone capable of effecting a political synthesis founded on an association between modernizing reason, mobilizing will, and equalizing justice." Ferry discusses the plea for a universal collective consciousness beyond "culturalist oppositions" to constitute a politically united community, with the goal being to form "the future European citizen."

For Wolton, it is difficult to speak of European space as a space of political production, due to the lack of political stakes and the experience of frequent debates among member states; consequently all networks tend to the formation of a "symbolic space." As for a public space that represents collective interests, Abélès shows that it is limited to institutional projects and the administrative world represented by the "practitioners of Europe (. . .) [who] claim to be the interpreters of a community of interest, wholly focused on a future that alone justifies its existence: European unification." Thus, the EU is being constructed as the world of an elite, not as the expression of a popular will nor thanks to the support of the European population as a whole, this also poses the question of whether European public space can be the space of political participation and representation, as well as the space of citizenship— which remains national for the time being. It is precisely this absence of "citizenship" born of a common political culture that gives content and pertinence to the concept of a "democratic deficit" in European construction. As Ferry rightly remarks, Europe is constructed from the accomplishments of national political cultures that have integrated the normative implications of democracy and the rule of law that we find in constitutions and in their conception of human rights. According to him, the precondition of a European public space lies in the articulation of three principles—civility, legality, publicity—which constitute the patrimony of European civilization: *legality* is the condition of its basic structure, *civility* assures its continuity in the concrete exercise of daily cooperative practices, the results of which are contested by the parties involved through the *publicity* of debates, thanks to the force of nonviolent constraint represented by the "third party" that is public opinion.

However, a European public space of another kind is visible, which is called transnational. The logic of supranationality produces a European civil society in which transnational networks compete and thus turn European space into a "communicational space," to use Habermas's phrase. Networks of information and media exchange (Wolton), networks of institutions (Hersant) and networks of solidarity and interests—whether presented as economic, political, cultural, or identitarian—constitute the web that covers the European space. Encouraged by supranational institutions, the actors involved in setting up such networks try to act directly through the commission in Brussels, consequently beyond the limits of nation-states. Thus there appears a new mode of political participation occasioned by a space open to the demands of both its citizens' and residents' interests and identities. This allows them to assert autonomy in relation to state systems that are territorially bounded. By the same token, transnational activity strengthens the demand of populations resulting from immigration now resident in European countries, for example, for equality of rights and treatment at the European level, as well as their struggle against racism; is a means of circumventing the assimilationist approaches of nation-states.[30] Transnationality, thanks to increasing interactions among actors from different traditions, might even become a means of socialization and training in a new political culture that one could truly call European. Transnationality thus introduces a practice of "European co-citizenship," in Etienne Tassin's words.[31]

However, according to Ferry, a transnational space "materialized" by networks of information or solidarity does not suffice to create or "recreate" the social fabric. The information society on which such a public space is founded evidently cannot replace "formation" through education, and so the transnational integration of Europe tends politically toward either the paradigm of the school, the medium of education, or the paradigm of the market, the medium of exchange. But a transnational public space, contrary to the nation-state, does not have "to translate a presumed identity and a common will."[32] In effect, the establishment of these networks is in large part the product of European institutions and not the result of a general European will. But one cannot ignore the engagement of actors in the consolidation of solidarities across frontiers. This engagement testifies to an ex post facto will to participate in the formation of a European identity that transcends national identities. Thus, as Lapeyronnie correctly stresses, "on one side is the space of rational action, economic development, and markets that corresponds for the citizen to participation, and on the other side, the space of cultural integration and collective identity that corresponds to the citizen's membership."

Engagement also poses the issues of belonging, allegiance, and consequently, citizenship.[33] Numerous debates about citizenship, nationality, and European identity have accompanied the gradual transformation of a common market into a Union that implies the emergence of a political space, stressing the multiplicity of identity references in the formation of a political Europe. Jean-Marc Ferry proposes a "postnational" model to describe the overcoming of the "nationalist principle" involved in the construction of a political Europe.[34] Habermas develops the concept of "constitutional patriotism" to underline the separation between the feeling of belonging implied by national citizenship and its legal practice in spheres beyond the nation-state. For him, citizenship is "conceived on the model of affiliation to an organization that assures a legal position and situates the individual outside the state." Ferry goes farther than the "classic version of constitutional patriotism" when he proposes the idea of "politics as culture," "beyond a consensus on the fundamental principles of democracy and the rule of law" due to the advent of a politically operative common sense—in contrast to a consensus, even authentic, about the various fundamental principles of universalist values. In another key, regarding the non-European populations arising from 1960s immigration, Yasemin Soysal defines as "postnational" the adoption of international norms referring to the person or residence and not to legal citizenship.[35]

These postnational conceptions of belonging feed normative discourses about the necessary definition of a new model of citizenship. But European legislation does not always move in the direction of these discourses. From a legal standpoint, the Maastricht Treaty maintains the link between national citizenship (hence nationality) and "citizenship of the Union." The E.U. citizen has the right to circulate and stay freely anywhere in the territory of member states, and even the right to vote in municipal and European elections in a member state from which he does not originate, simply as a resident. In fact, this practice introduces a notion of extraterritoriality of citizenship and challenges the adaptability of national citizenships within the European legal framework. Likewise, the registers of belonging and political engagement show that the practice of citizenship gives rise to a multiplicity of interests as well as a multiple kinds of belonging and allegiance within the European framework, detached from an entity that is exclusively national.

The political construction of Europe, in leaning on the supranational, is therefore opposed to the idea of the postnational. While the latter would involve recognizing cultural diversity and accepting pluralism as the foundation of European belonging, the supranational (for Ferry) is only a "redoubled nationalism in which only the geopolitical scale changes but not the philosophical principle of the nation-state." In effect, the supranational appears as a projection of the nation-state that is still incumbent on states. Moreover, while undermining the nation-state, it strengthens the role of states in constructing a political Europe.

This is one of the paradoxes of supranationality and consequently of European construction.[36] In effect, European institutions are a challenge to nation-states due to their autonomy in relation to national institutions and to the transnational activity they incite. But at the same time, by reproducing the national model in the legal definition of citizenship, they strengthen state power. The consolidation of transnational solidarities generally aims to influence states from outside. Even if transnational networks contribute, in certain respects, to the formation of "transnational communities," whether of interest or of identity, or both, the latter appear as the indispensable structures for negotiating with the public powers for recognition within contexts that remain national. This is more flagrant still in the case of immigrant populations: the cross-border structuring of associative networks has the long-term goal of strengthening their representativeness at the European level, but its practical aim is to achieve an equality of rights and to eliminate any discrimination at the national level. It is worth noting that militants, even those most active at the European level, represent the states as the sole "adversaries" with which they ultimately have to deal. State predominance is felt in the difficulty that associations have in coordinating their activities and their demands when the latter emanate from their own initiative.[37] Therefore Europeanization of activity does not necessarily lead to an Europeanization of demands—which remain national.

Toward a European "Multiculturalism"?

A European public space does seem perceptible outside nation-states, as demonstrated by the structuring of networks and the political engagement of actors, although for interests that are a priori particular. It is especially in the interpenetration between states and with the EU that political power and reciprocal influence are played out, and it is within nations that the general interest is expressed. This has led the states to be considered as the structuring force of European construction and the nation as the political space where, ultimately, "will" and citizenship are manifest (Lapeyronnie). In this sense, as Paul Thibaud stresses, "Europe remains an indeterminate political project that has not managed to legitimate itself independently of states"; according to him, within the EU "nations should see guaranteed the exercise of certain functions essential for their identity, in particular social and territorial solidarity and the defense of their cultures."[38] This appears as much in the production of cultural norms as in the production of European legal norms. For Hersant, it is unthinkable to define a European culture that amounts to ignoring the diversity of national cultures, languages, identities; and for Wolton, a European space cannot be constructed unless these identities are preserved as constitutive elements of a European public space, since "there is no communication without relations among mutually recognized identities," and "one of the greatest weaknesses of the current project is that it reproduces on a larger scale what exists within each nation-state." Similarly, among *"practitioners of Europe,"* reference to the community is not synonymous with a shared identity. For example, use of the national (or regional) language, despite the ambient pluralism, allows one to assert an identity that "is not confined to the cultural characteristics of the different countries but contains a political dimension" (Abélès).

In the legal realm, efforts to define a common legal space run up against "competing interpretations of the same principles and the same legal rules" (Ferry). The production of European legal norms, despite the quest for universality, especially with respect to human rights, shows that the states remain, in Weiler's expression, "the fundamental limits" in the creation of a European jurisprudence. These limits

apply to "the principle by which certain explicitly designated powers or authorities would guarantee that, in some domains, the human
communities would be free to make their own social choices without intervention from above." Even if the European Convention on
Human Rights defines a universal "hard kernel" transcending cultural
diversity, "human rights are almost invariably the expression of a compromise between competing social goods in the polity." According to
Weiler, they are consequently defined within the "fundamental limits"
and their essential values.

Similarly with regard to the right to protection of national minorities in Europe, Decaux shows that there seems an initial ambiguity
in the very definition of national minority and the uncertainties in
the establishment of legal forms for its recognition. In effect, is one
designating cultural, linguistic, territorial minorities that are officially
recognized as such (like Catalans and Basques in Spain) or rather referring to immigrant minorities that are equally officially recognized
(as in the Netherlands)? The definition offered by the Human Rights
Convention is very broad: "the term 'minority' refers to a group that is
numerically inferior to the rest of the population and whose members
are animated by the will to preserve their culture, traditions, religion
or language."[39] But it is the concept of minority developed in relation
to the social, cultural, and political realities of the countries of central and Eastern Europe, where the problem of democracy has arisen
since 1989 in terms of recognizing communities, that lies at the origin of the application of minority rights by European institutions to
other countries of Western Europe. In France, the term "minority" is
rejected, whether with regard to regional or religious identities or else
to collective identities expressed by immigrant populations. For example, the Council of Europe in November 1994 elaborated a convention
to guarantee the individual freedoms of minorities without injuring
the unity and cohesion of the state. But France did not sign it because
the minister in charge of European Affairs considered that the text
was "not compatible with the [French] Constitution." Thus, explains
Decaux, various declaration, charters, and conventions have oscillated
"between protecting the ethnic identity of persons and developing
conditions favorable to its promotion, thereby moving from individual
rights to collective ones, ending up at a 'relativism of situations' that
takes into account the diversity of national experiences and constitutional systems."

It is through the policies of asylum or immigration and integration that the force of the state is most strongly felt, leading to tension

between supranationality and the intergovernmental, tension between a tendency to unify European space and state sovereignty. Guiraudon notes that any supranational legal norm concerning the rights of immigrants is founded in national jurisprudence, and that the member states have always refused to transfer their powers to Brussels, preferring to move in the direction of intergovernmental cooperation as it has been institutionalized since Maastricht. For Leveau, signing the Schengen agreement on the entry and free circulation of foreigners within the EU meant nothing less than the establishment of an administrative network outside Brussels, which does not have the central power of a federation for democratic oversight. As for establishing a space of European security, the states prefer, he says, "multi-bilateral framework that did not call for definitive relinquishing of sovereignty."[40]

One line of thought on united Europe bears directly on overcoming statist models, understood as particularist, and on the means of linking the different juridical, cultural, and political spaces that comprise it. This presupposes a production of cultural and juridical norms in which the states' interests would be expressed, their principles and sovereignty protected, and their identity represented—in short, a model of pluralist society with a constitution founded on principles restructured by the recognition of different cultures to form a common European political culture. This would require ways of combining the plurality of national cultures with the political unity necessary to define a European identity. New forms of democracy would have to be imagined. Chantal Mouffe proposed a "plural democracy" that would take account of this multicultural vision of political realities, trying to find a new form of articulation between the universal and the particular.[41]

For Ferry, "Europe finds itself asked to invent an original method to edify its political unity." He adds that a "simple solution" consists in the adherence of member states and (virtual) citizens to a common constitution. He then wonders about the means to provide "European policy with substance" and asserts that the postnational substance of European policy must be the indispensable mediation between the cultural identities of member states, on the one hand, and the community politics and law, on the other. This condition itself presupposes opening and the structuring of a European public space, he says.

The dynamic of forming a political culture shared by the Union can only operate through confrontation among different national traditions. Already in national terms, the augmented relations among immigrant populations that are increasingly structured into communities bearing specific identities, testifies to a "political acculturation" (in Habermas's expression) in their forms of participation and adherence to the surrounding civic culture; this leads states into negotiations over identity that pose a challenge to political traditions on all sides in the hope of achieving a new historic compromise.[42] Meanwhile, in the European context, there is a need for a "reciprocal political acculturation among states" so as to create a common political culture, all the more so because European space is the space in which all identities are ultimately negotiated. Whether national, regional, linguistic, religious, majority, or minority, identities are redefined by the complex play of interaction and identification inside European space, an open space where "everything is in relation" (in Wolton's formula). It is precisely the whole set of these relations among the Union, the member states, and immigrants ("foreign" to European identity) that leads to a redefinition of the concepts of universality, particularity, nationality, and citizenship, concepts that are at the origin of the formation of a European identity.

For Wolton, the ideal would be to achieve "to create a symbolic political space in which people might believe." But it also means creating a European civic culture that respects identities. Politics as culture, says Ferry, also means making different cultural identities communicate with each other. For this, he adds, "you have to use procedures of civility, legality, publicity, that respectively codify the recognition of sensibilities, interests and the arguments of others."

However, the lack of European civic identity risks leading to a definition of a European "us" founded on a social order as a common good, but as a space of prosperity and security founded more on exclusion (based on ethnic and religious criteria) than on inclusion. Recent debates on the enlargement of Europe whose criteria are not clearly defined, as well as debates on immigration that have earned it the reputation of "fortress," underlie this image of unified space. This is all the more so in reference to a "clash of civilizations" in which Islam is considered to be an external threat and becomes a way of excluding the Muslim populations established in Europe (Leveau). This has contributed, he says, to "redefining both an internal and an external border that are supposedly uncrossable for cultural reasons." This can be translated into the rejection of immigrant populations who are constituted into diasporas feeling more solidarity with the external, especially countries of origin in North Africa or Turkey. Such a mechanism in defining European identity challenges notions of both universality and multiculturalism in European political visions.

Incontestably, European construction rests on combining of the one and the multiple. As Hersant points out, one has to learn to think of Europe "as simultaneously plural and one." Juridical experience, especially in the realm of human rights analyzed by Weiler, makes visible in Europe both the idea of uniformity and the idea of diversity: the very concept of human rights as a "fundamental right" is a universal concept yet also a source of differentiation among states. In practice, European institutions are the only political space in which this equation arising from a de facto pluralism appears so evidently. Marc Abélès shows that "European institutions are in effect machines for harmonizing, for inventing procedures to reconcile legislative forms that arise from political histories and cultural approaches that are sometimes far removed from each other," and "forms of political action are constructed to privilege the search for compromise."

Can "multiculturalism" provide the sought-for compromise? A multiculturalism that in Ferry's words would permit "reconciling the universality of its legal framework with the singularity of cultural identities so as to constitute a common political culture?" Multiculturalism as the foundation of political unity and that consider the cultural, political, and legal diversity that characterizes Europe—could this overcome the tensions and antagonisms among member states and between member states and Brussels, as thinking about a confederated Europe has suggested, resulting in a political unity that respects constitutional multiplicity as well as a diversity of identity across Europe?[43] Contrary to a federalism that rests on territorial and political unity and on the will of the native people to achieve a common constitution, multiculturalism takes the opposite route, beginning from the multiple and arriving at political unity, while seeking to establish a new equilibrium among culture, politics, and territory, arousing eventual identification by actors with this new political entity that would be endowed, according to Weiler, "with a constitutionally distinct identity and susceptibility and whose *constitutional ethos* should express, or at least take into account, a multiplicity of traditions." Weiler goes farther by asserting that this amounts to defining fundamental new equilibria, to redefining the "universal hard kernel" of human rights, even if this cannot be totally separated from the context in which the community finds itself. "Without a supranational state, the Union's political integration must be realized en route to shared political culture, without having to regard national cultures and languages as so many obstacles to communication" (Ferry).

Europe as a space of citizenship, engagement, and participation, as a space of belonging that is both regional and national, even ethnic and religious, will add a new element to the individual's choice of identity: thinking of oneself as European. Multiculturalism as the basis for negotiating multiple identities might solve problems of allegiance by enabling people to think of the EU not as a construct like the nation-state but as the coexistence among the identities that compose it. As Weiler stresses, "whatever the element that ends up dominating, it is much preferable that it be tempered by conflict between competing values."

In this hypothesis, multiculturalism might be the source of a European identity. Multiculturalism is probably one of the keys to the success (or failure) of the European project, thinks Wolton, but he prefers to speak of *cultural cohabitation* rather than multiculturalism. "To cohabit presupposes permanent adjustments, hence an open situation, whereas the idea of multiculturalism connotes a successful organization of relations among cultures." Of course, like any political model, multiculturalism runs up against limits and even its own paradoxes. In effect, multiculturalism risks, like nationalism, leading to a fractioning of European society into the multiple identities that characterize it, dividing the EU (like the nations that comprise it) into political unities and thereby skirting tribalism. Or else the strengthening of the role of the states in European construction might lead to a nationalism that leaves little space to other identities in the national societies (Lapeyronnie). Referring to the rights granted to minorities by European authorities, Decaux thinks that "each new political fracture, far from solving the question of minorities, creates at another level a cyclical process that is more and more destructive, multiplying minorities into more minorities." While the EU once seemed closely modeled on Switzerland, "today it has to avoid becoming a new Yugoslavia," he warns. European projects cannot ignore that states are caught and pulled between "nationalist passion and unitarian hope."[44] Thus a multiculturalist approach to Europe might one day make the EU into a political space in which the paradoxes of democracy are negotiated (Guy Hermet).

Notes

1. In the December 1993 issue of the French journal *Le Débat*, French historians debated on the best way to teach European history to high school students, on the themes to chose to highlight both the outlines of a variable geography and a culture that would unite national differences within territorial boundaries.

2. Edgar Morin. *Penser l'Europe*. Paris: Seuil, 1988: 168–169.

3. See John Rawls. *Political Liberalism*. New York: Columbia University Press, and more specifically pages 29–35 and Chapter VI, "The idea of public reason": 213–253.

4. See the debate on Charles Taylor in the volume edited by Amy Gutman. *The politics of Recognition*. Princeton, NJ: Princeton University Press, 1992 (1st edition).

5. See also Joseph Raz. "Multiculturalism: A Liberal Perspective." *Dissent*, Winter 1994: 67–79.

6. Jean Leca. "La démocratie à l'épreuve des pluralistes." *Revue française de science politique*, April–May 1996: 225–280.

7. The concept of minority should be considered with much precaution. First, minority in the European context equals a nation and refers to a people. On this particular topic, see the historical analysis on the birth of minorities: Guy Hermet. *Histoire des nations et du nationalisme en Europe*. Paris: Seuil, 1996. At the same time, its legal interpretation in European institutions is rather ambiguous.

8. See Joseph Raz. "Multiculturalism: A Liberal Perspective." See also Leca. "La démocratie à l'épreuve des pluralistes."

9. Charles Taylor. *Multiculturalism and the Politics of Recognition*. Princeton, NJ: Princeton University Press, 1992.

10. Philip Resnik. *Thinking English Canada* (see in particular Chapter 7). Toronto, Canada: Stoddart, 1994.

11. Samuel Huntington sees multiculturalist policies as a challenge to America's national identity, in *Who Are We: The Challenges to America's National Identity*. New York: Simon and Schuster, 2004.

12. See Nathan Glazer. *We Are All Multiculturalists Now*. Cambridge, MA: Harvard University Press, 1997.

13. Will Kymlicka distinguishes multinational States (States that are constituted of national entities that are defined in terms of language and territory) and polyethnic states (with several ethnic communities born from immigration), in *Multicultural Citizenship*. Oxford: Oxford University Press, 1995 (more particularly Chapter 2, "Politics of Multiculturalism").

14. For Switzerland, refer to Uli Windisch's works.

15. Refer to Frank-Olaf Radtke. "Multiculturalism in Germany: Local Management of Immigrants' Social Inclusion." *International Journal of Multicultural Societies* 5(1), 2003: 55–76.

16. He developed his ambitions and his intentions in a book he published in 1992. Daniel Cohn-Bendit and Thomas Schmid. *Heimat Babylon. Das Wagnis der Multikulturellen Demokratie*, Hamburg: Hoffman and Campe, 1992.

17. John Crowley. *Immigration, "relations raciales" et mobilisations minoritaires au Royaume-Uni. La démocratie face à la complexité sociale*. PhD in Political Science supervised by Jean Leca, Paris, 1994.

18. See the works by Harry Goulbourne, and "British Multi-culturalism and the Communal Option," presentation at the conference "Towards European Multiculturalism," Centre for International Studies and Research, Paris, March 1994.

19. Han Entzinger. "Y a-t-il un avenir pour le modèle néerlandais des 'minorités ethnique'?" in *Revue Européenne des Migrations Internationales* 10(1), 1994: 73–95.

20. Aleksandra Alund and Carl-Ulrik Schierup. *Paradoxes of Multiculturalism*. Aldershot: Avebury, 1991.
21. Radtke. "Multiculturalism in Germany."
22. Jacques Lenoble. "Penser l'identité et la démocratie en Europe," in Jacques Lenoble and Nicole Dewandre (eds.). *L'Europe au soir des siècles*, Paris: Seuil, 1992: 293–315
23. Marc Abélès. See his chapter in this edited volume.
24. Daniel Fabre. "L'ethnologue et les nations," in Daniel Fabre (ed.) *L'Europe entre cultures et nations*. Paris: Editions de la Maison des sciences de l'homme, 1996: 99–120.
25. See S. N. Eisenstadt and Stein Rokkan (eds.). 1973. *Building Nations and States*. Beverly Hills: Sage; Charles Tilly. *The Nation-State Formation, Reflections on the History of European State Building*. Princeton, NJ: Princeton University Press, 1973.
26. Jean Paul Jacqué. "Le labyrinthe décisionnel," in *Pouvoirs* 69, 1994: 23–34.
27. Bruno de Witte. "The European Community and Its Minorities," in Catherine Brölmann, René Lefeber, and Marjoleine Zieck (eds.). *Peoples and Minorities in International Law*. Dortrecht, Boston, London: Martinus Nijhoff, 1993: 167–185.
28. Yves Meny, Pierre Muller, and Jean-Louis Quermonne (ed.). *Politiques publiques en Europe*. Paris: L'Harmattan; see also Pierre Muller. "La mutation des politiques publiques européennes," *Pouvoirs* 69, 1994: 63–75; Jean Louis Quermonne. "De l'espace public au modèle politique," in Pierre Muller. *Politiques publiques en Europe*; see also "Interpréter l'Europe," *Cultures & Conflicts* 28, special issue directed by Christian Lequesne and Andy Smith, Winter 1997. Available online at: www. Conflits.org/index49.html (accessed on June 10, 2008).
29. Clifford Geertz. *The Interpretation of Cultures* (see in particular Chapter 11, "The Politics of Meaning"). Basic Books: New York, 1973: 316.
30. See Riva Kastoryano. "Mobilisation des migrants en Europe, du national au transnational," *Revue Européenne des Migrations Internationales* 10(1), 1994: 169–181. See also "Transnational Networks and Political Participation. The Place of Immigrants in the European Union" in Mabel Berezin and Martin Schain (eds.). 2003. *Europe without Borders: Remapping Territory, Citizenship and Identity in a Transnational Age*. Baltimore, MD: Johns Hopkins University Press: 64–89.
31. Etienne Tassin. "Europe, une communauté politique," *Esprit* 176, November 1991: 63–79.
32. Tassin. "Europe, une communauté politique."
33. For the issue of citizenship as a feeling of belonging and citizenship as an engagement, see Jean Leca "Individualisme et citoyenneté," in Pierre Birnbaum and Jean Leca (eds.). *Sur l'individualisme*. Paris: Presses de la FNSP. 1986: 159–213.
34. Jean Marc Ferry, "La pertinence du postnational," in Jacques Lenoble and Nicole Dewandre (eds.). *L'Europe au soir des siècles: Identité et démocratie*. Paris: Seuil. 1992: 39–59.
35. Yasemin Nuhoglu Soysal. *Limits of Citizenship, Migrants and Postnational Membership in Europe*. Chicago: University of Chicago Press. 1995.
36. Riva Kastoryano. "Participation transnationale et citoyenneté: les immigrés dans l'Union européenne," *Cultures & Conflicts* 28. 1997. Available online at: http://www.conflits.org/index2121.html (accessed on June 12, 2008). See also Christian Lequesne. "La Commission européenne entre autonomie et dépendance." *Revue française de science Politique* 46(3), June 1996: 389–408.
37. Kastoryano, "Mobilisation des migrants en Europe."
38. Paul Thibaud, "L'Europe allemande…Définitivement?" *Esprit*, May 1996: 53–65.
39. Article 2 of the convention proposition in 1991, quoted by Frédérick Sudre. *Droit international et européen des droits de l'homme*. Paris: Presses Universitaires de France, 1995: 156.
40. On this issue, see Didier Bigo. *Polices en réseaux. L'expérience européenne*. Paris: Presses de Science Po, 1996.
41. Chantal Mouffe. "La démocratie entre modernité et post-modernité: pour une démocratie plurielle," *Revue du MAUSS* 8, 1990: 14–30.

42. Riva Kastoryano. *La France, l'Allemagne et leurs immigrés. Négocier l'identité.* Paris: Armand Colin. 1997; and *Negotiating Identities. States and Immigrants in France and Germany,* Princeton, NJ: Princeton University Press, 2002.

43. For a discussion on the European constitutional system, see the special issue of *Political Studies,* vol. XLIV, 1996. See also Maurice Croisat and Jean Louis Quermonne. *L'Europe et le fédéralisme.* Paris: Montchretien, 1996.

44. Maurice Duverger. "L'Europe: balkanisée, communautaire ou dominée ?" *Pouvoirs* 57, 1991.

PART 1

*Cultural Production of
European Multiculturalism*

CHAPTER ONE

The Practitioners of Europe

MARC ABÉLÈS

For someone who studies the emergence of new European cultural actors, community institutions represent a privileged observatory. It is the supreme laboratory for Europe—so longed for by some and so despised by others. And it might be interesting for an anthropologist to penetrate a universe that has given rise to received ideas more than to serious research. Since I have done in-depth studies of two institutions, the parliament[1] and the commission,[2] I will present here some reflections about the relation of community actors to language and to culture. Second, I will deal with the impact of this cultural crossroads on administrative and political practices. To conclude, I will tackle some theoretical and methodological issues raised by an anthropological approach to the subject of the community.

If one asks bureaucrats and parliamentarians what their principal vocation is, there is every chance they will reply "our job is to construct Europe." This is in fact the objective fixed in the 1950s by all those in Brussels, Strasburg, and Luxemburg who patiently laid the foundations for an edifice that has today assumed considerable size. Europe, yes...but still...? How can you define an entity that is more than an encompassing economic space without constituting a state properly speaking?[3] The expression "community" has long been used to characterize Europe, and for which "union" has been more recently substituted, merits comment. For an anthropologist, it connotes the idea of a shared culture and incontestably presents a deepening compared to the notion of "common market" that characterized this enterprise in the 1960s. The notion of community implies more than material exchanges: a vision of the world, the adherence to values, and even the implementation of an overall project.[4] One might say the same for "union"—although it carries a voluntarist and implicitly more political connotation.

Terms are revealing, but they also function as subliminal images that operate beyond the consciousness of protagonists. Nevertheless, these words bear a concomitant ambiguity. On the one hand, we are dealing with a community under construction, whose boundaries are not yet— and won't be for a long time—decreed in stone. For more than a quarter of a century, it was defined by distinguishing itself from the East, the Communist glacis. Today it marks its specificity by claiming to measure itself against the giants of Asia and America. Yet it is a Europe of fluid contours, still in a state of becoming, that is facing the second millennium. On the other hand, one may wonder if "community" and "union" reflect the existence of an ensemble consisting of human relations, in which case Europe is indeed an unavoidable fact, or else whether it is an *ideological perspective*, which is assumed with more or less enthusiasm by various member states. For them, inscription in the nation-state constitutes the meaningful condition of access to citizenship. The limits of the communitarian experience are clearly seen: the tightening of economic ties and the interdependence this engenders have gigantic repercussions on production, trade, and the labor market in our societies. However, European *citizenship* is still in limbo, and community reference is not synonymous with a shared identity for the subjects of member states.

A Homogeneous Culture?

Let us turn now to those who work in the arcana of Europe. We are dealing with a specific experience, for there does exist a European public service that possesses a status that is different from its national homologues. These people work together, either for the commission or for other institutions (parliament, the court of justice, etc.). They come from different nationalities but all have the task of serving the European interest. This appears clearly in the behavior they adopt when they are confronted in the exercise of their duties with the representatives of national administrations: faced with a French civil servant, his European homologue also of French origin might make himself the interpreter of totally divergent positions. At the extreme, national belonging is effaced by consciousness of a communitarian interest, of which bureaucrats in Brussels are the living incarnation. If there is a European culture, even in gestation, then it lies among these practitioners of Europe—let us not call them "Eurocrats," a term laden with ambiguous connotations—which is where we should seek it.

The departments of the European Commission apparently present a strong homogeneity. One might compare this organism to our great national administrations: it is divided into Directorates-General (DGs) that are entrusted with the various domains of community activity: agriculture, domestic trade, the environment, transportation, research, regional policies, cooperation, and so on. Formerly gathered in a single building, the Berlaymont, the DGs are now dispersed in various districts of Brussels. The structuring of the offices is identical from one DG to another: a balance among nationalities, an internal hierarchy, and a functioning all obeying the same rules. The official working languages are English, French, and German, but in practice only the first two are commonly used. The DGs work under the leadership of European commissioners who divide up the different portfolios. Here again one may stress the analogy with national ministries, except that the commissioners function in the form of a college, each having the vocation to represent the commission as a whole, and having the right to consult the dossiers of his colleagues. Among commissioners, the president is only the foremost among equals.

We also note that each of the DGs possesses a specificity linked to its history as much as to its domain of competence. Agriculture (DG VI) has for a long time been the most important pole of the commission. It has always been directed by a French person, and this nationality has incontestably put its imprint on the functioning of its services. If the equilibrium among nationalities is the rule here as elsewhere, the dominant language in management meetings is French. Moreover, everyone is aware of the importance of this sector. It is with a certain pride that one official told me: "we weigh 36 billion *écus*, 52 percent of the Community budget." Seniority, power, influence: DG VI is a little like an empire within an empire. It seems like a giant in relation to DGs that are not in charge of managing a community policy. One detects a strong identification of officials with the style of the directorates to which they belong. The atmosphere is not the same in DG VIII (Cooperation and Development), very marked by postcolonial history, as in DG XVI (Regional Policies), created more recently and which has adopted a resolutely modern style of management.

Listening to the agents of the commission, one easily detects underlying oppositions linked to the vocation of the DGs: for example, DG XVI defines itself as more "social" than DG III (Domestic Trade). Regional policies in the community aim to remedy the disparities among regions: inversely, DG III develops a free trade perspective that consists of removing all obstacles to the great European market. In DG XI (Environment), they sometimes criticize the "planners" of DG XVI who are more concerned to encourage major infrastructure than preoccupied with the effects of their policy on the natural environment. Underneath the apparent homogeneity of "Community bureaucracy," one discerns a diversity that corresponds to both the relevant subjects and the traditions internal to each DG. The same could be said of styles of behavior. Rather great homogeneity is observed in external appearance, marked by sober clothing (suit and tie for men, trouser suits for women, in one or two styles and in discreet colors). But if some offices develop great conviviality, others privilege more formal relations among staff.

The practitioners of Europe are recruited by competition, according to the model of French public services: except for a limited contingent of experts on temporary assignment from member states (seven to eight hundred out of fourteen thousand), most of the agents have had to first pass the competitive exam and then be inscribed on reserve lists, before being appointed to a directorate of the commission. Without going into detail about professional careers, we note that above a certain level (reaching the grade of division head for officials of rank A), satisfying the balance among nationalities becomes a determining factor. According to context, a deserving official will obtain (or not) the decisive promotion that allows him or her to enter into the management circle of the organization. It is not rare to encounter excellent agents who complain of being blocked due to their nationality. Such frustrations may feed a certain tension inside departments. But everyone is obliged to accept the rules of the game, particularly since officials enjoy a comfortable income. The salaries without any doubt constitute a major motivation for those who sit the competitive exams. Unlike the veterans who used to define themselves as sorts of militants, as pioneers of Europe, today it is the prospect of stable and well-paid employment, as well as the visibility achieved by the institution under Jacques Delors, that attract young people.

Officials have generally been educated as lawyers and economists. Here again a certain uniformity reigns: "the spirit" of the commission bears the imprint of these disciplines. There are indeed sectors where one encounters veterinarians (DG VI) or medical doctors (DG VIII), and even diplomats (DG I), but economics and law are the best suited to the management and regulatory vocation of the European organization. Thus we may see a veritable Identikit of *homo communautarius*: motivations, behavior, expertise, and careers all contribute to unifying a group whose members are even invited to see themselves as interchangeable, since mobility among departments is encouraged. So should we speak of "new cultural actors?" At first sight, what seems prevalent is the insertion of individuals into a system of relations that assigns them a position, a status, tasks, a schedule—all as a function of its overall objectives. The commission seems concerned to present the customary profile of any large organization. Within it occurs the same type of division of labor as they have. As its organizational diagram (*organigramme*) bears witness, we are indeed dealing with an administration of the classic type. Those who have worked "centrally" in a French ministry feel in no way disoriented when they come to DGs placed under the tutelage of commissioners and their cabinet offices. The internal segmentation of DGs conforms to a well-known model. The same is true of the division that operates within certain services between "concept people" and "operational people," even between "office staff" and "staff on the ground."

At first sight, the culture of the commission might be defined therefore as the set of working representations shared by members of this collectivity: an administrative universe like so many others on the planet. In this sense, it is hard to see why there is so much animus against Eurocrats: as technocrats or bureaucrats, they are so neither more nor less than any national functionaries. Precisely, their detractors would say, for they are not nationals but "communitarians." This epithet, often employed in Brussels to characterize the people employed in European institutions, well summarizes the singular situation of the practitioners of Europe. They claim to be the interpreters of a community of interest, wholly focused on a future that alone justifies its existence: European unification.

Nevertheless the functioning of the commission cannot be understood without highlighting the importance of an ideal mechanism that is very vivid in the activities of its members. The idea of a Europe in construction, of a process to which each is contributing, and which should in the longer term profoundly transform the political and social situation on our continent, lies at the heart of this mechanism. Quite obviously, integrated Europe does not yet exist: and it is the whole specificity of institutions like the parliament and the commission to act more in the name of a projected entity than as representatives of an actual entity. In the discourse of European officials and Members of European Parliament (MEPs), one perceives a permanent tension between the weightiness of Realpolitik and the European ideal that animates community work. Europe is made day by day; the very future of institutions is closely linked to this evolution. Unlike national parliaments whose prerogatives have been (for the most part) clearly established for a long time, the European Parliament is still looking for its hallmark. At first meagerly endowed, it was able to nibble at new realms of competence, but nobody knows whether in the years to come it might undergo major mutations. One could say the same of the commission, whose excessive influence is criticized by some governments. Nothing excludes a redefinition of this body's role over time.

This very particular context distinguishes the European institutions from their national homologues. A temporality where the future dimension takes over from the traditions of the past; a sharp awareness of an evolution that is difficult to control; the definition of a communitarian interest that faces up to the plurality of national interests: such are the ingredients of the "culture" shared by the practitioners of Europe. The unity of the project and the homogeneity of the professional group assure a strong cohesion; there is a sort of "occupational culture." To the extent that "making Europe" appears a recent occupation, the expression "new cultural actors" might correctly apply to the communitarians of Brussels. But let us pursue the inquiry, for underneath the apparent uniformity of this European political and administrative function, a deeper diversity can be easily detected, provided one does not limit the notion of culture to its purely professional meaning.

The Plurality of Languages

One might assert that cultural pluralism is omnipresent in European institutions. The Palace of Europe in Strasburg, where the plenary sessions of parliament take place, offers the spectacle (sometimes disconcerting) of this encounter among national cultures. The corridors of the assembly buzz with various tongues, and it is rather delightful to see the nine languages of the Europe of the twelve[5] cohabiting in this way. For the observer, this is proof in action that the communitarian ideal is not a mirage: the parliament is daily proof of the possibility of a public space where linguistic and cultural differences are put at the service of an all-encompassing project. There is no artificial lingo like

Volapuk (a transliteration of the Cyrillic) or Esperanto: it is the parity of languages that has the force of law here. In this, respect for pluralism remains one of the intangible rules of the game of the community. But for the MEPs, the multilingualism practiced within the institution, the coexistence of different identities and cultural traditions, cannot avoid raising a certain number of problems. It is not only a matter of encountering the Other, like the voyager who in stopovers becomes familiar with a different culture and then loses fondness for it at the end of his journey. The exercise of politics implies verbal exchange above all. Isn't the mission of the parliament to deliberate, to be consulted, to cooperate with all the other European bodies?

The parliament questions; it offers its own answers in the form of amendments, resolutions, and opinions. Everything is transmitted through language—always and above all and before everything in speech. The place of language is crucial. But it is important to transcend particularisms and idiosyncrasies if one wants to advance the common effort. One of the essential legislative tasks is to *harmonize* national legislations. This requirement is confronted daily by the MEPs: such an enterprise, which sometimes takes very down-to-earth forms, also has an almost metaphysical aspect. The tribe of parliamentarians sacrifice to the god Europe, but at the same time each exhibits the insignia of its national identity. A strange universe where a subtle dialectic is permanently practiced between this identity and what lies beyond it, the community or "Union" to come, the destiny of which nobody can predict as yet. The strict respect for plurality of languages contributes to managing this space of uncertainty, and reducing the number of tongues, or at worst only accepting one of them, would already mean ratifying one conception of the future Europe by accepting surreptitiously a form of cultural ascendancy. The dream of a single common language presents the same flaw: would this not anticipate the pure and simple dilution of national contours and constrain the fate of Europe's evolution?

And so multilingualism remains; the daily exercise of confrontation among linguistic groups who to speak better together must speak each for itself. Concretely this poses the problem of translation: how best to organize a debate when each protagonist expresses himself in his language of origin? It is clear that the institution has tried to furnish the necessary services of interpretation and translation, though you might ask if multilingualism produces a particular form of political pathology. Can you measure the effects induced by the circulation of languages in the parliamentary precinct?

The geography of parliament illustrates the importance attached to the national. The most neutral space is that of offices, though you risk losing yourself in the maze of almost identical corridors. To get your bearings, it is best to listen to the surroundings. You quickly perceive that the zones attributed to each of the political groups are themselves divided among national delegations. Thus you pass through very different sound atmospheres but you are vividly aware of the contrasts. In the corridors and the bars, individuals tend to congregate among compatriots. Not that the MEPs are against any form of mixing: beyond the polite conversations between parliamentarians of different nationalities, links are knitted in the course of the activities of political groups and commissions. It would be overly unilateral to stress only spontaneous sociability among people from the same country.

However, you cannot minimize two essential factors: on the one hand, MEPs are most often dealing either with compatriots (electors, administrators, lobbies) requesting intervention on their part, or else with their national delegation within a political group; on the other hand, respect for linguistic pluralism implies that the deputy has access to all dossiers in his native language. An investigation into behavior in the news kiosks where the press is sold in Brussels and Strasburg demonstrates how much everyone favors reading national dailies and weeklies. In these conditions it is not surprising that parliamentarians are very attached to their language, which is not simply a vehicle but allows the assertion of an identity that is not confined to the cultural characteristics of the different countries, but contains a political dimension. It suffices to observe the importance given to a fair division of responsibilities among the nationals of different countries within groups and commissions to measure the political impact of the national identity issue.

Similarly, the example of Belgian MEPs, who use two different languages depending on whether they are Flemish or Walloons, is revealing. Moreover, above and beyond the regionalists of the rainbow group, certain MEPs vigorously demand the adoption of languages such as Catalan, Basque, and Irish, as unjustly excluded from community bodies. Irishwoman Mary Banotti, member of the Popular European Party, gave her first speech in her mother tongue, to the surprise of her colleagues. All these demands, however, have run up against flat rejections from the three great European institutions: only nine languages have a right to be there. But the interweaving of the political and the linguistic themes has implications for the forms of parliamentary organization relating to translation and simultaneous interpreting. In effect, assuring access to the nine community languages under any and all circumstances has necessitated major logistic efforts. In 1990, it was estimated that approximately 35 percent of the overall budget of parliament went to the costs of multilingualism. Apart from the existence of personnel specialized in interpreting and translating, one has to take into account the technical equipment linked to interpreting, as well as the impressive tonnage of printed paper required by the reproduction of parliamentary texts in nine languages.

To manage this cumbersome arrangement, the general secretariat long ago set up an infrastructure that has been beefed up with the extension of the community to twelve and then fifteen countries. Globally, interpreters, translators, and technical services linked to these activities represent almost half of parliament's administrative personnel. There is a "Directorate of Translation" that must answer a very high demand, for the regulations stipulate that the texts submitted to commissions and to the plenary cannot be taken under consideration unless they are translated into the eleven languages. Apart from the reports and amendments produced within the framework of procedures of consultation and cooperation, this arrangement covers a whole series of texts such as the resolutions proposed individually by MEPs, their questions, their statements, and so on. Amendments cannot be voted on by the plenary unless they figure in the twelve official languages. Although the majority of reports that are debated during the session are available at the latest on the Friday preceding the Strasburg week, it is acceptable for amendments to be distributed after the opening of the plenary. The President's office fixes for each session a deadline for tabling amendments as a function of the program adopted. To be debated, amendments and resolutions produced during this short lapse of time must be themselves printed in eleven languages. Of course parliament might infringe this rule: but a minority of ten members is sufficient to oblige the assembly to reverse course and require translation.

The log-jam of texts shortens the deadlines given for translation. Some feared that the quality of work might suffer from these exigencies. A text requires not only a translation, but also a revision. Among translators, the most experienced rise to the role of revisers, whose work consists of correcting the versions submitted to them. To respect the meaning and the technical nature of the originals, this work requires good knowledge of many domains and, if necessary, an effort of supplementary research. Each division employs researchers for this purpose, and sometimes a study group is asked to contribute. The activity of translators mirrors the rhythm of sessions. Two weeks out of four are particularly hectic, before and during the plenary. The final days preceding the session see a flood of texts. Translators work late into the evening, sometimes past midnight. The documents must be printed and loaded onto the trucks that shuttle between Luxemburg and Strasburg. During the session, amendments and resolutions arising during the debates must be translated immediately.

After translation, documents have to be printed and duplicated. A hundred people are employed for this purpose. Each document is printed in 1,000 to 1,500 copies. During the sessions in Strasburg, copying machines continuously work day and night to produce parliamentary imprints, but also other indispensable information, starting with the agendas and minutes of meetings. While the parliamentarians are discoursing in the amphitheatre, there is unceasing work in this document factory. The observer is overcome with a kind of vertigo at this continuous production and proliferation of texts. It has been calculated that in 1988, 3,089 documents were translated into 9 languages, meaning in total 27,801 texts, usually consisting of several pages and duplicated in at least a thousand copies. Enough to consume whole forests.

But let's leave figures aside and turn to the principal users: are the parliamentarians satisfied with the work accomplished? Everyone recognizes the extraordinary efficiency of this organization. "We obtain all documents on time and it is almost a miracle that we can learn in our language about amendments that have just been submitted to the Assembly," said a Greek deputy. At the same time, this inflation of printed texts is worrying and even perturbing. It is impossible to take in all this literature accumulating in the filing cabinets of parliamentarians, raising the subsidiary question of how to choose what to read beyond those documents that are strictly related to the commission's activity. This abundance has the effect of disorienting interested parties, who fall back on their habitual preoccupations. Some kind of regulation by limiting the tabling of amendments might be an important step to remedy such inflation in writing.

If translation contributes to the mountain of paper produced, it does have a very immediate advantage. Each person is from the start able to work in his language while being understood by his interlocutors. For this system to function, it is important that maximum transparency be achieved. Given the often technical nature of documents, word-for-word translation does not work; equivalent terms have to be inserted into cultural and legal contexts that are sometimes very remote from each other. Generally the translators can meet these requirements, but occasionally, like a grain of sand in a well-oiled machine, an inadequacy alters the general sense of the text. One example is that during the examination of a planned directive submitted to the Environment Commission about wildlife protection, the MEPs perceived after several weeks that the versions of the texts they possessed diverged from one language to another. Apart from the time wasted, the terms of the discussion had been falsified: amendments proposed by some had to be withdrawn upon reading the original. Such mistakes are not frequent; sometimes it is simply a coarse translation of a single word that can cause confusion—hence the quite special importance given to the work of revision in the linguistic offices.

When I conducted my study of the European Parliament, it was functioning in nine languages, which implied seventy-two possible combinations. It lacked personnel able to go between Danish and Greek or Spanish, or between Greek and Portuguese. To surmount this obstacle, they had recourse to "pivot" interpreters. For example, in the French booth, an interpreter translated Greek into French; it was this version that was used by other interpreters and retranslated into their own languages. This technique resolved the difficulty in acceptable conditions, but the pivot interpreter had a heavy responsibility. If he or she committed the least error, it would have repercussions in the seven other languages.

Recourse to interpreting and to translation affects not only the material organization of parliament by permanently mobilizing personnel and technicians, but it also creates a particular style of political communication between MEPs. As it is necessary to limit speaking time, rigor must prevail in all live speech. How can you have a chance of making yourself understood if you are incapable of condensing your remarks? In the space of a few minutes, everything must be said. A luminous chronometer counts the time of a speech; the president does not hesitate to interrupt loquacious MEPs. So you have to be as clear as possible, not get carried away by rhetorical flourishes or trying to be witty. Transmitting the message concisely is the sole preoccupation. The agency of interpreters is a factor making speech uniform: it turns parliamentary debate into a sort of continuous flow that sometimes creates among auditors a somnolence that is barely attenuated by the spectacle of the surrounding comings-and-goings.

Hence the paradox that plurilingualism, far from throwing into relief differences and complementarities, tends to neutralize, even crush, cultural particularities. In effect, recourse to the interpretation that punctuates the continuous passage from one language to another cannot take into account the dynamics proper to parliamentary debate. People no longer speak to each other; they state a viewpoint to an audience. European parliamentarism finds its maximum effectiveness in the reading of reports elaborated within commissions. But when it comes to discussion, it is a succession of monologues. The fragmentation of meaning observable in the amphitheater is only interrupted when parliamentarians of the same nationality call upon each other. Linguistic unity allows them to relaunch a coherent debate where they can refer to common assumptions. This is not only a matter of language, but also the fact of having homogenous conceptual reference points. So then veritable interlocution occurs, which contrasts with the uniform flow of a universe of discourse both totally depersonalized and opaque, due to the difficulty of grasping the overall sense and the political stakes in a situation of linguistic diversity.

The new parliamentary actors whom we see working in the assembly in Strasburg are obliged to invent a discourse without rhetoric, adaptable to the requirements of translation. It is well known that in any society, politics is an affair of language, and that language is the great affair of politicians. Plurilingualism postulates that it is possible to transmit a message that is pure and univocal. But this obscures the question of the cultural conditions of the enunciation in political debate. Everything happens as if those who did not submit to the principle of simplification ("be simple or you will not be translatable") were doomed to being misunderstood, not because interpreters are incompetent, but because they are being asked to realize an almost utopian objective: respect for the letter and exact transmission of the message emitted by each speaker.

To justify the requirement for simplification, even for the dulling of discourse, there is an alleged risk of the deformation of meaning due to overly complex statements. Working in real time, interpreters are never safe from mistranslation. They cite the old case of an Italian deputy who explained the importance of the job of *sostenitore* (supporter) in the mines. The French MEPs could not believe their ears when they heard that *souteneurs* ("pimps") were essential to life in the mine. They had to await the interpreter's correction to understand that it was in fact the job of "timber worker"; the mistake arose simply from poor knowledge of coal shaft specialties. Since then, technical terms have only multiplied and interpreters deserve great merit for recognizing them, but on the whole errors are relatively rare.

Is the obstacle only of a linguistic order? Would exchanges be made easier by improving the linguistic abilities of MEPs, or even by limiting the number of working languages? We cannot underestimate the fact that the language of those elected is inseparable from their history. Each language conveys traditions: the terms employed are inseparable from a culture that gives them meaning. Political language uses expressions and formula that presuppose immediate familiarity on the part of the auditor or interlocutor: "it goes without saying!" because one is inscribed in a common cultural filiation. But at the European Parliament, we are dealing with a quite different experience: underneath the plurality of languages proliferates a disparity of political cultures. At the same time, in the name of efficiency and rationality, it is a matter of creating conditions for a mode of expression that privileges homogeneity and attenuates differences. This quest is coherent with the fundamental goal of the assembly: to tackle questions in a spirit of harmonization.

Harmony and Differences

European institutions are in effect machines for harmonizing, for inventing procedures to reconcile legislative forms that arise from political histories and cultural approaches that are sometimes far removed from each other. The European "Union" would be only an empty word if it did not have the corollary and permanent practice of *negotiation*. I use this term deliberately to point out another singularity of European construction. It might be objected that this is not a diplomatic activity, in the classic sense, since Europe affirms itself as an already constituted community. In the effort to reconcile national legislations, Europe is in some ways only negotiating with itself. But this work proves indispensable to realize the eventual goal of harmonization. Forms of political action are constructed to privilege the search for compromise and to render increasingly obsolete traditional practice of regulated antagonism that previously characterized the parliamentary democracies of our old countries. More frequent recourse to expertise implies a profound transformation of the political universe in European arenas. Similarly, the imbrication between a democracy of compromise and diverse forms of lobbying characterizes the new community configuration.

In the parliament as in the commission, one can speak of a singular "culture" specific to the practitioners of Europe that mobilizes new kinds of *savoir-faire*, that incites people to adapt, even refashion, the dominant representations. Thus one sees the "common space of mediation" discussed by Pierre Muller, "an ensemble of networks that has produced its own language, its own codes, and its own operational modes."[6] Community actors live in a deterritorialized world; as an

Italian official explained to me, "due to living in Luxemburg, I have lost
the sense of my native language and when I go back there for vacations,
I no longer know how to make jokes." In constructing Europe, a new
identity is being created, signs of which may be perceived in the ways
of expressing and practicing the art of politics. The composite language
current in community bodies is significant of this. At the European
Commission, where the situation is simpler than in parliament since
the only two working languages are English and French (German is
rarely used), one witnesses a veritable condensation of the two idioms.[7]
In meetings, people slide from one to the other in the course of a sentence. "Eurospeak" or "franglais" engenders curious mixtures: *"on aura
recours à une démarche top down," "faut-il accepter l'opting out"*? Mixtures
of this kind occur daily. The lexicon of Volapuk grows all the time:
*"spill over," "méthode communautaire," "co-decision," "additivité," "complé-
mentarité," "subsidiarité," "comitologie," "juste retour."*[8]

The practitioners of Europe are so at ease with this jargon that they
forget the subtleties of their native languages. Here, too, there is a
strong element of cultural cohesion. Community language functions
as a sign of identity, not just as a vector of communication. At the same
time, insisting too much on the cultural identity of the functioning
of European politics and administration risks obscuring an essential
and paradoxical aspect of this "culture," which is to bear within itself
a constitutive and ineluctable pluralism. The European Parliament, as
we have seen, is the active manifestation of this pluralism. But in the
commission, too, under the homogeneous facade of a performative
administration, one discovers the coexistence of different administrative styles.[9] During their training in their countries of origin, civil servants have acquired methods and modes of evaluating others' work that
sometimes contrast with each other. French officials do not hesitate
to criticize the schematic and badly constructed notes written by the
British; inversely, the latter are ironic about the length and rhetorical
aspects of notes drawn up by their French colleagues.

In one of the offices I studied, a German official never stopped correcting, in the name of Germanic rigor, the notes transmitted by one
bureaucrat of Spanish origin writing in the English language, although
neither of them could boast of perfect mastery of that language. The
diversity of traditions, languages, and usages cannot disappear by magic
in the community melting pot. On the one hand, in life outside work,
Euro officials often cultivate a sociability that favors links among those
originating from the same country. On the other hand, in daily relations
at work, when tensions arise, as they do in any collective functioning,

they have a tendency to produce reactions that usually call on stereotypes. The kind of representations to which people resort in situations of conflict is rather limited, particularly to all the declensions of the well-known opposition between Northerners and Southerners: drinkers of beer versus drinkers of wine, chilliness versus warmth, rigorous versus easygoing. Similarly, protagonists drawn on the stock of received ideas attached to each nationality, whether about "the brilliant but hollow French," "the conscientious and hard-working Germans," "the disordered Greeks," the Spanish dubbed the "Prussians of the south," and so on. Stereotypes may become all the more redoubtable weapons because they refer to observable traits, even when they simplify reality outrageously. But the fact that everyone can use this weapon for his own purpose also generates disorder. Resorting to stereotypes works for confusion, increasing the possible orders of reference. Alterity is lodged at the very heart of identity: representation of the commission as unity is undermined by this emergence within it of a plurality of possible orders.

Occasionally agents are tempted to fall back on their respective cultural universes, especially in cases of conflict or when they feel they are not recognized at their true worth. Then the discourse of a superior in the hierarchy will appear not as the expression of the general norm but as a particular point of view. Stuck in his own cultural references, predetermined by a specific type of training, the superior could be reproached for not having "understood" what his subordinate wanted. Worse, he could be suspected of wanting to impose values and concepts that are the reflection of "his" culture. There is always the possibility of contesting the validity of a hierarchical injunction. Here we penetrate the world of the intercultural, where conceptual gaps, the coexistence of different value systems, may destabilize the norm of rationality underlying any bureaucratic enterprise. Rational organization may be imperiled by contact among cultures. Rather than producing the common identity in which the organization's culture would culminate, one sees a relativism that contrasts with a uniformity of procedures and with the stated project of increasing harmonization.

This tension between cultural singularities and the search for a "post national" unity[10] is characteristic of the community's politico-administrative system. At the commission as in parliament, the experience of deterritorialization simultaneously produces two contradictory tendencies: the first leads to creating a style of communication and action that is read with difficulty outside, since only an elite masters the indispensable codes and savoir faire and then it may identify itself

as truly bearing the European culture. The other tendency, equally
induced by the deterritorialization, is inversely characterized by reflex
and a reactivation of national belonging, feeding a relativist representation of the communitarian world. This dual movement reveals the
duality inhabited by the practitioners of Europe. They have to affirm
their autonomy of action in the face of other member states, but they
are constantly sent back to their national anchorage.

Anthropological Perspectives

This unprecedented experience is not always well understood by
citizens of Europe. Inasmuch as that the Brussels Commission presents
itself as a performative administration that plays a central role in
European affairs, it arouses some distrust. Read the criticism aimed at
"Eurocrats": esoteric Euro-language and Euro-texts seem opaque to
common mortals. At each important stage in the history of European
construction, the weight of the Brussels body has been challenged, for
example, during the debate aroused by ratification of the Maastricht
Treaty.[11] It seemed as if Euro-functionaries had got control of the
levers of command with the crazy ambition of bending reality to their
own norms. Perceived in this way, the new European actors might be
sorcerer's apprentices with a mechanism to crush cultural differences
in the name of an all powerful economy and market. This representation culminates in the stereotype of the Eurocrat that is so widespread
in public opinion. As partisan and partial as it may appear, it is symp-
tomatic, for it acknowledges the real gap existing between citizens and
those who are making Europe.

This gap relates not only to insufficient or inadequate communication, but also to the difficulty of apprehending the communitarian governance as a specific space where intercultural practice and the gestation
of an unprecedented politics are inextricably linked. To account for
this situation, a multidimensional analysis is indispensable: without it,
one runs the risk of being confined either to a culturalist perspective
(European construction as a problem of identity and communication)
or else of reasoning in purely political terms (about the stakes of power
and the democratic deficit in European construction). The interest of
an anthropological approach resides in its capacity to enlarge the field
and to articulate together and think about both the political order and
the cultural order as inseparable elements of the European puzzle. It is
not a matter of interpreting the establishment of political Europe as a

sort of Hegelian overcoming of national singularities. More prosaically, we are witnessing the difficult gestation of a logic of networks[12] where what matters are practices of negotiation and compromise, and where a dialectic between the communitarian and the identitarian permanently operates.

Anthropologists have studied in quite other contexts the contact between cultures; they have been especially interested in colonial situations where "acculturation" is the correlate of the domination exercised by Westerners. Acculturation may be translated into an "incorporation of foreign elements into the indigenous system," or inversely into a loss of identity corresponding to the adoption of the exogenous model.[13] Communitarian institutions offer the anthropologist an unprecedented terrain: the invention of Europe implies putting different national cultures into contact, but not in a way that relies on subordination: no one culture can claim to impose its hegemony on others. Moreover, cultural contact is inscribed in a voluntarist and concerted process: it is inseparable from a historic project. These two realizations highlight the specificity of the community's political configuration. This cultural universe of compromise conjugates unity with diversity, homogeny with difference, the universal with the relative. Here I have suggested a few speculations on this unprecedented conjuncture. It is up to the anthropologists to go farther in the study of this complex political society, its intercultural dynamics, and the tensions that shape it.

Notes

1. Marc Abélès. *La Vie quotidienne au Parlement européen*. Paris: Hachette, 1992.
2. Marc Abélès, Irène Bellier, and Maryon McDonald. *Approche anthropologique de la Commission Européenne,* miméo report, Brussels: European Commission, December 1993.
3. For an analysis of the original traits of the European system, cf. Stanley Hoffmann and Robert O. Keohane (eds.). *The New European Community: Decision making and Institutional Change.* Boulder, CO: Westview Press, 1991; Jean Louis Quermonne. *Le Système politique européen.* Paris: Montchrestien, 1993; William Wallace (ed.). *The Dynamics of European Integration,* London: Pinter, 1990.
4. On this theme, see Marc Abélès. "Virtual Europe," in Irène Bellier and Thomas M. Wilson (eds). *An Anthropology of the European Union: Building, Imagining and Experiencing the New Europe.* Oxford: Berg, 2000: 31–52.
5. The figures were collected between 1989 and 1995.
6. Pierre Muller. "La mutation des politiques publiques européennes." *Pouvoirs* 69; "Europe, de la Communauté à l'Union." Paris: Seuil, 1994: 63–74.
7. See the analysis by Irène Bellier, "Une culture de la Commission européenne?" in Yves Mény, Pierre Muller, and Jean Louis Quermonne (eds.). *Politiques publiques en Europe.* Paris: L'Harmattan, 1995: 49–60.

8. Philippe C. Schmitter gives a sample of the new political vocabulary in "Quelques alternatives pour le futur système politique européen et leurs implications pour les politiques publiques européennes," in Yves Mény, Pierre Muller, and Jean Louis Quermonne, *Politiques publiques en Europe*: 31–32.

9. Pascal Lamy. "Choses vues...d'Europe." *Esprit*, September 1991: 67–81.

10. Jean-Marc Ferry. "Pertinence du postnational." *Esprit*, September 1990: 80–90.

11. Dominique Wolton. *La Dernière utopie : Naissance de l'Europe démocratique*. Paris: Flammarion, 1993.

12. On this point, see Yves Mény, Pierre Muller, and Jean Louis Quermonne, *Politiques publiques en Europe*. See also Christian Lequesne. *Paris-Bruxelles: Comment se fait la politique européenne de la France*. Paris: Presses de la FNSP, 1993; Wolfgang Wessels. "Administrative Interaction," in William Wallace (ed.). *The Dynamics of European Integration*: 229–241.

13. Nathan Wachtel, "L'acculturation," in Jacques Le Goff and Pierre Nora (eds.) *Faire de l'histoire: Nouveaux problèmes*. Paris: Gallimard, 1974: 124–146.

CHAPTER TWO

Communication and Europe: From Multiculturalism to Cultural Cohabitation

DOMINIQUE WOLTON

The debate over multiculturalism that began twenty years ago in the United States has reached Europe, but with the risk of misinterpretation. For in effect, the conditions in which it has been discussed in North America do not have a lot to do with the way in which it should be posed here in Europe. Despite appearances, the arguments advanced across the Atlantic are scarcely useful for thinking through the same problem in Europe. Why? Because multiculturalism in the United States is made *within* a national community, defined with its frontiers, history, and sovereignty. There the question is: taking into account the *existence* of the United States, how should relations between cultures be organized? The European problem is the inverse: not how to preserve the diversity of cultures within a community, but first how to construct this community, this framework for them. The word "community" (correctly chosen since 1957) is in reality ahead of actual history. It expresses a voluntarism, a project, and designates more an intention than a reality. The prior problem is to manage to form, mark out, and identify this community—and make it live. The question of how identities cohabit inside this community does not come first, even if the two are linked. In reality, Europe is confronted with two simultaneous problems: to create a symbolic political space in which peoples can believe and to preserve their identities. In a certain way, to speak of multiculturalism presupposes that the problem is already resolved, whereas Europeans must invent resolutions for this problem; in the American experience, they do not easily find whatever help they often (in good faith) think they can use.

Europe and Communication at the Confluence of Three Different Problems

First, there is the political project that has been constant since the start of the Common Market, but has accelerated since Maastricht and the end of Communism: the construction of Europe. This is an immense gamble: to realize for the first time in human history, in a voluntary, democratic, and peaceful way, the largest democracy in the world, of 350 million people. And starting from long-standing peoples who were already governed by democratic regimes—and for a long time engaged in reciprocal conflicts! And meanwhile the two facts that used to justify this Pharaonic project have disappeared: the memory of world war and Communism. This ambition condenses both the will to conjure with history, and the desire to carry forward in an exemplary way the values of the Western democratic model to a scale never before attained.

Second, there is a profound sociological evolution, without any great relation with the first phenomenon, but which complicates it: the crumbling of great social structures, including social classes, the relation between city and country, the end of the rural and industrial living, and the breakdown and recomposition of the family. All this is taking place against the background of a profound movement to affirm individual freedom, of which feminism is one of the symbols. We have the emergence of what I call "the individualist mass society," characterized by these two contradictory and simultaneous dimensions: the assertion of the individual and the reality of a densely populated society with the emergence of mass democracy, as much on the sociological as political level. Within this evolution is located the movement of multiculturalism: society must organize (in a horizontal and not hierarchical way) the relations between cultures and communities. "Political correctness" is a reaction against this multiculturalism, even to the point of caricature, which is marked by a rigidifying of individual and inter-community relations. Political correctness is both the antithesis and the culmination of multiculturalism: the antithesis because it rejects it and the culmination because it encloses each community in its own identity, if not its own ghetto.

Third and finally, there is the explosion of technologies of communication. Appearing simultaneously with the social evolution centered on the individualization of social relations, they are seen to bring the necessary solution—that is to say, a communication solution for each community. The mass media for the greatest number of nonidentified consumers and segmented media for target groups, in phase with the most restricted communities, right down to the smallest scale, that of the individual. Isn't the "ideal" of communication in effect to bring to each person what he or she wants? Beyond the markets represented by communication, a sort of match seems to be established between a great political project, that is, Europe, which requires an increasing capacity for communication, and a social and cultural movement that on the contrary requires a matching with increasingly refined communications, right down to the individual relations.

The False Solution

From this situation to seeing the technologies of communication as the means of resolving two different and major problem—the construction of the symbolic space of Europe and the remedy for the crumbling of social relations consequent on the individualization of society—there is only one step, already taken by some. Communication technologies are claimed to be the solution to the dual issue of how to open up this new political space and how to animate the relations between culture and community. This false equation between using techniques of communication to construct Europe and the contradictions of individualist mass society assumes three aspects.

First, deregulation: since communication has become excessive, it is useless to keep regulatory and national barriers. The "user's freedom" is the best guarantee of regulation; individuals and groups in an open market know very well what they need to enter into relation with each other. The more the communication market is left fluid, the easier the match between communication needs and the technologies and services able to satisfy them. Even if in the short term this deregulation is, as always in history, favorable to the big ones, rather than the little ones.

The second aspect is a direct consequence of the preceding. It aims to play the card of communication on a European level. Opening borders as quickly as possible, favoring the creation of European television channels and media groups. In other words, finding in the very complete panoply of communication technologies the means of opening up borders and enlarging spheres of communication as a way of bringing European peoples, so long divided and separated, closer together.

The third aspect aims to couple new communication technologies and multiculturalism, that is to say, it presupposes a link between the increasing diversification of these technologies and the explosion of communities into multiple subgroups. The sought-for link would be the means of resolving the question of communication among communities and avoiding their closing in on themselves. The new communication technologies would permit multicultural communities both to express themselves and to remain in contact with each other. Technological fragmentation corresponds with societal fragmentation. Today we find this false solution in the valorization of two magical words of modernity: *network* and *community*. Thus everything that is community, and not society, is valorized like the idea of communication networks always appears preferable to the existence of mass media!

The network implies equality against hierarchy, and community implies free choice against the constraining nature of society. The meshing of communication in the form of networks constitutes the ideal infrastructure of relations among communities. And presto, the problem of multiculturalism is resolved!

The dual hypothesis of this correspondence between communication and multiculturalism is that (1) there is no hegemonic (or simply quarrelsome) dimension to multicultural demands and (2) there is no constraint on the functioning of these multimedia networks, either! In other words, there are no power relations between communities and no constraints on how communication networks function! This is a fallacy of peacefulness and lack of constraints, as if it were sufficient for the many communities and multiple medias to be matched up for conflicts to be resolved! Here is where a social ideology (community as utopia) and a technological ideology (technique as neutral tool) reinforce each other, creating a real risk of symbolic destabilization.

The Specificity of the European Problem

This idea of a correspondence between technology and a political project takes off alongside difficulties in constructing political space, in developing multimedia groups, and the proliferation of increasingly individualistic media. Alas, it is as false as finding in the construction of European public space a sequel to American multiculturalism! In reality, we are confronted with an anachronism. The historical context that gave rise to American multiculturalism has no direct relation with the problem posed today for Europe. In both cases, of course, the issue of relations among communities arises, but we cannot find in the American context some answer to the European problem. The principle of Europe's formation is far from being achieved, if only because in the last thirty years it has gone from six to twelve countries, and then fifteen—with twenty-seven on the horizon in 2007! Also the issue of cultural relations is not yet on the table. To speak of multiculturalism presupposes not only a principle of closure to the community, but also and equally the recognition and visibility of principles of the individuality of cultures. Moving too quickly past these two essential moments in the constitution of Europe—identification of a principle of closure and locating cultural identities and relations among them—risks leading to the impasses of the "supranational." This theme had a strong dynamic when there was no effective construction of Europe and the world was living according to the closed model—or at least in systematic noncommunication among cultural areas. But in a half century everything has changed. Practical construction has begun, immediately raising the problem of the role of cultural identities in this vast movement, as well as the opening of economies and societies to each other, thanks notably to the globalization of communication technology—all have changed the dominant model. Today the theme of "supranational" cannot have the same attraction or same meaning as it did a century ago. Moreover, a part of the world effectively became supranational; by starting to construct Europe's political and cultural space from an ineluctably supranational perspective, its authors discovered resistances from cultural identities. Passing from the ideal to reality, the principle of supranationality found its limits and difficulties, as we realize in rereading the very interesting writings of Denis de Rougemont, who was at that time one of the principal defenders of this model.

If the supranational model cannot resolve the essential question of multiculturalism for the future of Europe, the opposite solution of cutting territory up into regions as the correct basis for multiculturalism does not seem effective, either. First, because regions do not have the same status, the same history, or the same role in the various countries of the Union and also because what emerge as multiculturalist demands do not necessarily relate to regions. A region may be either too small or too vast, even if nobody denies that in most regions there is an essential component of multiculturalism. But regions and towns were constitutional units of multiculturalism within a closed European historical space, not identities corresponding to the current stakes of multiculturalism. Contrary to what is claimed today in favor of the region as an organizational basis for Europe, the region is probably not the unitarian principle of the new culturalism to be built. Although it was for a long time one of the essential cultural principles within a closed Europe defined by state sovereignty, that does not mean it will be so today! Not only because the world is more open, but also because there exists today a political project at work that, in trying to construct a political space whose area and characteristics outstrip the current superimposed regions, would completely upset the way of posing the problem. The role of the region will be easier to define once other identity principles truly able to structure European multiculturalism have emerged. In any case, it is often retrospectively that structuring principles appear. The realm of intercultural relations is one where political voluntarism most quickly finds its limits.

What do we find today within Europe? First, a common cultural space defined as much by religious traditions as by languages, history, economic trade, and common values. This common cultural space is obviously the prior condition for any European project, without which it could not take place, even if sustained by the memory of 100 million dead in two wars and the struggle against Communism. But this condition does not suffice to make a structuring principle of multiculturalism. There are plenty of public spaces linked to exchange of information, to cultural flow, but the obstacle of languages and history limit the force of this public space as an integrating principle. One does not move easily from the existence of public spaces to the existence of a public space—except perhaps for a tiny cultural minority that by its lifestyle and its presence in the media has a tendency to confuse its own situation with that of the great majority—and thus to generalize its own experience!

Finally, there is no political space due to the lack of common political stakes. Obviously, there are common political problems, but for the moment the 360 million Europeans have no *experience* of common debates, which is the precondition for the emergence of a political space.

Each time someone tries to find a concept able to characterize European multiculturalism, one falls into the same difficulty. The foundations of a multiculturalism are evident, visible on the ground, but they seem to evaporate each time one wants to be more specific about them.

As for communication, understood as the use of technologies to foster the expression of cultural identities and relations between them, it is not certain that in the current context, any structuring factor of multiculturalism can be seen.

Communication only plays its integrating role within nation-states or communities that are sufficiently constituted. If not, communication is not only insufficient to create a cultural dynamic, but it may even have a destabilizing effect. The existence of newspapers, radio stations, and television channels (even interactive ones) is not in itself sufficient to create movements of cultural exchange!

In any case, to play its role of exchange, communication presupposes that identities have been identified. There is no communication without relations between mutually recognized identities. And so we fall back on the problem of multiculturalism's presupposing a combination of such identities. This is precisely the difficulty confronted by nascent (or eventual) multiculturalism in Europe: what bases—language, history, symbols, values—distinguish mutually recognized identities, around which multiculturalism could be organized? In other words, to play on communication as a way of resolving the problem of European multiculturalism assumes that the problem is already solved! One always comes back to the point of departure: the multicultural problematic presumes two essential characteristics: a principle of closure and principles of identity. The whole difficulty of cultural Europe is that in an era of mass democracy, meaning of a more protean culture than that of the eighteenth- and nineteenth-century elites, these two principles currently have trouble emerging.

However, there is something to be done to recognize differences if one wants political Europe to succeed. If culture (in the wider sense) is obviously not the prime condition of the success of democratic Europe, over time it is probably one of its essential conditions. Beyond everything that separates Europeans, it is probably on the ground of common cultural values that the European project could popularly take root. But while Europeans can decide on common monetary, military, economic, and educational policies, they cannot do the same with culture, which in a certain way is the container, the precondition for all the other factors of European integration. The "structure" as much as the very "form" of Europe is at issue in this problematic of multiculturalism.

Directions for Research

If political voluntarism, communication technologies, and regional identities do not suffice to enable us to think about multiculturalism, what should we do, apart from waiting for events to establish multiculturalism concretely? Two simultaneous (and partly contradictory) movements can be envisaged.

The first is to locate and affirm cultural identities in all their forms. We may distrust identity movements, especially on the religious level, that often are transformed into a factor of exclusion. Irredentism and fundamentalism are increasingly considered as the result of identity movements that risk challenging the communitarian universalism on the basis of which the Western political model is conceived. Identity claims are most often considered as ambivalent and even dangerous, aiming in reality to move backward, whereas history by contrast translates into the overcoming of frontiers and identities. Thus we often hear an argument about where the project of democratic Europe would be if it aimed less to overcome or label cultures, if not enclose them in a static situation. As if a museum of "Popular Arts and Traditions" were Europe's sole ambition! The rebuttal appears radical. As much as identity is valorized on the individual level, so today it is suspect on the collective level. It remains to be seen if it is religious irredentism that creates this distrust, or whether the latter existed previously. This hypothesis should be contested for the two reasons already cited. Culture was first a phenomenon of opening and overcoming the identities of a closed universe. Today the situation is exactly the opposite: everything is open and in relation to everything else. Identity (especially cultural) is the condition for not getting carried away in the whirlpool of modernity and communication. The work of valorizing cultural identities is one of the best means of linking two essential characteristics of European anthropology, those of territory and frontier. Both have been violently upset by Europe's political project. Yet they are constitutive of our history over centuries, and it is difficult to believe that they are useless today. Thus identity is no longer a brake on openness and emancipation, but a means to avoid openness producing anomie. This reversal of the relation to identity from a cultural standpoint, valorizing it, is the first condition for this multiculturalism to emerge. A new landscape never appears out of nowhere, especially when it is a matter of bringing together very old peoples with rich and ancient cultures!

The second movement, quite the opposite, aims to foster work on political utopia. One of the greatest weaknesses of the current project is that it reproduces on a larger scale what exists within each nation-state; we find only institutions like a parliament, a court of justice, and an administration—not the stuff dreams are made on! How can you arouse the desire to create a new political space if there is not at least the perception of a rupture with the nation? European utopianism has consisted of believing in cooperation among nation-states; today it has broken down when it comes to inventing forms able to mobilize not the elites, but the general population. And utopianism in political thought is probably one of the most radical forms of cultural creation. Europeans are too timid about this, yet the movement of locating and valorizing cultural identities will not have a positive role to play in European multiculturalism unless at the same time this political utopianism emerges. If not, the danger is to slide from cultural identity to indifference toward the other, which is in large part the substratum of "political correctness." In the name of defending difference, the latter leads to enclosing people in clear-cut pockets.

We must not mistake the direction of this analysis. It is not the search for identities that kills political utopia and leads to withdrawal into communities, but the inverse. It is because utopianism has broken down that withdrawal is so strong. Political utopia is today largely giving way to the grip of the mode of economic and political rationality that dominates all reconstruction. This rationality is indispensable, but on condition of not being the sole instrument of European construction. And utopianism is all the more difficult to mobilize when it is not voluntarily decreed. Recent history has paid a sufficient price for everyone to be skeptical; it is understandable there is distrust about utopias. Yet it is this appeal to the imagination that will be the means of getting beyond the experience of political Europe simply as an institution and avoiding cultural policies turning identities in on themselves.

The difficulty comes from the necessity of doing both at the same time, and neither lends itself to voluntary and rational action! An example of utopian work is to find a word or concept able to account for the movement that is underway. Europe is not an empire, even if in its geographic area and the cohabitation of so many peoples make it resembles one. Today the word "empire" is forbidden in the dominant democratic culture, but two empires, the Austro-Hungarian and the Ottoman, are rich in history about intelligent organization: symbolic, political, cultural, and religious. Although democratic Europe cannot take direct inspiration from them, a little attentiveness to these two great political forms of the last four centuries proves how little Europeans are aware of the immense work to be done! To invent a democratic form on a large scale, at least one should analyze the qualities and limits of previous imperial and aristocratic forms.

Nor is Europe a nation. All its political organizations since the eighteenth century have been structured around the couple of nation-state (more or less bellicose). Democratic Europe is neither one nor the other, but least there should be theoretical work around the essential concepts of *territory* and *borders*. Technologies of communication have vanquished time and distance—they have apparently also vanquished space. Yet as communication shrinks the world, creating the false illusion of a "global village," the contrary ideas of territory and borders surge up again—more violently than peacefully. Europe is the corner of the world where people have decided to try to organize this new political space democratically. But space is not territory! How can you invent a new space if you don't take into account these two essential concepts, territory and borders, which are a means of overcoming the problematic of multiculturalism? The latter, in starting from the American example presupposes these issues have been resolved, but that is far from the case for Europe. Just think of ex-Yugoslavia.

Finally, Europe cannot be simply defined by the idea of citizenship referring back to France's Republican history, which is difficult to export to other countries—except perhaps by a symbolic *coup de force* (offensive action) that would not at all be assured of success!

This means that utopia, too, requires work on words to force the imagination while keeping history in mind. Rare are moments when peoples can innovate and try to invent other political forms, on condition that they at least have history in their dreams. Not to want to integrate it is to eschew a great ambition, underestimate the difficulty, and elaborate the new political form with an overly rationalist vision. The apparent movement of sociocultural differentiation that has been underway in Europe for a generation in the direction of reappropriating basic communities should not be viewed in the multiculturalist mode, or else its caricature, differentialism. For this amounts to fractioning, the opposite of unifying. Contrary to what some people think, basic communities will never be supplied by the panoply of communication technologies. Whatever their level of interactivity, these only link people on the basis of a preexisting political and social project. This is what is lacking in Europe. Technologies have never created any utopia, unless it is simply the technological paradise that disappears at the least blow from history. Today what can communication technologies do in ex-Yugoslavia or in the Balkans in general? Everybody knew everything, and yet this did not prevent the folly of history.

Conclusion

Multiculturalism is probably one of the keys to success or failure of the European project—with the difficulty that it is a totally unprecedented situation in the history of humanity. Cultural differences are just as much one of the strengths of Europe as one of the principal causes of the project's failure. Although it is possible to make a voluntarist policy in the domains of economics, military defense, and science, these forms of social experience are more malleable than culture. Especially if people say every day that it is the grand chance for Europe! The question of multiculturalism is posed in different terms from the European political project, for it has always existed in history, through wars, conflicts, trade—a de facto multiculturalism. But there is no central role that it can play tomorrow as the condition of the success of political democracy in Europe. Culture is not in itself linked to Europe, but to the ensemble of social and cultural changes that have been produced over a century, specifically the dual contradictory movement of the individualist mass society discussed earlier: valorization of the individual, hence of difference, and the constraint of the greatest number, linked to universal suffrage.

   It is the democratic nature of the European political project that obliges us to reopen the issue of the role of culture. If this were an aristocratic political project, the problem would have been much simpler. In effect, since the seventeenth (or perhaps the eighteenth) century, a form of "European culture" has existed, linked to elites. Today the difficulty is not to organize the multiculturalism of elites but to organize it on the scale of the greatest number! Thus it is its character as mass democracy that obliges Europe to postpone *without immediate solution* the question of culture's role in the construction of this symbolic edifice. To mark the awareness of the immense complexity of this situation, it is preferable to speak of *cultural cohabitation* rather than of *multiculturalism*. The former is more modest, and it reminds us that the relation between cultural forms is by no means resolved. This word also has the advantage of a certain dynamism, for "cohabiting" assumes permanent adjustments, hence an open situation, whereas the idea of multiculturalism connotes a successful organization of intercultural relations. To cohabit assumes that neither the problem of identity nor that of managing differences are resolved and that it is not an option to turn to miracle words like "community," "region," or "communications." Yesterday Europe was organized on an aristocratic mode, more often warlike than pacific, of multiculturalism. The opening of the building site of democratic Europe obliges to totally rethink the problem in a short time, keeping all the contradictions in sight. If speaking of cultural *cohabitation* does not in itself resolve this aporia, at least it has the advantage of recalling, contrary to *multiculturalism*, that everything is to be done. And on another scale than yesterday's innumerable yet misleading references to "multicultural Europe."

Bibliography

Badie, Bertrand. 1995. *La fin des territoires*. Paris: Fayard.

Banniard, Michel. 1989. *Génèse culturelle de l'Europe*. Paris: Seuil-Point.

Barber, Benjamin. 1993. *L'expérience et l'égalité*. Paris: Belin.

Bibo, István. 1993. *Misères de petits Etats de l'Europe de l'Est*. Paris: Albin Michel.

Corm, Georges. 1989. *L'Europe et l'Orient: De la balkanisation à la libanisation. Histoire d'une modernité inaccomplie*. Paris: La Découverte.

Débat (special issue) *Nation: entre le dépassement et reviviscence*, n°84, March–April 1995. (See articles by Coqueret, Guiomar, Luthy, Mann, and Paqueteau).

Duroselle, Jean-Baptiste. 1990. *Europe: A History of Its Peoples*. Translated by Richard Mayne. New York: Viking.

Elias, Norbert. 2001. *The Society of Individuals*. Edited by Michael Schröter. Translated by Edmund Jephcott. New York: Continuum.

Esprit (special issue) *Le spectre du multiculturalisme américain*, June 1995. (See articles by Barber, Feher, Todorov, and Walzev).

Foucher, Michel. 1995. *The New Faces of Europe*. Strasbourg: Council of Europe Press.

Foucher, Michel and Potel, Jean Yves (eds.). 1993. *Le continent retrouvé*. Paris: Ed de l'Aube.

Hermes no. 8/9, 1990: *Frontières en mouvement*. Paris: Ed. du CNRS.

Hermes no. 10, 1991: *Espaces publics, tradition et communautés*. Paris: Ed. du CNRS.

Labasse, Jean. 1991. *L'Europe des régions*. Paris: Flammarion.

Magris, Claudio. 1985. *Danube*. Translated from the Italian by Patrick Creagh. London: Collins Harvill.

Meyer-Bisch, Patrice. 1993. *Les droits culturels. Une catégorie sous-développée des droits de l'Homme*. Fribourg, Switzerland: Ed de l'Université de Fribourg.

Poupard, Paul (Cardinal). 1994. *The Church and Culture: Challenge and Confrontation: Inculturation and Evangelization*. Translated by John H. Miller. St. Louis, MO: Central Bureau, CCVA.

Segalen, Martine (ed.) 1989. *L'Autre et le Semblable: regards sur l'ethnologie des sociétés contemporaines.* Paris: Ed. du CNRS.

Taylor, Charles. 1994. *Multiculturalism: Examining the Politics of Recognition.* Princeton, NJ: Princeton University Press.

Thual, François. 1994. *Géopolitique de l'orthodoxie.* Paris: Dunod.

————. 1995. *Les Conflits identitaires.* Paris: Ed. Marketing.

Touraine, Marisol. 1995. *Le bouleversement du monde: le géopolitique du XXI siècle.* Paris: Seuil.

Wolton, Dominique. 1993. *La dernière utopie: Naissance de l'Europe démocratique.* Paris: Flammarion.

CHAPTER THREE

Against Euroculture

YVES HERSANT

The word "culture" seems to flow from everybody's lips these days—even those of civil servants who are nastily referred to as Eurocrats. No doubt we should be glad that the new builders of Europe, unlike the founding fathers, seem to reserve an evergrowing place for the "cultural"; so much the better if they discover problems other than customs, borders other than policy ones. It is better if they pay more attention to the great common situations that, to use terms of Milan Kundera, "gather people together and always regroup them differently, inside imaginary and always changing borders, where the same memory, the same experience, the same community of tradition all subsist."[1] But we must resist intellectual comforts, like the temptations of propaganda. We are submerged in conventional statements, soothing declarations, incantatory speeches; and we must really wonder if European culture does not have much to dread from those who proclaim themselves its defenders.

With variable zeal, no doubt, all the peoples of the Old World have taken up the study of their spiritual geography in Husserl's expression. Attached as they are to a "special something" that is "almost nothing," aware of a Europeanness that they designate in turn as an idea or as a spirit, as civilization or as culture, it is a paradoxical specificity, both individual and collective, that they are trying more than ever to grasp. A hard task, especially when people claim to assume it inside the continent; it might be more tempting to "think Europe" in geographical or historical, socioeconomic, or scientific terms. Especially since in seeking the unity of one's culture, one discovers its variety; wanting to objectify it, one only manages to dissolve it; any assertion about it may turn into its contrary. From Julien Benda to Edgar Morin, from Valéry to Derrida—to mention only the French who are relatively close to us—many intellectuals have noticed the evanescence of the notion. Nevertheless, however difficult clear and distinct analysis may appear, at least the enterprise does not seem impossible. European culture is today a major theme of reflection, a "common place," in the strong sense. A space explored tirelessly by newspapers and publishing, as much by the universities as museums; and a terrain where even politicians, formerly so skittish, no longer fear to tread. The community of values, in polyglot dissertations, becomes an obligatory reference. Why? Either because the words "Europe" and "culture," employed in an equally vague way, are easy to bracket together; or because political uncertainties, like economic problems, incite us to seek refuge in "values of the spirit"; or else that people take pleasure, to better repel Marxism, in locating the real infrastructure in what is cultural—whatever the case, within political parties as in community bodies, there is no longer any debate about Europe that does not invoke its culture, nor any cultural project without a European dimension.

A Small Historical Reminder

In this sense, the wish of the delegates to the Congress in The Hague in 1948 seems partially realized. From "summits" to "Bluebooks," from informal meetings to conferences, "cultural" initiatives have spectacularly increased—even if precautions remain numerous, as required by the susceptibilities of partners and by respect for the Treaty of Rome. Cooperation develops, legislations get harmonized.[2] Despite recurrent worries over national disparities—the centralism of France, the federalism of Germany, the cultural liberalism of the British or Danes—a quantity of measures have been taken and innumerable recommendations adopted, which tend to facilitate exchanges: the free circulation or works of art, aid for translation, struggle against audiovisual piracy, support for the culture industries, and so on. Thus, under the impetus of "Eurocrats," an Eurocultural activity is developing whose merits cannot be denied—but it is good to challenge the ideology underlying it. For in transforming itself into Euroculture, European culture is threatened with decline. In the official rhetoric, its principal function is to fabricate consensus; the more bitter the debates on the price of butter or mutton, the more comforting it is to agree on grand but hollow notions. It is precisely this vacuity that calls for vigilance, much more so than the striking contrast between ambitions and means. It is not in euros that the stakes are measured, and poverty is revealed less in the budget than in the actual practices.

The evolution of these practices, since the signing of the Treaty of Rome, has taken place in three stages. From 1957 to about 1973, the European Community did not perceive or describe itself as a cultural entity; supposed to arise from politics, culture remained the affair of nation-states, who jealously guard it; it was up to each to defend its wealth, linguistic or artistic, philosophical or scientific. After 1968, on the contrary, another conception prevailed: "Europe is not only industrialists, cultivators, and technocrats"; the new themes of "social Europe" and "regional Europe," no less than the difficulties of economic cooperation, favored the emergence of culture among community preoccupations. Witness the adoption at the Copenhagen Summit of 1973 of a Declaration on European Identity: an identity defined by "attachment to common values and principles," by the "rapprochement of conceptions of living," by the "consciousness of possessing specific interests in common." In the minds of the signatories, it was to preserve itself both as civilization and as culture that Europe should be constructed; defending the patrimony, even outside national frameworks, became a mission of salvation. There has been a noble valorization of the cultural, but in practice, it has allowed the member-states, incapable of agreeing on other plans, to dissimulate their dissension. Culture, without disengaging in the slightest from the tutelage of politics, becomes a sector of the economy.[3] Then, presented at summits as the very soul of Europe, culture appears to the commission as a market to be developed. This is a contradiction that a new Declaration in 1983 in Stuttgart wanted to resolve: the principle of cultural cooperation, which has remained in force ever since, gives a communitarian allure to agreements concluded by states. Without shaking up national frameworks, it respects the great theme of identity, especially since cultural cooperation invites treating as a "space" what had been only "sectoral." Along comes the time of "networks": Euroculture is conceived on the model of circulation and exchange, and henceforth the Union's programs function on that basis. For example, there is Erasmus, a program of university exchanges whose bureaucratic ponderousness does not seem to harm its success.

Sometimes a stake in competition between states, sometimes an economic sector ripe for development, sometimes a simple flow of exchanges to be managed more or less well: Euroculture is always a reduction of European culture. Today more than ever, its promoters are confronted with formidable contradictions: it is through culture that they legitimize the unification of the Continent, but on bringing the commerce of minds down to the commercial level, they confine their designs to creating a grand market. Although they are always inclined to vaunt the diversity of the "patrimony," the search for consensus pushes them to reject differences (to take only one example, the Iberian corrida is not at all prized by the people of Brussels). Finally, they never stop invoking the culture of all of Europe, but de facto they privilege that of a Western minority. That their activity is not exempt from hegemonic temptations is suggested by actual events: in the dialogue with the East as conducted by so many good apostles, the reminder of common values is only an arrogant call to order. "The Community, by its dynamism and its influence, is the European entity to which the countries of Central and Eastern Europe now refer, wishing to maintain close links with it"; or else "In this period of profound and rapid changes, the Community constitutes and must remain a pole of reference and influence. It is the cornerstone of a new European architecture and, in its wish for openness, an anchor pier for a future European equilibrium."[4] What does this rhetoric of "influence (*rayonnement*)" express if not a refusal to listen to the other? In point of fact, the East once invited us to question our certainties; voices were raised on that side, whose skeptical tones contrasted sharply with the optimism of our officials. "I believe," wrote Vaclav Havel in the era of his dissidence, "that regarding its relations with totalitarian systems, the biggest mistake that Western Europe might commit is the one that threatens it most: not understanding them as they are in the last analysis, that is to say, as a magnifying mirror of modern civilization as a whole and an urgent invitation—perhaps the last one—to a general revision in the way this civilization conceives of itself."[5]

European Mythology

Thus we see two great cultural options take shape. Henceforth a choice must be made: either culture as love of self, as lyrical exaltation of the European genius, or else culture as critique and as radical questioning.

Adopting the first option means accepting as such a myth that Europeans have forged for themselves. As they correctly repeat, the Old Continent is the home of an exceptional civilization, to which the world owes democracy and reason, science and humanism; in its crucible was formed a happy synthesis between Jewish and Christian, Greco-Latin and Germanic traditions; the pantheon of its artists, the achievements of its thinkers, are unequalled on the planet. Cervantes and Shakespeare, Descartes and Kant, Vermeer and Chopin, are glorious items in a bottomless fund of culture that people do not fear overexploiting (on the lines of "Mozart Year") and may be shown to all humanity as an example. European culture inscribes the universal in the singular (a secular universalism which it alone has invented). Moreover, in Edgar Morin's expression, it has "Europeanized the globe and globalized Europeanism,"[6] not only because its states dominated the planet for centuries, but also because those who were dominated, to liberate themselves from its tutelage, had to adopt its concepts. So Europe fulfilled, even in its decolonization, the civilizing mission that had long before been assigned to it by Leibniz and by Vico.

Choosing the second option by having a more demanding conception of culture is not to refuse the grand founding myth as a whole, but to try to strip it of the mystifications that accompany it. For if the myth does speak true in its own way, it also lies by omission. It evacuates from our culture the intimate contradictions that cut through it, the antagonisms that tear it, the immense role of the negative, and critical and ironic thought (essential to the "patrimony": no European culture without perpetual questioning of the conditions of knowledge, without shaking every limit). In parallel, the legend censures the folly that has been deployed in our history: from Europe has issued people's freedom and rights, but also genocides, frenzies of racism, and the worst enemies of humankind. The European heritage includes the perverse effects of reason, subservience to technology, and totalitarian abuses. To quote Edgar Morin again:

> In Europe has been concocted the mixture of barbarism, technicity, and science that spreads in our planetary iron age.... Totalitarianism is a European invention three times over. Nuclear extermination itself, although American by birth, is of European genealogy, and it is the genial European pacifist, Albert Einstein, who urged the President of the United States to make the first atomic bomb. Thus what Europe has produced that is most original is today universalized for better or worse. Reason has spread in the form of critical rationality, in the form of rationalization in the service of myths, and in the form of instrumental rationality in the service of barbarisms. Humanism has spread, and has been

able to introduce human rights in many places, but it has also lent
its name again to the oppression of people.[7]

If one wants to pose as heir, it is necessary to assume the whole heritage.
To simplify this complex past is not the best means of constructing
Europe; a European education cannot be founded on forgetting this
history, which on the contrary should be meditated on—not to enter-
tain a sterilizing guilt, but to maintain an always lively and responsible
memory and to sharpen awareness of the ambivalences of our *logos*.

To refuse the comfort of myth, of the simplified representation that
our culture gives of itself, one has to perceive it as paradoxically one
and plural. It is historically one because the peoples of Europe have
shared the same regulating principles (freedom of thought, pure pursuit
of knowledge, theoretical ambition to overtake the finite), the same
intellectual movements (Christianity, humanism, rationalism), the same
conceptual categories (particular/universal, faith/reason, individual/
collective, etc.). And it is sociologically one because today more than
ever the European fabric is homogeneous: the development of middle
classes, the economic level, freedom of expression, relative social protection, and quality of life all appear to be factors in the reduction of
differences. Europeans, moreover, have in common the same problems, including drugs and unemployment, the crisis in the state and
the integration of immigrants; among the youngest, the way of life
is becoming uniform; and in its relations with the rest of the world,
it even happens that Europe expresses itself with a single voice. This
well-known evolution seems to force the conclusion that "the countries of the European Community are definitively following the route
to unity...they will soon have a common history, made of the same
experiences (positive or negative), lived with the same interests and the
same expectations."[8]

Arguments supporting the contrary thesis are no less strong; European
cultural life is played on quite different levels. It is easy to prove that
the great transnational cultures (Latin, Slavic, or Germanic) are not
interchangeable; that the very diversity of languages differentiates the
traditions of each nation; that particularism flourishes everywhere as
precious residues in our provinces of the great work of history. Each
country, each region can claim to be exceptional; in fact, the gap is
more marked between Spain and Denmark, or between Alsace and
the Limousin, than between California and Illinois. The diversity of
customs, of local knowledge and folklores make the Old Continent
appear a mosaic of microspaces. In becoming aware of this variety that

enriches their patrimony, Europeans surely risk yielding to a narrow form of chauvinism or to a cultural relativism that places handicrafts on the same level as cathedrals. At least by affirming their polyculture, they would be better equipped to resist the leveling technicism and the standardization that threaten them. And they also now threaten the countries of Central Europe. As Philip Roth told Ivan Klima in 1990: "As Czechoslovakia becomes a free and democratic consumer society, you writers are going to find yourselves assailed by a lot of new adversaries—from which, rather strangely, repressive and sterile totalitarianism had protected you. Particularly dangerous will be the adversary who is the sworn, omnipresent, and all-powerful enemy of literature, literacy, and language. I can guarantee that no rebellious crowd will ever gather in Wenceslas Square to overthrow its tyranny. I am speaking of that universal vulgarizer, commercial television."[9]

Today it is no longer a matter of asking whether Europe is one or multiple, but of learning to think of it as simultaneously plural and one (in this respect, the defunct Republic of Letters is rich in lessons to teach). It is in the nonidentical that its identity is discovered; shot through with otherness, it should remain open and multiform. In which case, among the consequences would be a duty to resist any simplification of a culture whose complexity constitutes its value. Particularly suspect in this respect are:

- Nation-states, when in the name of defending "their" language they transform it into a stake in fierce competition. It would be better to spread the idea that the European citizen is a polyglot and give each person the means effectively to become so.

- The culture industries, which the opening of markets to the East makes people so hungry for, and whose marketing imperatives lead to a standardizing of their products. (Intellectuals, journalists, and teachers are exposed to similar temptations.)

- The power of television, relayed or not by satellite, that imposes its mold on millions of Europeans. An example has been "Sky Channel" broadcasting generalist fare (in English, with the same entertainment shows and the same advertisements), indistinctly beamed at Italians as at Danes. Other more effective cable strategies diversify programs according to national demands, Europeanizing only the financing. These transborder apparatuses should worry us on several counts; imposing moral or aesthetic norms, reducing the level of intelligibility ("dumbing down"), subjecting all discourse to the needs of efficient and immediate communication. Their prime objective is the search for audience ratings and commercial profitability; rather than a modern agora where they might exchange ideas, they demagogically establish sites of facile consensus.

It is not a matter of contesting the major media conglomerates, nor the culture industries, which have had a very positive role in the democratic process. On the contrary, it is a matter of making sure they do not arrogate an exclusive cultural power to themselves, by everywhere imposing the same norms and same models of discourse. Hence there is a double and contradictory necessity, as Jacques Derrida remarked, to avoid both dividing culture up into parcels (intellectual provincialism, particularist withdrawal) and the homogenizing of culture by an authoritarian centralism. We must refuse standardized culture, but "without cultivating for their own sakes minority differences, untranslatable idiolects, nationalist antagonisms, chauvinism about idiom."[10]

Critical Proposals

But it is time to stress that the "defenders of culture" are not all defending the same thing, and the terms they use lend themselves to many equivocations.

For example, many experts follow an Anglo-German tradition and designate under the term "culture(s)" practices and tastes, behavior and lifestyles that singularize social groups and make their particular genius. In the Latin tradition, by contrast, the same word designates what "civilization" means for the Germans: an ensemble of values, able to be generalized and exported, that may be communicated from one people to another in the name of universal reason. This distinction cuts across another, which it would be wrong to think of as academic: rather loosely defined as everything that is transmitted socially, the cultural is the opposite of the natural. Meanwhile, appreciated from the double viewpoint of aesthetics and ethics, culture is opposed to barbarity. This is why there have been so many misunderstandings in the East-West dialogue: in the West, "cultures are considered in the plural, and their equal dignity is proved by their equal complexity, whereas over there culture is being defended in the singular. [...] So-called Eastern Europe believes that beauty exists, that there are aesthetic judgments, and that this is natural."[11] To increase even more the various risks of quid pro quo, Europeans varyingly refer, more or less explicitly, to three conceptions of the cultural, whose coexistence is difficult. Thus we should distinguish among:

- A patrimonial model, which we may call that because it assimilates culture to hereditary wealth. Composed of monuments and documents that must be preserved, it constitutes a patrimony that is received and bequeathed; as the metaphor suggests, it relates less to being than to having. Quantifiable and measurable, the domain of the cultural requires a policy that ensures its integrity; fearing innovation, whether internal or foreign, this system refuses dialectic as a factor of change.

- A biological model, implying that culture functions like an organism. It is "cultural life" that people speak of, and they admit that it evolves; endogenous or exogenous, the system tolerates variations, as long as they do not threaten its health.

- A dialogic model, illustrated by Edgar Morin in *Penser l'Europe*.[12] Under this stark lighting, our culture is defined as an incessant confrontation between antagonistic currents: "It is interactions between peoples, cultures, classes, and states that has woven a unity that is itself plural and contradictory." In itself as in its relations with the world, European culture puts to work a dialectic, a wish for dialogue, a radical self-negation that prevents conceiving of it as a stable and fixed reality; far from being presented as an accumulation of values, it must now be described as a perpetual "whirlpool," a "tumultuous worksite"—unless you prefer Morin's metaphoric pun: "the *bouillon* [mixture] of European culture was and still is a *brouillon* [rough draft]."

It seems that the first of these models is preferred by the civil servants of culture; the second by a majority of citizens; the third, by a minority of intellectuals. For the latter, our cultural situation cannot be presented either in simple terms or lived in comfort. Because in truth, Europe has always been a *problem*.

Even and first of all in the etymological sense—promontory, projection, advanced—this is the first meaning Greek gives to *problema*. Before signifying what is "pro-posed" to controversy, what one puts under discussion, the word designates what is thrown before oneself, what is launched and juts out. The advanced point of a continent, it is already in its geographical position that Europe seems to have inscribed its intellectual project.

Problematic, we know how it also has been so historically, and how difficult was the emergence of the European idea. To mention only the recent past, it took two world wars and the ruin of the Old World for a communitarian project to be reborn; it would take grave external threats, strong pressure from the economy, a laborious decolonization, to convert to Europeanism many intellectuals who had been until then traumatized by the Nazi aberrations of "new Europe," or too dazzled by Communism to adhere to a community of another kind. And no doubt it will take new upheavals for the peoples concerned to lift the obstacles to their union.

Europe is never only a project, nor is problematization the essential trait of its culture. If in each era it is inventing, and in prodigious quantity, new ideas and new signs, new theories and new forms, it is to contest the following era and the principles that founded it. In the Renaissance, it dislodged the intellectual unity of the Middle Ages; separating faith from reason, mankind from nature and from the divine, it invented modern science and humanism; but the following centuries were charged with shaking those foundations. Science believed it was able to establish its theories on observation and experiments, reason was high on certitude and logic, humanism was persuaded that man might order the whole universe; but these hopes and these principles, contested in turn, soon yielded to others.

Perhaps we should define European culture, what is most precious about it, as a horror of dogmatic slumber, as the capacity to not persevere in eternal certainty, as the refusal to "accept any achieved identity," as Kolakowski said, adding: "The aptitude to put oneself in question, to abandon (not without strong resistance, of course) one's own fatuousness, is at the source of Europe as a spiritual force."[13] Thus Europe would never be Europe so much as when it is not closed in on itself, when it knows how to put itself in perspective: that is to say, to confront its own conceptions with those of other times and other cultures. To come to some problems of the present, from that result two consequences and one doubt.

The first consequence is that if European culture is characterized by openness, by noncoincidence with itself, it has much to fear from technicist rationalism. Nothing is more contrary to the skeptical spirit than a kind of thought reduced to calculation. Until now, Europe has not ceased oscillating between two rational modes: between the idea of a universal science and the play of irony, between mastery of the real and the desire to evade it. Today we see only too well where the preference lies. Our discourse is regulated by the scientific model, over which our universities labor, on which our very leisure is organized. Everywhere the serious and the logic of the marketplace reign; being is conceived as production. Culture is administered according to an economic rationality that measures its profits; this is how the experts triumph. Nobody doubts that Europe needs a growing number of engineers, but if it must conserve one of the specificities of its culture, it must also be careful about maintaining the tradition of self-criticism—at the risk, as Granel brutally says, of an "American end to Europe, a metaphysico-scientistic end to logic, a total extinction in our foreseeable future of the glimmer where the clarity of Greek daylight still used to shine."[14]

The second consequence is that if Europe is characterized culturally by the aptitude to integrate what it is not (and to make other what it is), it must remain open to what is not and will never be Europe. In this respect, the inadequate teaching of languages, intellectual nationalism, and resistance to translation may prove no less disastrous than political measures dictated by xenophobia. Although Europe has renounced imposing on the world the supreme norms of humanity, while it has abandoned any pretension to posing as the centre of the universe, it is still well placed to contribute something by "dialogical" exchanges to the free spreading of cultures.

Finally, the doubt: but what if it is already too late? If the constant reference to culture, its constant invocation (in fifteen years, we have gone from everything-is-political to everything-is-cultural; the political question of meaning cedes to the cultural question of the sign) being precisely the mark of a culture in anguish. Perhaps this doubt is tonic. Nobody expresses it better than Milan Kundera in this historical summary (*The Art of the Novel*):

> In the Middle Ages, European unity rested on the common religion. In the Modern Era, religion yielded its position to culture (to cultural creation), which came to embody the supreme values by which Europeans recognized themselves, defined and identified themselves. Now in our own time, culture is in turn yielding its position. But to what and to whom? What sphere will provide the sort of the supreme values that could unify Europe? Technology? The marketplace? Politics involving the democratic ideal, the principle of tolerance? But if that tolerance no longer has any rich creativity or any powerful thought to protect, will it not become empty and useless? Or can we take culture's abdication as

a kind of deliverance, to be welcomed euphorically? I don't know. I merely believe I know that culture has already yielded. And thus the image of European unity slips away into the past. European: one who is nostalgic for Europe.[15]

Notes

1. Milan Kundera. "Un Occident kidnappé, ou la tragédie de l'Europe centrale." *Le Débat* 27, November 1983: 14.
2. For a survey of this subject, see the analysis by Anne-Sophie Perriaux. *Revue de synthèse* 3, July–September 1990.
3. For example, Simone Weil's remark: "One can think that in the course of the decades to come, it is in the cultural sector that the most jobs will be created."
4. December 1989.
5. Speech given in 1984, partially quoted by Lionel Jospin. Text available at: http://www.vie-publique.fr/cdp/983002978.html (accessed on April 14, 2008).
6. Edgar Morin. *Penser l'Europe*. Paris: Gallimard, 1990 [1987]: 143.
7. Morin. *Penser l'Europe*: 143–144.
8. Sergio Romano, "Le poids de l'histoire," in Dominique Schnapper and H. Mendras, (eds.) *Six manières d'être européen*. Paris: Gallimard, 1990.
9. *Conversation à Prague*, Paris, 1990.
10. Jacques Derrida, "L'autre cap," Liber/Le Monde, n°5, 1990. A fuller version was published under the same title by Editions de Minuit in 1991.
11. *Le Messager européen*, n°4, 1990.
12. Morin. *Penser l'Europe*: 143.
13. Leszek Kolakowski. *Le Village introuvable*. Paris: Complexe, 1989.
14. Quoted by Michèle Gendreau-Massaloux, "Un lieu philosophique," http://www.iisf.it/francese/unesco.pdf (accessed on April 14, 2008).
15. Kundera, Milan. *The Art of the Novel*. New York: Grove Press, 1988: 127–128.

PART 2

Juridical Production of European Multiculturalism

CHAPTER FOUR

Fundamental Rights and Fundamental Boundaries: Common Standards and Conflicting Values in the Protection of Human Rights in the European Legal Space*

JOSEPH H. H. WEILER

Introduction: Fundamental Rights and Fundamental Boundaries

No area of "legal production" better illustrates the themes of uniformity and diversity and of European multiculturalism than the area of judicial protection against violation of fundamental human rights.[1] It is an area of "legal production" par excellence since in this area, since the treaties were silent, it was the court of justice that constructed the entire legal architecture. Thus it is an illustration of how legal actors, with little guidance from political sources, have tried to grapple with the issues of diverse cultural norms.

The classical vision regards a commitment to fundamental human rights as a unifying ideal, one of the core values around which the people and peoples of Europe may coalesce. When the court, in the very well-known story, held itself out as the guarantor of fundamental human rights in the field of community law, it was, on this view, merely giving judicial expression (and teeth!) to that core value.

But judicial protection of fundamental human rights by the European Court of Justice (ECJ) may operate as a source of both unity and

*The two articles by Joseph H. H. Weiler were originally published before the most recent constitutional developments in the legal order of the European Union. We have decided to retain them because of their theoretical and philosophical importance which transcends the specificity of the positive law on which they are based.

74 Joseph H. H. Weiler

disunity in the dialectical process of European integration. It is worth focusing on its "disintegrative" effect.

First, and this goes to the heart of this chapter, beyond a certain core, reflected in Europe by the European Convention of Human Rights (ECHR), the definition of fundamental human rights often differs from polity to polity. These differences, I will argue, reflect fundamental societal choices and form an important part in the different identities of polities and societies. They are often that part of social identity about which people care a great deal. What menu and flavor of human rights are chosen in the community context matters and can become a source of tension even absent direct conflict of norms. The choice of human rights is about the choice of fundamental values so the stakes are rather high. In the first part of this chapter, I shall explore these situations of conflict and tension and, from a distance, try and explain how the ECJ has attempted to mediate the tensions and blunt the conflicts.

Second, judicial review of community measures but especially member state measures can be seen, and have been seen, as part of a relentless and highly problematic extension of Union jurisdiction into areas of social regulation that are, or ought to be, the prerogative of the member states. I will deal, in some detail, with this extension of jurisdiction and its roots.

I should clarify that my focus is not on the problems that result from the fact that it is judge made law—an issue with which I have dealt elsewhere. I am concerned with the meeting of European rights with national rights. In this chapter, I shall remain firmly within the liberal rights paradigm leaving for another occasion the rights-critique apparatus.

Before turning to the actual jurisprudence, I will explore a little deeper the notion of human rights as societal values and their potential for conflict in the European architecture.

Modern liberal states, taking their cue principally from the American rather than British democratic tradition, increasingly acknowledge a higher law—typically a constitution, and in more recent time, international treaties—which bind even the legislature of the state. In an increasing number of modern democracies the higher law is backed up by courts and a system of judicial review that give it, so to speak, teeth. Within this constitutional ethos judicial protection of fundamental human rights has a central place. Constitutionalism, despite its counter-majoritarian effect is regarded as a complimentary principle to majoritarianism rather than its negation. One formulation that describes the complex relationship between the two is the notion of protection against a tyranny of the majority—seemingly an oxymoron. I think the appeal of rights has to do with two roots. The first of these two roots regards fundamental rights (and liberties) as an expression of a vision of humanity that vests the deepest values in the individual that, hence, may not be compromised by anyone. Probably one of the oldest and most influential sources of this vision is to be found in the Pentateuch: *And God created man in His own image, in the image of God created He him* (Genesis 1:27). With this trademark, what legislator has the authority to transgress the essential humanity of the species? Naturally, there are secular, humanist parallels to this vision a plenty.

The other root for the great appeal of rights and part of the justification even if countermajoritarian looks to them as an instrument for the promotion of the per se value of putting constraints on power. Modern democracy emerges, after all, also as a rejection of absolutism—and absolutism is not the prerogative of kings and emperors. Similar sentiments inform the great appeal of fundamental boundaries in nonunitary systems such as federal states and the European Union (EU). I use the term Fundamental Boundaries as a metaphor for the principle of enumerated powers or limited competences that are designed to guarantee that in certain areas communities (rather than individuals) should be free to make their own social choices without interference from above. If you wish, if fundamental rights are about the autonomy and self-determination of the individual, fundamental boundaries are about the autonomy and self-determination of communities. The appeal of fundamental boundaries rests as well on two parallel roots. First as an expression of a vision of humanity which vests the deepest values in communities (potentially existing within larger polities) that, thus, must be protected. This community vision of humanity derives from an acknowledgment of the social nature of humankind, as a counterbalance to the atomistic view of the individual that is reflected in the concept of individual rights and liberties. It too finds a powerful Biblical expression in the Pentateuch: *And the Lord God said: It is not good that man should be alone* (Genesis 11:18). Fundamental boundaries around communities-of-value become the guarantee against existential aloneness—the protection of the Gemeinschaft against the Gesellschaft. Its second root is a reflection at the level of social organization of that same per se value of nonaggregation of power. Fundamental boundaries constitute and thus ensure different realms of power.

At first blush it would seem that these two basic principles need not clash at all. There could be, it would seem, a neat, tidy way to situate fundamental rights and fundamental boundaries within the constitutional architecture of Europe. For example, one set of norms and institutions, national-constitutional and/or transnational, would take care of human rights: ensuring that no public authority at any level of governance would violate the basic autonomy and liberty of the individual. Another set of norms, national-constitutional and/or transnational, would take care of boundaries: ensuring that transnational governance would not encroach on fundamental societal choices of, principally, states.

The adoption of the ECHR by the member states of the Council of Europe is a reflection of this tidy arrangement: The High Contracting Powers of the convention retain their full prerogatives as sovereign states. State boundaries constitute thus par excellence fundamental boundaries that guarantee full autonomy of their respective national societies. The one self-limiting exception concerns the core fundamental human rights given expression in the ECHR that may not be transgressed in any of these societies. Thus, the universalism of human rights and the particularism of fundamental boundaries may rest together like the Wolf and Sheep.

You will note, however, that I used the term "core fundamental rights" in drawing this idyll. The neat arrangement that the ECHR may be said to represent can only work in relation to a core that gives expression to these "rights," or to these "levels of protection," which are said to be universal, transcending any legitimate cultural or political difference among different societies in, at least, the universe of Europe. The ECHR is premised on this understanding.

Critically and crucially the ECHR does not exhaust the spectrum of human rights. By its own self-understanding, whereas the ECHR provides the "minimum standard" of protection "below" which no state may fall, the High Contracting Parties are free, perhaps even encouraged, to offer "higher" standards of protection to individuals. Indeed, part of the uniqueness of states, part of what differentiates them from each other may be the very way they give protection beyond the core universal standard.

Thus, the commitment to, and the acceptance of the ECHR as a universal, culturally transcendent core of human rights is, surely, an expression of a very important aspect of the political culture of a state, which brings it together with other states and societies. When this is backed up by submission to transnational machinery of enforcement the commitment is all the more expressive.

But the differences in the protection of human rights in these societies within the large band that exists beyond the universal core is no less an important aspect of the political culture and identity of societies. Human rights constitute, thus, both a source of, and index for, cross-national differentiation and not only cross-national assimilation. Here is a banal example to illustrate the point. Freedom of expression is a fundamental right in relation to which a transcendent universal core of protected speech may be defined across national divides in the framework of the ECHR. But there is, evidently, a large margin for rights discourse beyond that core of protected speech. In America, a band of neo-nazis may march with full regalia in the neighborhood of Holocaust survivors. An attempt by the local authorities to ban such a march will be struck down as compromising the fundamental right to freedom of expression of the marchers. In many European countries, and clearly in, say, Germany, such speech would be prohibited without that prohibition being construed in violation of core freedom of expression. I would make three comments on the example.

1. First, we do not capture the contrast of values inherent in this example by simply saying that in America you get a little bit more protection of freedom of expression than in, say, Germany. Often, there is much more to these differences. It is through these differences, and others like them, that societies at times define some of their core values that go to their very self-understanding—their particularized identity rooted in history, and social and political culture. America is saying something very important about itself (good and/or bad) when it insists on the right of the individual to engage in such extremist, even injurious speech. Germany says something very important about itself (good and/or bad) when it would deny the individual such a right. It may even be saying something rather profound about a different emphasis on individualism and communitarianism in the respective polities.

2. There is another sense in which it would be simplifying these societal choices to articulate them as a "mere" difference between level of protection of human rights. Human rights are almost invariably the expression of a compromise between competing social goods in the polity. In liberal democracies, the most typical is an accommodation between, on the one hand, the various interests of the collectivity represented by governmental authority and, on the other, the interest of the individual in autonomy and individual liberty. Society may find it very important to empower the individual against government authority. That is how we normally think of human rights. But society may find it very important too to empower government authority against the individual. The fight against crime comes, perhaps, first to mind.

Alternatively, in the context, say, of rights to private property and land reform, differences between capitalist-liberalism and the gamut of socialist world views is a good context in which the need to look at human rights as a looking-glass reflection of government or public rights is self-evident. The extent of government power (as well as the desirability) to interfere with private property rights (e.g., programs for nationalization) was for long a dividing line between governments of left or right persuasion within European liberal democracies.

Critically, when a society strikes that balance between these competing interests and characterizes that balance as a fundamental right or liberty (to property, to free speech etc.) it is the balance that is fundamental: The fundamental right of the individual to be protected against government power, set against the fundamental right of the public through government to act in accordance with the general interest. Note, that it is as injurious to the social choice involved in this balance to compromise the right of the individual as it would be to limit the rights of government. This balance is an expression of core values, of basic societal choices. This is the point where the distinction between rights and boundaries collapses since fundamental rights— beyond the core—become an expression of the kind of particularized societal choice of which fundamental boundaries are an expression. Fundamental boundaries are designed, thus, to allow communities and polities to make and live by those difference balances that they deem fundamental. Beyond the agreed core, to foist a fundamental right on a society is, arguably, to tamper with its fundamental boundaries.

3. Finally, the position of the ECHR in relation to this tension is, once more, worth defining. Imagine that the example of the neo-nazi march were transported into Europe. Imagine further one ECHR state following the American solution. So now we would have one state prohibiting the march and one state protecting it. The jurisprudence of the ECHR would not hold the prohibition on the march as a violation of freedom of expression protected by the convention. But, in this type of case, it would also not interfere with the state that protected the rights of the marchers. In relation to freedom of expression, the ECHR would be concerned to define a core of protected speech, a minimum level of protection. Once it was decided (for good or for bad) that the neo-nazi hate speech did not fall within this core, states would be free to protect it or to ban it and to part define themselves and differentiate themselves in terms of the choice they made on this issue. This is part

of the famous margin of appreciation that the ECHR allows. States might, as I mentioned, even constitutionalize such a choice, and make it a "fundamental" part of their self-understanding. The difference between the states would thus become fundamental. By contrast, in relation to speech found to be within the core protected by the ECHR, states would not be able to make that choice. They would be bound by a shared view, that the protection of that particular speech vindicated a right which was transcendent and to which all were bound. In this case the commonality between the states would be fundamental.

Another way of describing the play of the ECHR in this context is to say that it defines the margin within which states may opt for different fundamental balances between government and individuals. It defines the area within which fundamental boundaries may be drawn. However, certain balances, tilted too much in favor of government are not permitted. It is against this background that I turn now to the protection of fundamental rights in the legal order of the Union.

Human Rights in the Union Legal Order

Judicial Protection of Fundamental Human Rights and European Community Measures: The Conundrum of "High" and "Low" Standards

Neither the Treaty of Paris nor the Treaty of Rome contained any allusion to the protection of fundamental human rights. And yet, once the ECJ put in place its constitutional jurisprudence in cases such as *Van Gend en Loos* and *Costa v. ENEL,* it became legally and politically imperative that a way be found to vindicate fundamental human rights at the community level. How could one assert the direct effect and supremacy of European law—vesting huge constitutional power in the political organs of the community—without postulating embedded legal and judicial guarantees on the exercise of such power? After all, the effect of direct effect and supremacy would be to efface the possibility of national legislative or judicial control of community law. This imperative was all the more urgent given the notorious democratic deficiencies of European governance, in some respects more acute in the 1960s than in the 1980s and 1990s. How could one expect the constitutional and other high courts of the member states, especially of those member states with national constitutional orders and judicial review such as, at the time, Germany and Italy, to accept the direct effect and supremacy of community norms without an assurance that human rights would be protected within the community legal order and, critically, that individuals would not lose any of the protections afforded under national constitutions?

Protecting human rights became a joined legal and political imperative. The response to this imperative, the story of *Strauder* and *Nold* and all the rest has been told so many times as to obviate the necessity of recapitulation. Likewise, of equal tedium, is the investigation into the legal basis and formal constitutional legitimacy of this act of so-called judicial activism by the ECJ whereby the court put in a place, or discovered, an unwritten Bill of Rights against which to check the legality of community measures.

It is the perspective of Rights-as-Values that is of interest to me in this chapter. The issues can be drawn out at their sharpest by imagining the European Court's jurisprudence as a dialogue with, or a monologue at, its national counterparts.

Let us take the *Hauer* case as our basic factual matrix: Imagine (following *Hauer*) a community measure, say a Regulation, which restricts the use of agricultural land, prohibiting its exploitation as a vineyard by its owner, a German national, and, thus, arguably compromising her right to "private property." States differ in the extent to which they will protect private property against governmental authority. Imagine therefore further, merely for the sake of argument, that in Germany the constitutional norm and practice affords greater protection to private property than, say, in Italy and that both offer more protection than the core guaranteed under the ECHR. Let us, finally, imagine that Germany affords protection of private property greater than any other member state in the community.

Direct effect and supremacy mean that the national legal orders must uphold the community measure restricting the use of agricultural land and potentially compromising the fundamental human right to private property. It therefore fails to the ECJ to check the community regulation. The potential conflict of values emerges, classically, in response to the question: Which standard of protection should the ECJ adopt? Given the legal and political imperatives I suggested earlier, there would seem to be a ready and easy answer: The court should adopt the high, German, standard.

Several reasons argue for this "maximalist" approach. First, it may be argued with an idealistic turn that the community should always seek to adopt the highest standard of human rights around. If, in the field of property rights it is a German standard, so be it. After all, it is often asserted in the regulatory area that European political decision making creates the danger of a race to the bottom, of lowest common denominator choices. Why, then, not have in the field of human rights a race to the top? Idealism would, in this instance, be complemented by expediency: How would you expect the German Constitutional Court to accept less? From the German perspective, it would not be enough that the European Court undertake in principle to scrutinize community legislation for violation of human rights. Its yardstick for scrutiny must be "up to standard"—the German standard. It is only the combination of the procedural with the material, of the institutional with the constitutional, that will give the assurances necessary to accept supremacy and all the rest.

The virtue of the maximalist approach goes even further since, it is argued, while it would satisfy the German legal order, it would not dissatisfy the other legal orders.

For, if the court were to adopt the "high" German standard in this area—what would be the reaction of, say, the Italian legal order and that of the other member states? They, the argument goes, would not and should not object since the measure to be judged by the high German standard would be a community measure. There own legislation would not be touched. And, in other areas the European Court would be looking to their standards, always choosing the highest around.

Yet, the maximalist approach does not work, cannot work and, for good reason, has been rejected by the court. The maximalist approach would be satisfactory neither from an individual member state perspective nor from a community or Union perspective. In some cases, it is not achievable at all.

To explain why, consider first another hypothetical. Imagine a member state like Ireland, with relatively little heavy industry. Imagine further that the member state adopts a constitutional amendment that introduces a fundamental human right to clear air that was then interpreted by the domestic constitutional court as requiring a very high level of purity. To impose these standards on, say, heavy coal and steel industries would be to render them economically nonviable, but this is a matter which need not concern the Irish political and legal policy maker since Ireland has no coal and steel industries. Imagine now that at some stage the community adopts an industrial policy that in combination with its environmental protection policy allows certain levels of factory emissions that exceed the strict ("high") Irish standard. If, at this point, the European policy were challenged before the European Court, would it, under the maximalist approach be obliged to adopt the Irish standard for the entire community and strike the policy down? Let us now move beyond the hypothetical case and articulate in more abstract terms the high-low conundrum.

If, on the one hand, the community's constitutional architecture that includes direct effect and supremacy should not compromise the protection of individual rights guaranteed in the various member states; and if the court is to secure and maintain the loyalty of its national counterparts to the EU constitutional structure, it would seem, the court would have to adopt the maximalist approach—in each case it would have to choose the highest level of human rights protection that exist among the member states.

No wonder that the court in *Hauer* said the following:

> [F]undamental rights form an integral part of the general principles of the law, the observance of which it ensures; that in safeguarding those rights, the Court is bound to draw inspiration from constitutional traditions common to the Member States, *so that measures which are incompatible with the fundamental rights recognized by the constitutions of those States are unacceptable in the Community,* and that, similarly, international treaties for the protection of human rights on which the Member States have collaborated or of which they are signatories, can supply guidelines which should be followed within the framework of Community law. (Recital 15, emphasis added)

If, on the other hand, the court were to adopt in each case the highest standard of protection it would mean, as in our "Irish" hypothetical, that it would be subject to the constitutional dictate of individual member states even when these national standards of protection may be considered as entirely unsuitable for the community as a whole.

No wonder that in the same case the court said as follows:

> [T]he question of a possible infringement of fundamental rights by a measure of the Community institutions can only be judged in the light of Community law itself. *The introduction of special criteria for assessment stemming from the legislation or constitutional law of a particular Member State would, by damaging the substantive unity and efficacy of Community law, lead inevitably to the destruction of the unity of the Common Market and the jeopardizing of the Cohesion of the Community.* (Recital 14, emphasis added)

The problem is even more complex calling into question the very utility of using the "high" and "low," maximal/minimal nomenclature in this context.

Consider first the situation when at issue is a fundamental human right that seeks to protect rights as between individuals inter se. No clearer is the case in relation to abortion as recently emerged in the *Grogan* case. *Grogan* provides a classic illustration why the maximalist approach was rejected and why it cannot both as a matter of policy and logic be accepted in this type of case. In Ireland there was a very "high" level of protection for the unborn. What if in another member state, the "opposing" right of a woman to autonomy over her body was constitutionally guaranteed, including the right to abort a fetus in certain circumstances? Which of the two rights would the court choose to recognize as a community right? Is there any meaning to a maximalist approach in this situation? In the case of abortion, how can the court recognize the near absolute right of the unborn in the Irish constitution and at the same time uphold a woman's right to self-determination, which, say, in another member state permits abortion in some situations?

It could, however, be argued that the abortion situation is special, pitting as it were one individual against another. In most situations, it could be argued, the philosophy of rights pits the individual against public authorities. In those cases, the vast majority, it still does make sense to talk about high and low standards of protection, and, consequently, the maximalist approach would be feasible and desirable. To understand the fallacy of this argument, we have to recall the introductory remarks on human rights as an expression of a fundamental balance between rights of the individual and rights of public authorities. To say, as we did in our hypothetical case based on Hauer that Germany has the highest level of protection of private property among the member states is also to say that Germany, in this area, places the largest number of restrictions on public authorities to act in the general interest. The rights of the public at large have the "lowest" level of protection. Even if this is so, we could still ask, why it would matter to the Italian legal order that in the areas of private property rights the ECJ adopt the "high" German standard? After all, as we already mentioned, that choice does not interfere with the conduct of Italian socioeconomic policies by Italian public authorities.

This very question represents a failure to grasp that what is fundamental in fundamental rights is the balance struck between individual and public interests.

If this is understood, surely the answer to the question is that it could and should matter to the Italian legal order that the court adopts the German standard simply because it is the "highest." The fallacy rests in the unstated assumption that "higher" standards are always desirable. But we know better. We know that to adopt the "higher" German standard (or that of another member state, as the case may be) is to adopt for the community as a whole the societal Weltanschauung struck in a particular member state between individual and the public at large. It is to adopt for the community as a whole the fundamental values of a particular member state. At least two things are problematic with such an outcome.

The community is comprised of many member states and peoples. Its basic values should be an expression of that melange. The maximalist approach would always privilege the core values of one member state, the one which happened to accord the "highest" level of protection to the individual, the "lowest" level of protection to the public and the general interest.

Further, when applied across the board, the "maximal" approach could lead to an interesting result. In all member states, there would tend to be a balance among different human rights—some privileging the individual others the public and the general interest. If the court were to adopt a maximalist approach this would simply mean that for the community in each and every area the balance would be most restrictive on the public and general interest. A maximalist approach to human rights would result in a minimalist approach to community government. This, in the eyes of some, would be a fine choice of socioeconomic values. It may be so, or may not. But it should not happen as the unintended consequence (nonworkable) of protecting human rights.

How can one solve, if at all, this conundrum? How can one square the need to ensure that the Union constitutional architecture not be bought at the expense of compromising individual rights hitherto protected by national constitutions that points toward a maximal standard policy with the realization that such a policy is inherently flawed, and in some instances simply not workable? How has the court sought to square this vicious circle? Again *Hauer* can provide the clues. Let us here move from the hypothetical to the actual decision and see how the court attempts to resolve the conundrum.

The court first repeats its basic philosophy and methodology in this specific context:

The right to property is guaranteed in the community legal order in accordance with the ideas common to the constitutions of the member states, which are also reflected in the first Protocol to the (ECHR, Recital 17). Whereas earlier it said that *measures which are incompatible with the fundamental rights recognized by the constitutions of those States are unacceptable in the Community*, there is now a subtle change—the court is insisting that the right to property will be guaranteed in accordance with *ideas* common to the constitutions of the member state. I interpret that as the court itself edging away from the vocabulary of standards. Interestingly, the court deals first with the protection afforded through the ECHR. After citing article 1 of the Protocol.

> Every ... person is entitled to the peaceful enjoyment of his possessions. No one shall be deprived of his possessions except in the public interest and subject to the conditions provided for by law and by the general principles of international law. The preceding provisions shall not, however, in any way impair the right of a State to enforce such laws as it deems necessary to control the use of property in accordance with the general interest or to secure the payment taxes or other contributions or penalties.

The court simply notes that the Council Regulation would come within the right of the State "to enforce such laws as it deems necessary to control the use of property in accordance with the general interest." Further, the provisions in the convention, in the eyes of the court, do not enable a sufficiently precise answer to be given to the question submitted by the German Court (Recital 19).

It is clear that for the purposes of its decision the court regards itself subject to the requirements of the Protocol despite the fact that the community as such is not a signatory. Second, it is in my view evident that the court regards the convention and its Protocols as mere starting points, as the first and not most difficult steeplechase which the community regulation has to pass. It is hugely important to note that although the court regards the community as bound by the convention, it does not regard the convention as setting "The" standard of protection for the community. Like a state, the community may not violate the convention but may go beyond it.

The court then moves to define its own balance. Its starting point seems to respect the rhetoric employed earlier:

> [I]n order to be able to answer [the question], it is necessary to consider also the indications provided by the constitutional

rules and practices of the nine [as they then were] Member States (Recital 20).

In practice, the court gives only three textual examples (from the German, Italian, and Irish constitutions) but then goes on to declare that

> In all the Member States, numerous legislative measures have given concrete expression to [the] social function of the right to property [namely] that those rules and practices permit the legislature to control the use of private property in accordance with the general interest.
>
> [I]n all the Member States there is legislation on agriculture and forestry, the water supply, the protection of the environment and town and country planning, which imposes restrictions, sometimes appreciable, on the use of real property. More particularly, all the wine-producing countries of the Community have restrictive legislation, albeit of differing severity, concerning the planting of vines [etc.] . . . [which is not] considered to be incompatible in principle with the regard due to the right to property.

This, in my view, is the most critical juncture in its decision. If all the court was doing was to ensure that measures which are incompatible with the fundamental rights recognized by the constitutions of those states are unacceptable in the community, it could have reached a rapid conclusion to its decision at this point. Surely the above analysis proves beyond doubt that the community regulation in question is not incompatible with the fundamental rights recognized by the constitutions of the member states. But there would have been a huge price to pay had the court ended its decision at this point. The implication could have been that had it discovered that a similar measure was held unconstitutional in one of the member states, than the community measure too would have to be struck down. At a stroke we would be back to the Maximal Standard trap.

Instead, the court reverts to the second strand in its reasoning that the right to property is guaranteed in the community legal order in accordance with the ideas common to the constitutions of the member states. The constitutional practices of the member states are not used by the court as a test for the constitutionality of the community measure but simply as a source for culling the "ideas" inherent in the right to private property.

This the court defines, not surprisingly, as a requirement that interference with private property correspond to objectives of general interest pursued by the community and, in a cumulative test (though the court uses the word "or") the measure must not constitute a disproportionate and intolerable interference with the rights of the owner, impinging upon the very substance of the right to property.

These two tests of substantive and procedural policy bona fide and proportionality are of course known in virtually all systems of administrative and legislative review. It is worth noting that in substance the court has not really developed criteria that are in any way more precise than those enumerated in the ECHR and which it had earlier dismissed rather curtly as not enabling it to give an answer.

Since we are not interested in the substance of property law in the EU, it is not necessary to go into the detailed assessment by the court of the aims of the agricultural policy on the basis of the contested regulation nor into its assessment of the reasonableness of the measure itself save to make some general comments on the method as a whole.

First it is clear that in assessing what is the "general interest" which the measure must serve the court makes reference to the *community* general interest and not to an aggregate or cumulative member state interest. In adducing the general interest, the court looks at the preamble of the regulation and at the general objectives of the Common Agricultural Policy as enunciated in the treaty.

Proportionality is also discussed in terms of the community policy. The court makes reference to the temporary nature of the regulation and the conjunctural situation of the community as a whole suffering from a surplus in the vine sector. In the light of its analysis of these factors, the court concludes:

> [T]he measure criticized does not entail any undue limitation upon the exercise of the right to property. Indeed, the cultivation of new vineyards in a situation of continuous overproduction would not have any effect, from the economic point of view, apart from increasing the volume of the surpluses; further, such an extension at that stage would entail the risk of making more difficult the implementation of a structural policy at the Community level in the event of such a policy resting on the application of criteria more stringent than the current provisions of national legislation concerning the selection of land accepted for wine-growing.

[T]he restriction . . . is justified by the objectives of general interest
pursued by the Community and does not infringe the substance
of the right to property in the form in which it is recognized and
protected in the Community legal order.

What does this have to tell us on the way the court addresses the issue
of "high" and "low" standards? The following is my interpretation of
this case and the general jurisprudence. It is clear that the court rejects
the maximal approach. To repeat:

[T]he question of a possible infringement of fundamental rights
by a measure of the Community institutions can only be judged
in the light of Community law itself. *The introduction of special criteria for assessment stemming from the legislation or constitutional law
of a particular Member State would, by damaging the substantive unity
and efficacy of Community law, lead inevitably to the destruction of the
unity of the Common Market and the jeopardizing of the Cohesion of the
Community.*

But the court's move is even bolder. It rejects, in my view, any attempt
at some mathematical averages approach to this issue. In its dialogue
with its national counterparts, its claim is jurisdictional: Only the ECJ
is in a position to determine the compatibility of a community measure
with fundamental human rights.

I will explain this in two steps. Assume first that the court were to
adopt the "German" Standard (or that of any other member state). It
would still have to apply that standard to the facts of the case and to the
material, geographic, social, and other matrix of the community which
is different from that of any member state. Imagine that the German
Government were to pass an identical measure restricting the growth
of vineyards in its territory. Imagine further that on the German market planting such a vineyard would make economic sense. It is conceivable that German Constitutional Court would find that the state could
not prove a sufficiently strong general interest to outweigh the interest
of the individual in his or her unrestricted use of their private property.
But in the community geographic and socioeconomic context, it is
possible that planting the vineyard in Germany could put someone out
of work in Sicily. The courts first claim is that only it, given its position, is able meaningfully to assess the claims of general interest and
proportionality in the community as a whole.

The second implicit claim in *Hauer* is even bolder. The language of the constitutional provisions it cites from the German, Italian, and Irish constitutions are as bland as the text of the ECHR protocol. It is the respective court in each of these systems that translates the bland language into the societal choice, the fundamental balance between individual and the general public. To the best of their ability, judges will give expression to the constitutional ethos of the constitutional text and of the polity in those decisions. Why we should entrust such a fundamental choice to our judges is a different question, but that we do so entrust them with the task is beyond dispute. The care we take in choosing judges to constitutional courts is an acknowledgment of that function we give to them.

The first claim of the European Court is a claim about process and jurisdiction. It is an assertion that the similarity of the European judicial process to its national counterpart and the integrity of that process affords it a normative legitimacy. But the integrity of process cannot—should not—paper over the potential conflict of values.

The second, deeper, implicit claim of the European Courts goes to the issue of values. The claim in *Hauer* is that the community legal order can do no better or worse than its national counterparts. It inevitably falls to a court, itself, to make that fundamental balance for the community legal order. But clearly the European Court, when fleshing out the bland language of general interest and proportionality should try and give expression to a constitutional ethos that derives from its controlling texts—not the constitution of one member state but of all of them. Just as in the geographical-political sense, the community constitutes a polity different from its member states with a general interest that must include Bavaria and Sicily, so too its constitutional ethos should reflect the various member state constitutions as well as the Unions own founding treaties. It is a new polity the constitutional ethos of which must give expression to a multiplicity of traditions. The implicit claim of the European Court is that in the field of community law a balance will have to be struck that derives from the specificity of the community. The court is calling on its national counterparts to accept that it, the European Court, will do, has to do, within the community legal order what they, national courts, do, have to do, within the national realms. It is not about high or low standards. It is a call to acknowledge the community and Union as a polity with its own separate identity and constitutional sensibilities that has to define its own fundamental balances—its own core values.

Protection of Fundamental Human Rights:
Review of Member State Measures

My starting point here is the well-known development in the jurisprudence of the court from a practice that focused on community measures to a jurisprudence that is willing to scrutinize some member state measures too.

Here too the general story is well-known. The material landmarks are *Rutili, Cinetheque, Klensch, Wachauf,* A. G. in *Grogan, ERT.* I do not consider it necessary to recapitulate fully the faces of these cases or their principal holdings. Briefly stated, the court who regards its duty to ensure the protection of fundamental rights within the field of community law has construed that field to include member state measures implementing community law as well as member state measures adopted in derogation from the prohibition on restricting the free movement of the four factors of production.

In the first part of this chapter, we saw how even the review of community measures may create a tension with fundamental values of the various member states. Here the "assault" is more direct since at issue are member state measures normally thought to be subject to the scrutiny and control of member state courts.

And, to return to the issue of standards: In relation to community measures we saw the possible concern of member state courts was that the community standards not be high enough thus letting stand community measure that, but for the doctrine of supremacy would be struck down by national courts. In relation to member state measures the principal concern would be reversed. That in reviewing member state measures, the ECJ strike down acts authorized by the domestic jurisdiction and possibly even sanctioned by the ECHR.

The first and most pressing issue that has to be addressed in this context is the very justification for review of member state measure by the European Court. If, as I argued in the introduction to this chapter, constitutionally protected human rights express core societal choices as to the balance between individual and community interests (and visions), an "encroachment" by the ECJ would be a direct challenge to the fundamental boundaries of the member state. There already has been some considerable protest in this regard. What then is the justification for this jurisdictional drive?

The court has extended, so far, the exercise of its human rights jurisdiction to member state measures in two types of situation: (a) The Agency situation—when the member state is acting for and/or on behalf of the community and implementing a community policy (*Klensch Wachauf*); and (b) When the state relies on a derogation to fundamental market freedoms (ERT). How is this to be evaluated from a narrower "legal" point of view?

The Rationale for "Agency" Review

All of us often fall into the trap of thinking of the community as an entity wholly distinct from the member states. But of course, like some well-known theological concepts, the community is, in some senses, its member states, in other senses separate from them. This, as two thousand years of Christian theology attest, can at times be hard to grasp. But in one area of community life it is easy. In the European community system of governance, to an extent far greater than any federal state, the member states often act as, indeed are, the executive branch of the community. When, to give an example, a British customs official collects a community imposed tariff from an importer of noncommunity goods, he or she are organically part of the British customs service, but functionally they are wearing a community hat. If the court's human rights jurisdiction covers, as it clearly does, not merely the formal legislative community normative source, but its *mise-en-oeuvre* (application), is it not really self-evident, as Advocate General Jacobs puts it in *Wachauf*, even on a narrow construction of the court's human rights jurisdiction, that it should review these "member state" measures for violation of human rights. In this case, the very nomenclature that distinguished member state and community acts fails to capture the reality of community governance and the community legal order. Not to review these acts would be legally inconsistent with the constant human rights jurisprudence and, from the human rights policy perspective, arbitrary: If the commission is responsible for the *mise-en-oeuvre* review will take place but if it is a member state, it will not?

The Rationale for ERT Type Review

The development in *ERT*, foreshadowed by the opinion of the advocate general in *Grogan* is more delicate. The treaty interdicts member state measures that interfere with the fundamental free movement provisions of the treaty. This interdiction applies to any member state measure, regardless of its source. The mere fact that the interference may emanate from a constitutional norm is, in and of itself, irrelevant. Likewise, the fact that the constitutional measures may be an expression of a deeply held national societal more or value is, in and of itself, irrelevant. If, say, a member state, even under widespread popular conviction and support, were to adopt a constitutional amendment that, "in the interest of preserving national identity and the inalienable fundamental rights of our citizens" prohibited an undertaking from employing foreigners, including community nationals, ahead of member state citizens or to purchase foreign goods ahead of national products, such a constitutional provision would be in violation of community law.

Community law itself defines two situations that may exculpate such a national measure from the treaty interdiction. First, the national measure itself must be considered as constituting an illegal interference with the market freedom. The treaty is very vague on this and the court has developed a rich case law in this regard. Not every measure which on its face seems to interfere will necessarily be construed as a violation of one of the market freedoms. Second, even a national measure which on its face constitutes a violation of the interdiction may, under community law, be exculpated if it can be shown to fall under derogation clauses to be found in the treaty. Article 36, for example, speaks of measures "justified" on grounds of public morality, health, and the like.

The crucial point is that defining what constitutes a violation of the basic market freedoms is, substantively and jurisdictionally, a matter of community law and for the court to decide, as is the exculpatory regime. Substantively, the court will interpret the language of the treaty often opaque: What, for example, does (or should) "justified" mean? or "public order," and so on. Jurisdictionally, the court (in tandem with national jurisdictions) will supervise that the member states are in fact fulfilling their obligations under the treaty.

One way of explaining the "extension" of human rights jurisdiction to member state measures in the ERT situation is simple enough. Once a member state measure is found to be in violation of the market freedoms, *but for* the derogation it would be illegal. The scope of the derogation and the conditions for its employment are all "creatures" of community law, treaty, and judge made. Now, it could be argued in opposition, and I would not consider this a specious argument, that one should look at the derogations as defining the limit of community law reach. I am not persuaded. Even from a formalist perspective, the structure of, say, article 30–36 indicates the acceptance of the member states that the legality or otherwise of a measure constituting a prima facie violation of the prohibition on measures having effect to quantitative restrictions becomes a matter for community law. From a policy perspective, it could hardly be otherwise. Imagine the state of the common market if each member state could determine by reference to its own laws and values—without any reference to community law—what was or was not covered by the prohibition and its derogation. Surely how wide or narrow the derogation is, should be controlled by community law The concomitant consequence of this is that once it is found that a member state measure contravenes the market freedom interdictions such as article 30, even if it is exculpated by a derogation clause in the treaty, the community's legislative competence is triggered, and it may become susceptible to harmonization.

Let us illustrate this by taking the most telling instance: The Rule of Reason doctrine developed principally in *Cassis de Dijon* of which *Cinetheque* is an example. Here the court has carved out new circumstances, not explicitly mentioned in the treaty derogation clause, which would allow the member states to adopt measures that otherwise would be a violation of article 30. I do not recall any protest by member states complaining about the courts rather audacious construction of articles 30–36 in this regard. But, obviously the member states are not given a free hand. The court will have to be persuaded that the member state measures seeking to benefit from the Rule of Reason are, for example, as a matter of community law, in the general interest and of sufficient importance to override the interest in the free movement of goods, that they are proportionate to the objective pursued, that they are adopted in good faith and are not a disguised restriction to trade. So, the ability of the member states to move within the derogations to the free movement provisions are subject to a series of limitations, some explicitly to be found in the treaty, others the result of judicial construction of the treaty.

In construing the various community law limitations on the member states' ability to derogate from the treaty and in administering these limitations in cases that came before it, should the court insist on all these other limitations and yet adopt a "hands off" attitude toward violation of human rights. Is it so revolutionary to insist that when the member states avail themselves of a community law created derogation they respect too the fundamental human rights, deriving from the constitutional traditions of the member states, given if the European community construction of this or that right differs from its construction in this or that member state? After all, but for the judicially constructed Rule of Reason in Cassis, France would not be able to justify at all its video cassette policy designed to protect French cinematographic culture. To respect the community notion of human rights in this scenario appears to us wholly consistent with the earlier case law and the policy behind it.

It could be argued that in supervising the derogation the court should not enter into the policy merits of the member state measure other than to check that it is proportionate and not a disguised restriction to trade. Human rights review, on this reading, is an interference with the merits. Again, I am not persuaded. First it must be understood that the doctrine of proportionality also involves a community imposed value choice by the court on a member state. Each time the court says, for example, that a label informing the consumer will serve a policy adequately compared to an outright prohibition, it is clear that at least some consumers will, despite the label, be misled. There are ample studies to demonstrate the limited effectiveness of labels. Thus, in the most banal proportionality test "lurks" a judicial decision by the ECJ as to the level of risk society may be permitted to take with its consumers.

Second, even if Human rights review may be more intrusive than proportionately in some cases, it need not always interfere with the actual merits of the policy pursued and could still leave considerable latitude to the state to pursue their own devices. Provided they do not violate human rights, the court will not interfere with the content of the policy. Admittedly this may sometimes thwart their wills, but that, after all, would also be the case under the ECHR. That on some occasions it might give teeth to the European convention in those countries that have after decades not yet incorporated it into national law must, we assume be welcomed by those who profess to take rights seriously.

The Double Scrutiny of Member State Measures: Institutional Considerations and the Question of Standards

Even if there is a doctrinal and policy justification for extending human rights review to this category of member state measures, would it not be overly transgressing the prerogatives of member state courts? This very question might suggest a view that sees the relationship between the European Court and its national counterparts in the area of human rights as consisting of a zero-sum game (powers granted to one are taken away from the other) or, worse, confrontational. It suggests perhaps a view that considers a tug-of-war between a *Transnational* court and a *National* court. This might be so in some instances, but the relationship is far more complex and in some cases could, and in my view should, be seen as involving a transnational *court* and a national *court*: A cooperative relationship wherein the critical sense of identity results not from one body being national and the other transnational but from their sense of both belonging to the judicial branch, not confrontational but mutually reinforcing their ability to uphold the law (as they see it). Not, then, a zero-sum game, but a positive sum game with both parties better off.

The institutional dimension is particularly intriguing in relation to the domestic application of the ECHR especially in those states, like the United Kingdom, in which the convention has not been incorporated into domestic law. Consider, for example, the United Kingdom.

By extending its jurisdiction to member state measures, the court may be stepping into areas that previously were reserved to a national court. But that domain may be more illusory than real. What was reserved to UK courts previously? The "power" to tell hapless individuals that, for example, since successive British governments for their own reasons have refused to incorporate the ECHR into domestic law, courts were unable to give them relief (except, *a la Wachauf*, as an aid in interpretation) even in the face of egregious violations of the convention to which their country is a party? One can, of course, take the view that British constitutional arrangements and the denial of power to British courts to apply the ECHR are matters that should be left to Britain. But in anybody's book that would hardly qualify as a position that takes human rights seriously. Moreover, is not the extension of jurisdiction of the ECJ, at least in some respects, an empowerment of the UK national courts and a strengthening of the protection of human rights in Britain in that at least in those areas coming within the scope of community law as defined by the ECJ, British domestic courts would have gained the right and the power, hitherto denied them, to give human rights relief to individuals?

What then of the issue of standards of review? What are the potentials here for conflict of fundamental values? My reflections in this respect are very speculative—suggesting at most a possible interpretation of the scant case law. More realistically, they should be taken as prognosis of future developments. Let us examine first the *Wachauf* situation, review of a member state measure implementing or acting for the community. This review arises only in those situations when the community norm or policy leaves some discretion to the member state so that national authority are choosing from several possible executing or implementing options.

Human Right Standards in the Wachauf Situation

Scenario A: The measure is in violation of the ECHR. Result: It should be struck down either by the national court or by the European Court. There would be no conflict of values since both community and member state regard the ECHR as a basic core that cannot be transgressed.

Scenario B: The measure clears the ECHR hurdle but is in violation of a more stringent member state standard though it would not be in violation of the community standard. Result: The measure should be struck down by the national court. Since the community gives the member state discretion in execution or implementation, provided the community norm is executed or implemented by one way or another, community law does not require that member state standards be violated. There is no conflict of values either.

Scenario C: The measure clears the ECHR hurdle, clears national standards of human rights but fails the community standard. Result: The measure should be struck down. There is a conflict of values since the public authorities of the member state are prohibited from exercising a power in a manner, which under domestic constitutional standards would be permitted. The conflict is not acute since the member state public authorities are, ipso facto and *ipso jure* acting for and on behalf of the community.

Human Rights Standards in the ERT Situation

Scenario A: The member state measure violates the ECHR. Result: The measure should be struck down either by national court or by the ECJ. There is no substantive conflict of values since both legal orders accept the ECHR as a basic core that cannot be transgressed. There could, of course, be a difference in interpreting the ECHR minimal standard. The mistake will inevitably fall in favor of human rights.

Scenario B: The member state measure clears the ECHR standard but violates the national standard though it would clear the community standard. I would submit that the result should be a striking down of the measure. There is no community interest in overriding a national human rights standard applied by a national court against a member state derogating from the treaty.

Scenario C: The member state measure clears the ECHR, clears the member state standard but violates the community standard. I have come to believe that in the ERT situation, the community should not impose its own standard on the member state measure but allow a wide margin of appreciation, insisting only that the member state not violate the basic core encapsulated in the ECHR. This seems to be consistent with the Opinion of A. G Van Gerven in *Grogan*. Unlike the *Wachauf* situation where the member state is merely the agent of the community and the member state measure is in truth a community measure, here we are dealing with a member state measure in application of a member state policy. The interest of the court and the community should be to prevent a violation of core human rights but to allow beyond that maximum leeway to national policy. This would essentially equate situation C with situation A with practical effects limited essentially to those jurisdictions, such as the United Kingdom, where national courts are not empowered to enforce under national law the ECHR. They would, as suggested earlier, be empowered through EU law. It would also mean that should the community harmonize disparate member state derogation measures to, say, article 30, the standard of human rights review of the harmonized measure may be higher than the standard applied by the court to reviewing the previous member state measures.

Concluding Remarks

Finally, in the ERT situation and more generally, even when the standard for review imposed by the court may be no different than that applying in the member state I confess to a bias, rebuttable to be sure, in favor of human rights judicial review by courts not directly part of the polity the measures of which come under review. That is why, for example, I favor accession of the community to the ECHR that would subject even the jurisprudence of the ECJ to a second outside scrutiny. As I noted in the introduction, transnational protection of human rights frequently involves the painful tension between the universal and the particular. So far I have insisted on the value of the particular as encapsulating a fundamental choice of the polity. It is trite to recall, however, that regularly, states defend alleged human rights violations on the grounds of respect for deeply held local cultural practices. Sometimes there is merit in the argument. Often, as in the case of, say, the Southern states in the USA defending in the 1950s and 1960s discrimination against blacks, or some countries today defending the ghastly practice of female mutilation, or corporal punishment of adults (hand chopping) and children (whippings, canings, and the like) the defense is specious, a mockery of the transcendental notion of human dignity. In our impressionistic view, local courts, close to local culture, are over susceptible to this type of argument. We are particularly suspicions of these claims when they emanate in contexts, such as Europe, of considerable common cultural affinity among peoples and a shared concept of the state and public authority. Adjudicating these competing claims between the particular and the universal is never easy and may not ultimately have a "right" answer. On balance, from the perspective of my own human rights sensibilities, I prefer, in this respect, the bias of the transnational forum to that of the national one, tempered as it is by the doctrine of margin of appreciation and mindful that the transnational forum is, as noted, often a second bite at the apple, the national jurisdiction having already had its say.

By way of conclusion, I would like to set out in tabulated form the principal permutations of review for violation of human rights and the relationship between the different standards of review.

Table 4.1   Principal permutations of human rights review in Union legal order

Type of measure	*Conformity with ECHR*	*Conformity with EC Human Rights Standards*	*Conformity with National Human Rights Standards*	*Constitutionally Correct Result*
Community measure	Violates	(Necessarily) violates	(Necessarily) violates	Should be struck down by ECJ
Community measure	Does not violate	Violates	Does not violate	Should be struck down by ECJ
Community measure	Does not violate	Does not violate	Violates	Should be upheld and not struck down by either ECJ or member state court
Member state measure: Agency situation where member state has discretion	Violates	(Necessarily) violates	(Necessarily) violates	Should be struck down by ECJ or member state court
Member state measure: Agency situation where member state has discretion	Does not violate	Violates	Does not violate	Should be struck down by ECJ or member state court

continued

Table 4.1—*continued*

Type of measure	Conformity with ECHR	Conformity with EC Human Rights Standards	Conformity with National Human Rights Standards	Constitutionally Correct Result
Member state measure: Agency situation where member state has discretion	Does not violate	Does not violate	Violates	Should be struck down by member state and implemented another way
Member state measure: ERT situation	Violates	(Necessarily) violates	(Necessarily) violates	Should be struck down by ECJ or member state court
Member state measure: ERT situation	Does not violate	Violates (i.e., EC Standard when applied to community measure goes beyond core ECHR)	Does not violate	Should not be struck down. ECJ should not enforce own standard beyond ECHR core
Member state measure: ERT situation	Does not violate	Does not violate	Violates	Should be struck down by member state court and implemented another way

Notes

1. A similar version to this chapter has been published in Nanette A. Neuwahl and Allan Rosas (eds.), *The European Union and Human Right*. The Hague: Kluwer Law International, 1995: 51–76. Republished with permission of the author.

Bibliography

Cases

Case 1/58 Stork (1959) ECR 17.
Case 2/92 The Queen and Ministry of Agriculture, Fisheries, and Food, ex parte Dennis Clifford Bostock, Decision of March 24, 1994.
Case 4/73 J. *Nold, Kohlen and Baustoffgrosshandlung v. Commission of the European Communities* (1974) ECR 491.
Case 11/70 *Internazionale Handelsgesellschaft* (1970) ECR 1125.
Case 12/86 *Demirel* (1987) ECR 3719.

Case 29/69 *Strauder* (1969) ECR 419.

Case 44/79 *Liselotte Hauer v. Land Rheinland-Pfalz* (1979) ECR 3727.

Joined Cases 60 and 61/84 *Cinéthèque* (1985) ECR 2605.

Secondary sources

General

Cassese, Antonio, Andrew Clapham, and Joseph Weiler (eds.). 1992. *European Union. The Human Rights Challenge*, vols. I, II, and III. Baden-Baden, Germany: Nomos Verlagsgesellschaft.

Coppel, Jason and Aidan O'Neil. 1992. "The European Court of Justice: Taking Rights Seriously." *CML Rev* 29: 669–692.

Schermers Henry G. and Denis Welbroeck. 2001 (6th ed.). *Judicial Protection in the European Communities.* London: Kluwer Law International.

Weiler, Joseph H. H. 1986. "Eurocracy and Distrust: Some Questions Concerning the Role of the European Court of Justice in the Protection of Fundamental Human Rights Within the Legal Order of the European Communities." *Washington Law Review* 61: 1103–1144.

Weiler, Joseph H. H. and Nicolas J. S. Lockhart. 1995. "Taking Rights Seriously. The European Court of Justice and Its Fundamental Rights Jurisprudence. *Common Market Law Review* 32: 51 (Part 1) and 579 (Part 2).

On human rights as value system and on cultural relativism

An-Na'im Abdullahi Ahmed (ed.). 1995. *Human Rights in Cross-Cultural Perspectives.* Philadelphia: University of Pennsylvania Press.

Dundes Renteln, Alison. 1985. "The Unanswered Challenge of Relativism and the Consequences for Human Rights." *Human Rights Quarterly* 7(4): 514–540.

Weiler, Joseph H. H. (1985–1992). "Thou Shalt Not Oppress a Stranger: On the Judicial Protection of the Human Rights of Non-EC Nationals—A Critique." *European Journal of International Law* 3: 65–91.

On European Human Rights application by national jurisdictions

Arnull J. 1993. "Applying the Common Rules on the Free Movement of Persons—the Role of the National Judiciary in the Light of the Jurisprudence of the European Court of Justice," in Schermers H. G. (ed.), *Free Movement of Persons in Europe.* Dordrecht: Martinus Nijhoff Publishers.

Bingham, Sir Thomas. 1992. " 'There is a World Elsewhere': The Changing Perspective of English Law." *International Comparative Law Quarterly* 41: 513–529.

———. 1993. "The European Convention on Human Rights, Time to Incorporate." *Law Quarterly Review* 109 (July): 390–400.

Brown W. 1992. "The Infiltration of a Bill of Rights." *Public Law*, Autumn: 397–410.

Drzemczewski, Andrew Z. 1983. *European Human Rights Convention in Domestic Law: A Comparative Study.* Oxford: Clarendon Press.

Laws, Sir John. 1993. "Is the High Court of Justice the Guardian of Fundamental Constitutional Rights?" *Public Law*, Spring: 59–79.

Weiler, Joseph H. H. 1987. "The European Court at a Crossroads: Community Human Rights and Member State Action," in Pierre Pescatore, Francesco Capotorti (eds.) *Du Droit International au Droit de l'Intégration: Liber Amicorum.* Baden-Baden, Germany: Nomos.

On relations between Human Rights and European Integration

Frowein, Jochen, Stephen Schulhofer, and Martin Shapiro. 1985. "The Protection of Fundamental Rights as a Vehicle of Integration," in Mauro Cappelletti, Monica Seccombe, and Joseph H. H. Weiler (eds.). *Integration through Law: Europe and the American Federal Experience*, vols. I, II, and III. Berlin: Walter de Gruyter.

Mancini G. F. 1989. "A Constitution for Europe." *CML Rev* 26: 595–611.

Pescatore, Pierre. 1981. "The Context and Significance of Fundamental Rights in the Law of the European Communities." *Human rights law journal* 2 (3/4): 295–308.

On relations between community protection, Human Rights, and the European Convention on Human Rights

Cohen-Jonathan Gérard. 1977. "La Convention européenne des droits de l'homme et la Communauté européenne," in *Mélanges Fernand Dehousse*, vol.1: 164 ss.

De Salvia I. 1979. "La Protezione dei diritti dell'uomo nel quadro della Convenzione europea e second ail dirritto comunitario: interferenze e problemi di coordinamento." *Diritto comunitario e degli scambi internazionale* 489.

Grief, N. 1991. "The Domestic Impact of the ECHR as Mediated through Community Law." *Public Law*, Winter: 555–567.

Macdonald Ronald. St. John. 1990. "The Margin of Appreciation in the Jurisprudence of the European Court of Human Rights," in Andrew Clapham and Frank Emmert (eds.), *The Protection of Human Rights in Europe, I/2. Collected Courses of the Academy of European Law*: 95–161.

Pipkorn Jörn. 1993. "La Communauté européenne et la Convention européenne des droits de l'homme." *Revue trimestrielle des droits de l'homme* 221: 232–242.

CHAPTER FIVE

Human Rights, Constitutionalism, and Integration: Iconography and Fetishism*

JOSEPH H. H. WEILER

Introduction: Mirror, Mirror on the Wall— Who Is the Most Beautiful of All?

The advent of the Charter of Fundamental Rights of the European Union has made it into the so-called constitution.[1] For many this is the center piece, indeed the only justification to call this treaty a constitution. It is appropriate that fundamental rights (German preference) or human rights (French preference) should be at the center of such constitutional discussion. But it is also appropriate that one does not allow the normative complexity of the trinity of human rights, constitutionalism, and integration to be obscured by our enthusiasms for all three. This chapter is meant, thus, to highlight some of the darker aspects of the ongoing debate.

There is an undeniable celebratory tone to our human rights discourse. We brandish human rights, with considerable justification, as one of the important achievements of our civilization. We hail our commitment to human rights and their embedment in our legal systems among the signal and mature proofs of Europe's response to, and overcoming of, its inglorious recent past in World War II. We consider human rights, alongside democracy, as a foundational value of our political order, something it is even worth fighting for. The recent "adoption" of the EU Charter is a final apotheosis of this discourse.

*The two articles by Joseph H. H. Weiler were originally published before the most recent constitutional developments in the legal order of the European Union. We have decided to retain them because of their theoretical and philosophical importance which transcends the specificity of the positive law on which they are based.

Human rights have undoubtedly achieved an iconographical position in European culture. And though we distance ourselves, with disdain, from the more vulgar expressions of American end-of-history triumphalism that gushed forth with the fall of the Soviet empire, that very disdain cannot but conceal Europe's sense of its cultural superiority and hence its own brand of self-satisfaction and triumphalism. We raise the mirror of human rights, as evidenced by both national and transnational instruments before our collective face, and smile with satisfaction: Yes, WE are the most beautiful of all. But, as we know, the mirror, if only we look carefully, does not hide our warts, blemishes and, at times, downright ugliness. At least it returns a more nuanced picture to the self-admiring gaze.

The following are three central features in the debate on human rights, constitutionalism, and integration.

1. First, human rights are part of a broader discourse of, and commitment to, constitutions and constitutionalism, often to the thick, hard version of constitutions and constitutionalism found in, say, the German and Italian legal orders, which embody the notion of constitution as a higher law. Such developments are noticeable even in countries such as Denmark, Belgium, France, and others that had a softer version of constitutionalism and a long tradition of skepticism toward American style judicial empowerment. For its part, the EU already has a very robust version of constitutionalism and the EU Charter is, as noted, perceived by many as the first element in a would-be European Union formalization of that brand of constitutionalism.

Concomitantly, human rights also signify the ever increasing acceptance of (and resignation to) the central role of courts and judges in public discourse. Courts are most audacious in asserting their power when they garb themselves in the mantle of guardians of the human rights guaranteed by constitutional documents. They are, too, most successful in mobilizing support for and legitimating their power in the context of human rights. Europe adds an interesting nuance to this phenomenon too. First, one should not forget this little element of self-serving and self-interest as the European Court of Justice (ECJ) rushes to embrace the charter into its jurisprudence, a charter which pointedly was not made part of the European legal order by those whose political and democratic legitimacy is much higher than that of the European Court. Second, whilst there have always been and there is currently perhaps an even increasing specific critique of the so-called activism of the ECJ and it has even been couched, from time to time, in the language which objects to a *Gouvernance des Juges*, a more careful look at such criticism usually discovers that it issues from a nationalist sentiment worried more about the loss of national sovereignty to Europe than of popular or parliamentary power to judges. If the European Court were "activist" in the opposite direction, namely slashing European Union power (and make no mistake, this too would be a form of judicial activism) you would find the same critics celebrating the ECJ. In other words, most of the critique is not of the judicial empowerment as such, but of the content which it embraces. Significantly, when national courts, in acts of *national judicial empowerment,* claiming to protect *nationally defined human rights,* strike out at the ECJ (and there have been quite a few such expressions in recent years) they are celebrated as protecting national values and identity and sovereignty. Few seem to protest that it is the judiciary, often in ways constitutionally shielded from parliamentary challenge, which is deciding fundamental issues that define the relationship of a member state to the Union.

2. Second, beyond constitutionalism and its concomitant commitment to, or acceptance of, courts and judges as such, there is in the discourse of human rights a great faith in the *judicial protection* of human rights. We may call this the Habeas Corpus syndrome. The point I wish to make is simple enough: Increasingly, the measurement of the efficacy of these documents, of their very reality as meaningful legal instruments is in their invocability by individuals and their enforcement, at the instance of individuals, against public authority by courts. It is the *Writ* of Habeas Corpus that solidified its position in legal history. In today's world, documents and declarations which do not have such a quality are oft derided as "hortatory," aspirational, embryonic, all awaiting realization of their potential by arriving at the promised lands of individual invocability and judicial enforceability.

3. Finally, human rights have become an important part of European Integration and European identity discourse. This debate takes place at two levels. The first is the bland affirmation of human rights as being part of a common patrimony et cetera, good stuff for politicians to drone on about, something akin to Beethoven's Fifth or the Blue Flag with the Golden Stars. But there is a more serious dimension to this prattle. As the polity grows, as the ability of national mechanisms and instruments to provide democratic legitimacy to European norms is

increasingly understood as partial and often formal rather than real, the necessity of democratizing decision making at the European level become ever more pressing. Such democratization requires, in its turn, the emergence of a polity with social commitments, allegiances and ties which is a *conditio sine qua non* for the discipline of majoritarian decision making. No demos, no democracy. Europe rightly shies away from an ethnic, religious, or any other thick form of organic self-understanding and political identity. The only normatively acceptable construct is to conceive the polity as a community of values, much in the original spirit (though not practice) of Post-Revolution France and the United States. When one grasps for a content for such a community of values, the commitment to human rights becomes the most ready currency. Here are values around which, surely, Europeans can coalesce (and celebrate).

There is much truth and much value to our polities in our commitment to constitutional orders that celebrate democracy, human rights, and the rule of law; in the seriousness with which we take this commitment as evidence by our willingness to make human rights a veritable legal instruments, often of superior normative value, opposable by individuals against public authorities and adjudicated and enforced by our courts; and in our placing human rights, alongside markets and economic prosperity as defining the values of our emerging European polity. But there are shades, nuances, warts, and downright ugly aspects to this picture too which is also worth bearing.

Constitutional Patriotism: The Last Refuge of the Scoundrel?

Why is it that we give such importance to the constitutional integrity of our legal orders? Why is it, that despite the fact that the European Union has a functional legal order there are strong voices that would like to root it in a formal constitutional document? Why is it that we talk of crisis when national and European constitutionalisms conflict, not least in the area of human rights?

There is, of course, no one answer to this question. But any answer would, I believe, have to include at least a shade of the following.

We consider the integrity of our *national* constitutional orders not simply as a matter important to the good functioning of government and an orderly distribution of political power but of moral commitment and identity. Our national constitutions are perceived by us as doing more than simply structuring the respective powers of government and the relationships between public authority and individuals or between the state and other agents. Our constitutions are said to encapsulate fundamental values of the polity and this, in turn, is said to be a reflection of our collective identity as a people, as a nation, as a state, as a community, as a Union. When we are proud and attached to our constitutions we are so for these very reasons. They are about restricting power, not enlarging it; they protect fundamental rights of the individual; and they define a collective identity that does not make us feel queasy the way some forms of ethnic identity might. Thus, in the endless and tiresome debates about the European Union constitutional order, national courts have become in the last decade far more aggressive in their constitutional self-understanding. The case law is well known. National courts are no longer at the vanguard of the "new European legal order," bringing the rule of law to transnational relations, and empowering, through EC law, individuals vis-à-vis member state authority. Instead, they stand at the gate and defend national constitutions against illicit encroachment from Brussels and Luxembourg. They have received a sympathetic hearing, since they are perceived as protecting fundamental human rights as well as protecting national identity. To protect national sovereignty is *passé* (outmoded); to protect national identity by insisting on constitutional specificity is *à la mode* (fashionable).

On this reading, modern liberal constitutions are, indeed, about limiting the power of government vis-à-vis the individual; they do, too, articulate fundamental human rights in the best neo-Kantian tradition; and they reflect a notion of collective identity as a community of values that is far less threatening than more organic definitions of collective identity. They are a reflection of our better part.

But, like the moon, like much which is good in life, there is here a dark side too.

It is, first, worth listening carefully to the rhetoric of the constitutional discourse. Even when voiced by the greatest humanists, the military overtones are present. We have been invited to develop a *patriotism* around our modern, liberal, constitutions. The constitutional patriot is invited to *defend* the constitution. In some states, we have agencies designed to protect the constitution whose very name is similar to our border defenses. In other countries, we are invited to *swear allegiance* to the constitution. In a constitutional democracy, we have a doctrine of a *fighting* democracy, whereby democratic hospitality is not extended to those who would destroy constitutional democracy itself. To be a good constitutional liberal, it would seem from this idiom, is to be a constitutional nationalist and, it turns out, the constitutional stakes are not only about values and limitations of power but also about its opposite: the power that lurks underneath such values.

Very few constitutionalists and practically no modern constitutional court will make an *overt* appeal to natural law. Thus the formal normative authority of the constitutions around which our patriotism must form and which we must defend is, from a legal point of view, mostly positivist. This means that it is as deep or shallow as the last constitutional amendment: In some countries, like Switzerland or Germany, not a particularly onerous political process. Consequently, vesting so much in the constitutional integrity of the member state is an astonishing feat of self-celebration and self-aggrandizement, of bestowing on ourselves, in our capacity of constituent power, a breathtaking normative authority. Just think of the near sacred nature we give today to the constitutions adopted by societies, great segments of which were morally corrupted, of the World War II generation in, say, Germany, Italy, and elsewhere.

A similar doubt should dampen somewhat any enthusiasm toward the new constitutional posture of national courts that hold themselves out as defending the core constitutional values of their polity, indeed its very identity. The limitation of power imposed on the political branches of government is, as has been widely noticed, accompanied by a huge dose of judicial self-empowerment and no small measure of sanctimonious moralizing. Human rights often provoke the most strident rhetoric by courts. Yet constitutional texts in our different polities, especially when it comes to human rights, are remarkably similar. Defending the constitutional identity of the state and its core values turns out in many cases to be a defense of some hermeneutic foible adopted by five judges voting against four. The banana saga, which has taxed the ECJ, the German Constitutional Court, the Appellate Body of the World Trade Organization, and endless lawyers and academics is the perfect symbol of this farce.

Finally, there is also in an exquisite irony in a constitutional ethos that, while appropriately suspicious of older notions of organic and ethnic identity, at the very same time implicitly celebrates a supposed unique moral identity, wisdom, and, yes, superiority, of the authors of the constitution, the people, the constitutional *demos*, when it wears the hat of constituent power and, naturally, of those who interpret it.

It was Samuel Johnson who suggested that patriotism was the last refuge of a scoundrel. Dr Johnson was, of course, only partly right. Patriotism can also be noble. But it is an aphorism worth remembering when we celebrate constitutional patriotism, mostly embodied in human rights national or transnational.

The Charter and the Judicial Protection of Fundamental Human Rights

The European Charter is with us, and we should make the best of it. But it is still worth asking whether Europe really needed it: Will it actually enhance the protection of fundamental human rights in the Union? European citizens and residents do not, after all suffer from a deficit of judicial protection of Human Rights. Their human rights in most member states are protected by their constitution and by their constitutional court or other courts. As an additional safety net, they are protected by the European Convention on Human Rights (ECHR) and the Strasbourg organs. In the community, they receive judicial protection from the ECJ using as it source the same convention and the constitutional traditions common to the member states.

So why a new Charter at all?

Most important in the eyes of the charter promoters was the issue of perception and identity. Ever since Maastricht, the political legitimacy of the European construct had been a live issue; the advent of Europe Monetary Union (EMU) with its barely accountable European Central Bank added fuel to a perception of a Europe concerned more with markets than with people. It may be true that the European Court guarantees legal protection against human rights abuses, but who is aware of this?

A charter, its supporters said, would render visible and prominent that which until now was known only to dusty lawyers. In addition, the charter, as an important symbol, would counterbalance the Euro and become part of the iconography of European integration and contributing to both the identity and identification with Europe.

Has this been born out? Only time will tell, but for now the evidence is that it has been lost in the tens of thousands of words that constitute the new "Constitution." In the debate about the constitution,

I do not hear any voice suggesting that voting No in the impending referenda will weaken the protection of human rights European citizens enjoy. Indeed—and this is a critical point—the charter within the constitution is seen as much part of a liberal project that has little real socioeconomic soul; An American style protector of liberty instead of protector of welfare.

Clarity was a second justification often invoked to justify the exercise. The current system of looking to the common constitutional traditions and to the ECHR as a source for the rights protected in the Union is, it is argued, unsatisfactory and should be replaced by a formal document listing such rights. But would clarity actually be added? Examine the text. It is, appropriately drafted in the magisterial language characteristic of our constitutional traditions: Human Dignity is Inviolable and so on. There is much to be said for this tradition, but clarity is not one of them. When it comes to the contours of the rights included in the charter, I do not believe that it adds much clarity to what exactly is protected and what is not.

Note however, that by drafting a list and perhaps one day fully incorporating it into the legal order, we will have jettisoned, at least in part, one of the truly original features of the pre-charter constitutional architecture in the field of human rights—the ability to use the legal system of each of the member states as an organic and living laboratory of human rights protection that then, case by case, can be adapted and adopted for the needs of the Union by the European Court in dialogue with its national counterparts. The charter may not thwart that process, but it runs the risk of inducing a more inward looking jurisprudence and chilling the constitutional dialogue.

Drafting a new charter, it was said, would give the chance of introducing much needed innovation to our constitutional norms that were shaped by aging constitutions and international treaties. Issues such as biotechnology, genetic engineering, privacy in the age of the Internet, sexual identity and, most importantly, political rights empowering the individual could be dealt with afresh placing the charter at the avant-garde of European constitutionalism.

I leave it to the reader to judge whether the charter has introduced such innovation. In some instances the language used by the charter risks "deconstitutionalization" of certain rights. The formula quite frequently used of rights "...guaranteed in accordance with the national laws governing the exercise of these rights" may turn out to do considerable damage to constitutional protection of human rights. Whilst it is a formula one finds in constitutional orders of the member states and international treaties, and whilst it is possible to develop a jurisprudence that separates the existence of a right from its exercise, in the particular circumstances of the community, it will be very difficult ever to challenge constitutionally a community (let alone a member state) measure that replicated the existing law in this or that member state. This may turn out to be a very regressive development for the protection of human rights.

Another regressive scenario is one under which there will be great pressure on the court to reject any progressive interpretations of various formulae found in the charter if this turns out to have been rejected by the convention that drafted the charter. For example, a proposal to introduce to the charter "the right for everyone to have a nationality" was rejected during the drafting process. It will be difficult for the court to articulate such a right. Likewise, Genetic Integrity was dropped from article 3 on the Integrity of the Person. This too might have subsequent interpretative consequences. Many more examples can be found. In general, it will be much harder for the court to crystallize a community right when such was considered and rejected by a political constituent assembly. In some areas the charter actually cuts down on protection now offered in the legal order of the community. Article 51(1) actually reduces the categories of member state acts that would be subject to European scrutiny, and article 53 at least raises problematic issues on the supremacy of community law in this area.

But most troubling of all is the fact that the charter exercise served as a subterfuge, an alibi, for not doing that which is truly necessary if the purpose was truly to enhance the protection of fundamental rights in the Union rather than talk about enhancing such protection.

The real problem of the community is the absence of a *human rights policy* with everything this entails: A commissioner, a directorate general, a budget, and a horizontal action plan for making those rights already granted by the treaties and judicially protected by the various levels of European Courts effective. Much of the human rights story, and its abuse, takes place far from the august halls of courts. Most of those whose rights are violated have neither knowledge nor means to seek judicial vindication. The Union does not need more rights on its lists, or more lists of rights. What is mostly needed are programs and agencies to make rights real, not simply negative interdictions that courts can enforce.

The best way to drive the point home is to think of Competition Policy. Imagine our community with an article 81 and 82 interdicting Restrictive Practices and Abuse of Dominant Position, but not having a commissioner and a DG4 to monitor, investigate, regulate, and prosecute violations. The interdiction against competition violations would be seriously compromised. But that is exactly the situation with human rights. For the most part the appropriate norms are in place. If violations were to reach the court, the judicial reaction would be equally appropriate. But would there be any chance effectively to combat antitrust violations without a DG4? Do we have any chance in the human rights field, without a similar institutional set up?

One reason we do not have a policy is because the court, in its wisdom, erroneously in my view, announced in Opinion 2/94 that protection of human rights is not one of the policy objectives of the community and thus cannot be a subject for a proactive policy.

Far more important than any charter for the effective vindication of human rights would have been a simple treaty amendment that would have made active protection of human rights within the sphere of application of community law one of the policies of the community alongside other policies and objectives in article 3 and a commitment to take all measures to give teeth to such a policy expeditiously.[2] Not only was such a step not taken, but article 51(2) made absolute that such a development would be even more difficult to take in the future.

Human Rights and Integration

As mentioned earlier, the classical vision regards a commitment to fundamental human rights as a unifying "universal" ideal, one of the core values around which the peoples of Europe may coalesce in a shared patrimony. When the European Court held itself out as the guarantor of fundamental human rights in the field of community law, was it not merely giving judicial expression (and teeth!) to a common heritage rather than contending with cultural diversity? The answer to this question is "Yes, but..."

Beyond a certain core, reflected in Europe by the ECHR, the specific definition of fundamental human rights often differs from polity to polity. Even in a relatively homogeneous cultural zone such as Western Europe, these differences might reflect fundamental societal choices and form an important part in the different identities of polities and societies. They are often that part of social identity about which people care a great deal. Often people might consider that these values as an expression of their specific identity should be respected against any unifying encroachment. Given that the rights are considered fundamental, so would be the differences among them. When the court has to choose this or that variant of a right "for Europe" it is making, implicitly, a choice about the cultural identity of Europe. The stakes, thus, are high. They are even higher if we consider that many would consider that the *autonomy* of different societies (certainly nation-states) to make these identity choices is as important as the choice actually made and that this autonomy should be protected by boundaries as fundamental as the rights themselves. In essence, the exercise of European judicial protection of human rights inevitably manifests the inbuilt dilemma of a multination and multicultural polity—that of reconciling the vindication of universal fundamental rights with the vindication of national autonomy guarded by fundamental boundaries.

Whence this strong appeal of human rights? I think it has to do with two roots. The first of these two roots regards fundamental rights (and liberties) as an expression of a vision of humanity that vests the deepest values in the individual that, hence, may not be compromised by anyone.

The other root for the great appeal of rights and part of the justification even if countermajoritarian looks to them as an instrument for the promotion of the per se value of putting constraints on power. Modern democracy emerges, after all, also as a rejection of absolutism—and absolutism is not the prerogative of kings and emperors.[3]

As I have argued, the differences in the protection of human rights in these societies within the large band which exists beyond the universal core, is no less an important aspect of the political culture and identity of societies. Human rights constitute, thus, both a source of, and index for, cross-national differentiation and not only cross-national assimilation.

There is no dramatic conclusion to this final consideration. It is simply meant as a sobering reminder when we reflect on the import of the various instruments of human rights. In the process of integration, human rights become the perfect vehicle both for our celebration and hopes as well as for our hesitations and fears.

Notes

1. This chapter has previously been published in 2001 in International Law Forum 3(4): 227–238. Published with the permission of the author.

2. For a full-fledged discussion of the need and content of such a policy, see Philip Alston and Joseph. H. H. Weiler, An "Ever Closer Union" in Need of a Human Rights Policy: The European Union and Human Rights Harvard Jean Monnet Working Paper 1/99 www.law. harvard.edu/programs/JeanMonnet/ (accessed on June 19, 2008).

3. For further developments on this issue see previous chapter, Joseph H. H. Weiler, "Fundamental Rights and Fundamental Boundaries: Common Standards and Conflicting Values in the Protection of Human Rights in the European Legal Space."

CHAPTER SIX

The New Legal Frameworks for National Minorities in Europe

EMMANUEL DECAUX

The upheavals experienced in Europe since 1989 have given new urgency to the question of the right of national minorities. Drawing lessons from the failure of the League of Nations, the protagonists of the postwar system intended still to found the protection of individuals upon a universalist conception of human rights, bypassing the notion of "minorities" in the name of equal rights for all and of their being guaranteed against discrimination. Still today, the term "national minorities" might seem inappropriate and pejorative, corresponding neither to constitutional situations in Western Europe where diverse communities seek to cohabit on equal footing (Switzerland, Belgium, Spain), nor to the new minorities that appear in Eastern Europe within a group that has been long dominant (like Russians or Russophones).

A fortiori this problematic appears unsatisfactory in the case of France, where the nation-state has constituted itself for centuries by the assimilation of contributions from many places. In this sense, the French position is not the result of finicky legalism, but much rather the outcome of a choice by society, marked by refusal of exclusion and discrimination, of both ghettos and communitarian withdrawal. In this sense, France has formulated a declaration bearing on article 27 of the International Pact on civil and political rights, not to deny the various rights enumerated by this article, but rather refusing to sanction a minoritarian logic by granting collective rights to a group defined as such, instead of guaranteeing the effectiveness of individual rights for all, in conformity with the principles of article 2 of the French Constitution.[1]

Apart from this reference to article 27 of the pact, positive right has long been very thin. To speak of the "right of minorities" is ambiguous. Without going into the doctrinal controversies on the nature of international law and the possibility of an emerging *jus cogens*[2] of the right of minorities,[3] I would like to offer an inventory. The recent evolution of minority rights has been in two phases, profoundly different in nature: a declaratory phase that showed its limits, and then a normative phase that remains uncertain.

The Limits of the Declaratory Phase

This first phase, composed of political commitments and general declarations was not without afterthoughts and mental reservations on all sides, and it proved increasingly repetitive. Several international organizations were concerned, without it being easy to determine what was the most appropriate site for such a legal exercise. The United Nations framework presented the advantage of universalism, but the diversity of historical and political situations, notably in the Third World where the great powers were particularly hesitant—one thinks of China, India, and so on,—which made progress difficult in this domain, all the more so because the debate on national minorities interfered with that over indigenous populations, not only for the young African nations but for the Latin-American states where the Indian question was not resolved.

With respect to Europe, it is the competition among initiatives that is striking. Long constituting a homogeneous juridical space founded on a strong culture of human rights, the Council of Europe was able to consider that the problems of national minorities was largely external to its zone. But thanks to a politics of openness that has made the number of member states rise from twenty-three to forty-five, the Council of Europe today finds these problems in its interior, with an urgent need for a solution, or else the whole Strasbourg system will be threatened.[4] The new internal balance of the Council of Europe has allowed it to go farther than the United Nations or the Commission on Security and Cooperation in Europe (CSCE), where the counterweight of the major powers—notably the United States—had played a full role. Similarly, the risks of France's isolation are greater inside restricted bodies, often dominated by political bargaining, than inside universal bodies. However, the general conception of the rights of minorities seems to have found a point of equilibrium that it would be difficult today to challenge.

The CSCE's References

From the start, the CSCE made a place for national minorities in the principles of the *final act of the Helsinki Conference*. Principle VII on human rights specified that "The participating States on whose territory national minorities exist will respect the right of persons belonging to such minorities to equality before the law."[5] The point of departure is clear: a commitment limited to certain states—those with territory on which are found, for historical reasons, some minorities—that aims to assure to individuals, taken as such ("persons belonging to national minorities"), a complete equality of rights, in full respect for human rights.

The debate would not really be relaunched until June 1990, in Copenhagen, on the occasion of the second meeting of the Conference on the Human Dimension of the CSCE. The text adopted includes a chapter (IV) on minorities that to be more precise was inscribed within this general framework. The *Charter of Paris for a New Europe* in November of the same year marked a real turning point, since the heads of state at the summit "affirm that the ethnic, cultural, linguistic and religious identity of national minorities will be protected and that persons belonging to national minorities have the right freely to express, preserve and develop that identity without any discrimination and in full equality before the law."[6] Moreover, in its "guidelines for the future," the text stressed the necessity that "conditions for the promotion of that identity be created."

Suddenly passing from an individualist conception, based on nondiscrimination and the effective guarantee of human rights to a collective conception that makes a place for "ethnic identity" as such (which the summit was careful not to describe), the charter thought it important not only to "protect," but also to "promote" through positive discrimination. However, we may read the development of the *Charter of Paris* as a complement to the Helsinki Act, not as questioning its principles of relativism and individualism.

This work to synthesize approaches would be given to experts on national minorities, meeting in Geneva in July 1991. Some have spoken of this meeting as a failure, but this is a partisan judgment. In fact, the meeting ended up adopting by consensus a text—written within the

NATO framework—that was the exact outcome of tensions internal to the conference. On the one hand, there were maximalists, sometimes demanding all or nothing; we might suppose that this was the tactic of Yugoslavia on the verge of decomposition. On the other hand, there were minimalists, often sheltering behind a caricature of the nation-state as "one and indivisible." And there existed a third group that shared the same fundamental principles founded on an individualist conception of pluralist democracy and human rights, despite dissimilar legal traditions (including the United States, the United Kingdom, and France, the traditional countries of immigration). Their rejection of positive discrimination also expressed the financial preoccupations of both the British and the U.S. Republican administration, concerned to avoid any concrete commitment in this domain.

The Geneva text is characterized by great flexibility that takes into account the diversity of national situations. As in the Helsinki Act, in effect, the formula "States on whose territory national minorities exist" makes relativism explicit. The logical complement of this statement is the reminder that "not all the ethnic, cultural, linguistic or religious differences necessarily lead to the creation of national minorities." It was the individualist perspective that prevailed, through numerous references to "persons belonging to national minorities," contrary to the wishes of participants like Germany, Austria, and Hungary, which wished to consecrate collective entities to better defend the rights of minorities within a given state. Thus the rights of minorities pertain to the framework of human rights and "real" democracy. Finally, the text took into account "the diversity of situations and constitutional systems" in presenting its proposals, stressing that there was no "single approach" applicable everywhere, but that "positive results" might be obtained through "appropriate democratic channels."[7]

This flexibility was also translated on the diplomatic level, with the setting up of the high commissioner for national minorities, charged with finding concrete solutions for situations that attracted his attention. After a decision in principle adopted during the Helsinki Summit of July 1992, Max van der Stoel, a former Dutch Minister of Foreign Affairs (in addition, special envoy to the Commission of Human Rights) was appointed starting on January 1, 1993; he exercised this office, after several extensions of his initial mandate of three years, until July 1, 2001. These seven years were decisive for fixing the bases and modes of a wide mandate that implicated a personal diplomacy at a very high level, through discrete preventive actions and the cooperation of the states concerned, to avoid juridical antagonism crystallizing.[8] The success of this first experience made the task particularly heavy for his more retiring successor, a former Swedish diplomat, Rolf Ekéus, who stressed that "the HCMN is the OSCE's High Commissioner on National Minorities and not for National Minorities." At the end of his second mandate, Mr Ekéus made a visit in some Western countries, like France, in spring 2006, to study the situation of "new minorities" outside of his mandate, at the request of the parliamentary assembly. His report was published in July 2006 with title *Politics on integration and diversity in some OSCE Participants States.*[9] On July 2007, Knut Voellebaek, a former Minister of Foreign Affairs of Norway, was appointed for a first mandate of three years.[10]

One of the tools of the high commission has been to establish recommendations, taking inspiration from good practice found on the ground; this led to the publication of four documents: the Hague's recommendations on the rights of national minorities in the realm of education (1996), the Oslo recommendations about the linguistic rights of national minorities (1998), the Lund recommendations on effective participation by national minorities in public life (1999), and finally, in liaison with the representative of the CSCE responsible for freedom of the media, on the use of minority languages in the media (2003).

The U.N. Declaration

The work undertaken within the United Nations in this area had reached a standstill before finding new vigor due to the CSCE's efforts. France, though, did not take part in the group writing a draft declaration on national minorities except on the occasion of the second reading of the text in 1991. On this occasion, it enjoyed noticeable influence on the final version of the document, through a series of compromises.[11]

The title of the declaration was amended to become *Declaration on the Rights of Persons Belonging to National, or Ethnic, Religious and Linguistic Minorities*, thus marking a bridge between the notion of "national minorities" and the three elements retained under article 27 of the pact. The French position was reaffirmed before the working group,[12] and since this text included a precise line of argument, it was judged sufficient to recall the fundamental French conception and adopt a constructive attitude toward the finalization of the text. However, this well-known position was in fact not recalled during the adoption by consensus of the declaration, whereas Germany made a motion at the last moment to exclude foreigners from the definition of national minorities; Turkey, too, made a motion deploring the absence of definition in the resolution.

With this resolution, adopted by the General Assembly on December 18, 1992 (Res.47/135), the plinth of principles was well established. The protection of minorities is inscribed within the framework of respect for borders and for state sovereignty—as well as the ensemble of goals and principles of the United Nations, to which article 8 of the declaration refers—but the equality of rights of citizens pertains to an individualist approach aimed at "persons belonging to national minorities." It is even specified in article 3 that "no disadvantage shall result for any person belonging to a minority as the consequence of the exercise or non-exercise of the rights set forth in the present Declaration." The influence of CSCE's debates is very clear when the first article of the declaration mentions a formula like "States shall protect the existence and the national or ethnic, cultural, religious and linguistic identity of minorities within their respective territories and shall encourage conditions for the promotion of that identity." Logically, it was difficult for states to refuse this concession to collective rights within the U.N. framework, after having ratified it within the CSCE. Once this equalization of principles from one body to another was accomplished, some people thought it was now suitable to extend the debate to the terrain of constraining obligations and no longer stick to "pious wishes."

Should they now move from the declaratory, or even the incantatory, to the normative? The United Nations (like the CSCE) did not make this move of privileging concrete mechanisms to be applied. The experience of the high commissioner of the CSCE had been particularly conclusive, as we have seen. For its part, the U.N.'s Commission on Human Rights had set up a working group of the sub-commission, presided over by the Norwegian expert A. Eide, starting in 1995.[13] The haunting temptation to go farther and to codify principles and practices did remain, however. Thus, during the session of the sub-commission in 2004, it was proposed to study an additional protocol to the International Pact relating to civil and political rights, despite calls for prudence from several experts, notably the Chinese and the French. With the reform of the Commission on Human Rights, and incidentally of its sub-commission, a new mandate was instituted, with the nomination of Gay McDougall (United States), as independent expert of the HRC on minorities issues. Mrs McDougall made a short visit in France in September 2007 and published a very harsh and candid report.[14]

The Ambiguities of the Normative Phase

On this new terrain, states apparently rediscovered the certitudes of their own voluntarism, whether guarantees for the "persistent objector," or the legal modes of treaties. There was a shift from false unanimity, with the always-difficult choice between forced consensus and deadlock, to the autonomy of the will. Moreover, relativism in treaty law implies adaptation to concrete situations, which is more useful than general declarations.

Yet the trap of upping the ante subsists. Although the issue primarily concerned the countries of central and Eastern Europe, some states could maintain a maximalist attitude by demanding a general legal regime that was applicable to all participants to avoid any "unequal treaty," any disequilibrium between states subject to international tutelage and the rest. Increasingly in international negotiations on human rights, the remark was heard that there are only two categories of states, the "lesson-teachers" on one side, and the "bad students" on the other. It was evident that in the West, communitarian integration, social mobility, and cultural standardization—which could be deplored just like the domination of a subculture—did not permit the debate being posed in the same terms as in the East, where the temptation of identitarian withdrawal and exclusion of the other were triumphing, in the still fragile context of democratic transition.

Amidst all these uncertainties, we must examine one by one the various legal guarantees aiming to protect minorities. By all the logic, domestic law should offer the best guarantees in the framework of a "veritable democracy" while respecting the sovereignty to which states remain fiercely attached. The best examples of protection of minorities in the postwar period correspond to this scheme, with the regime of special status planned by the Italian Constitution of 1947. Thus, in case of a latent international conflict like that between High-Adige and South-Tyrol, Italy claimed carefully that it was dealing only with the Germanophone population of the region and not with Austria, even though the latter noted measures taken in favor of the local population, and the two ministers of foreign affairs sent parallel letters notifying the Secretary General of the United Nations of the end of the argument. We may also recall that the accord of 1955 between the Federal Republic of Germany and Denmark took the form of an exchange of "declarations," and not of a bilateral treaty, in the strict sense. The Austrian Constitution of 1955 remains a good example of unilateral protection of minorities, even if Austria sought to challenge, in the name of multilateralism, these shackles imposed on it by the victors. But incontestably, it is the recent Hungarian law that offers a "window" on what it is possible to do for minorities regarding constitutional protection, even if this exemplariness is evidently aimed to project it into the international order by calling for reciprocity in favor of Hungarian minorities abroad. Hungary has undertaken to establish a network of bilateral treaties with neighboring countries.[15]

Toward a Network of Bilateral Treaties

The idea of good neighbor treaties—guaranteeing borders and minorities—also corresponds to the objective of resolving difficulties as much as possible by adapting to local situations. Since the fall of the Berlin Wall, many treaties of this type have been negotiated and concluded, sometimes addressing specifically the question of national minorities.[16] Still, we must note the public warning made on this subject by the representative of the Holy See during the CSCE meeting on the application of humanitarian commitments held in Warsaw in October 1993: this practice risks creating new forms of discrimination not only by means of "unequal treaties" imposed by a strong party on a weak party, but also through differentiation between minorities protected by a powerful neighbor and orphan minorities that might become doubly discriminated against. The experience between the world wars showed the dangers of partial protection of minorities. Searching for a mixed solution in which bilateral treaties would be inscribed within a more general framework of principles and guarantees aims to answer this objection.

This is also in part the sense of the initiative by Mr Edouard Balladur, in his capacity as French Prime Minister, in favor of a pact on stability in Europe. After the launching conference of May 1994, two "regional tables" of negotiation were set up, one for the Baltic region, the other for central and Eastern Europe. Their goal was to encourage the states concerned to agree on being good neighbors and to include them in the pact's "basket," for which the CSCE would be the "depository," according to modes that remained uncertain. Thus, according to statements by Mr Balladur, "in the effort to organize the European continent that is its own, the European Union wished for the Stability Pact to have a close relation with the CSCE. I wish for the method and process of the Pact to contribute to the dynamism and efficacy if the CSCE, to which France is very attached. Our continent needs such an institution where all its members might agree on common norms and favor preventive diplomacy and the maintenance of peace." The objective remains to guarantee borders and to protect minorities by favoring "good neighborliness" among all European countries.

This initiative, taken up by the fifteen, resulted in a conference convened in Paris in March 1995 to adopt a framework in which the European powers might support this set of bilateral treaties. Negotiations were prompted by the EU, which to foster a good neighbor agreement had ended up lending its full financial support. Most agreements placed "in the Pact basket" were preexisting.[17] A new Stability Pact for the Balkans has widened European objectives, putting the accent on the consolidation of legal states and cross-border cooperation, apart from any juridical debate. But the strategy of preadhesion was the main asset of the EU regional initiatives, without being able to find a diplomatic solution to the crisis in Kosovo, neither in 1999, with the military intervention of NATO, nor in 2008, with the unilateral declaration of independence of Kosovo.[18]

Initiatives from the Council of Europe

Uncertainties also remain due to the mandate given to the Council of Europe on the occasion of the first summit by heads of state and government held in Vienna in October 1993.[19] Several proposals were already on the agenda, coming notably from the Venice Commission "democracy by law," specifically Professor Malinverni's plan for a convention to give national minorities a general status,[20] but also from the parliamentary assembly, with its idea for an additional protocol for the European Convention on Human Rights (ECHR) (Jean-Pierre Worms wrote the report).[21] During the Vienna summit, the heads of state were unable to endorse such ambitious projects, but by a compromise that remained open about the future, they distinguished three elements: specifying measures of trust, elaborating a convention-framework, and preparing a protocol for the Human Rights Convention. I will examine them in turn.

The idea of measures of trust in this area had been developed a while before by the Council of Europe. We may also mention several "collateral" conventions that already offered concrete possibilities for cooperation and reform without tackling head-on the issue of the qualification of national minorities. But we must note that these instruments remain overly neglected by states that make abstract claims without putting into effect the practical measures at their disposal. *The European Outline Convention on Transfrontier Co-operation between Territorial Communities or*

Authorities (n°106) had gone into force back in December 1981 and anticipated considerations by the CSCE on the importance of good neighbor contacts to avoid the isolation of national minorities; by the end of 1997, it linked only nineteen participating states. Ten years later, there were thirty-three participating states and three signatories. Apart from peripheral cases like Great Britain, progress was significant: Cyprus, Greece, Macedonia, Serbia-Montenegro, Bosnia-Herzegovina (signatory), and also on the periphery of Russia, with Estonia and Georgia. We note ratification by Russia in 2002, Rumania in 2003, Armenia in 2003, and Azerbaijan in 2004, Croatia and Slovenia in 2003—all expressing the political dynamic of the treaty.[22]

With respect to the *European Charter for Regional or Minority Languages* (n°148) (adopted on November 5, 1992), it went into force on March 1, 1998, and ten years later, gathered twenty-three ratifications, with ten signatures in suspense—and other states keeping their distance: Belgium, Greece, Ireland, Portugal, and Turkey, as well as former Communist countries like Albania, Bulgaria, Estonia, Latvia, Lithuania, and Georgia. The simple signatories are also weighty, like France (which signed the charter on May 7, 1999, but found itself tied by a decision on June 15, 1999 from the Constitutional Council), Italy, Poland, and Russia. It remains to be seen if these signatures have reached an impasse, as in the French case, or are en route to ratification. By its very flexibility, the charter offers a means adapted to diverse situations to protect the regional languages that constitute an element of our cultural patrimony: the charter allows each state to specify the languages concerned and to modulate its commitments by choosing a certain number of gradual provisions. However, the possibility for states themselves to specify languages might remove from the charter a great portion of its scope, as with the restrictive declaration by Germany that targets only a few historic minorities to the detriment of the languages of immigration.

During the first 1993 summit of the Council of Europe in Vienna, states seemed to rush things by advocating "to draft with minimum delay a framework convention specifying the principles which contracting States commit themselves to respect, in order to assure the protection of national minorities. This instrument would also be open for signature by non-member states."[23] This instrument was supposed to be open to non-member states. The appendix on national minorities of the Vienna Declaration already stipulated several paths when it indicated that "States should ensure the respect of the principles which are fundamental to our common European tradition: equality before the law, non-discrimination, equal opportunity, freedom of association and assembly as well as to participate actively in public life." We note that these principles seem to go without saying and to be assumed already guaranteed domestically and within the European Convention.[24] Regarding "participation" in public life, one wonders if this implies questioning the democratic principle, founded on "majority rule," as determined by pluralism and alternating political parties, to consecrate a system of electoral quotas, separate legislatures, or reserved seats—all of which are barely acceptable in old democracies.

The Framework convention,[25] as it was adopted on February 1, 1995 disappointed a parliamentary assembly that continues to claim adherence to its resolution 1201 and to impose it on new member states as a condition of membership, whereas this resolution is in contradiction with the compromise position adopted by the Committee of Ministers. Moreover, reference to resolution 1201 is found in the text of the bilateral treaty between Hungary and Slovakia, while it was Romania's refusal of this mention that made the attempted agreement with Hungary fail during the conference on the Stability Pact. The Framework convention went into force on February 1, 1998 and ten years after links thirty-nine member states, with four more signatories. Thus the effect has been fully felt, despite radical opposition from France and Turkey. The attitude of the signatories might seem uncertain (Island and Luxembourg since 1995, Greece since 1997, and Belgium since 2001), as if external pressure were encountering strong domestic resistance. The third Parties, like France and Turkey are strongly in the defensive position of "persistent objector." The parliamentary assembly of the Council of Europe, like the European Commission against Racism and Intolerance (ECRI), constantly serves notice on recalcitrant states, playing the trump card against state sovereignty.

Basically, it is a relatively detailed text marked by the idea that "a pluralist and genuinely democratic society should not only respect the ethnic, cultural, linguistic and religious identity of each person belonging to a national minority, but also create appropriate conditions enabling them to express, preserve and develop this identity." However, the notion of "national minority" is not defined, nor the forms of legal eligibility. It is specified in article 3.1 that "Every person belonging to a national minority shall have the right freely to choose to be treated or not to be treated as such and no disadvantage shall result from this choice or from the exercise of the rights which are connected to that choice," but this is putting off the thorny issue of who should decide whether a person belongs to a national minority?

On many issues, the Framework convention merely makes an inventory of human rights that are already guaranteed, going so far as to specify in a rather curious legal formula: "The rights and freedoms flowing from the principles enshrined in the present framework Convention, in so far as they are the subject of a corresponding provision in the Convention for the Protection of Human Rights and Fundamental Freedoms or in the Protocols thereto, shall be understood so as to conform to the latter provisions" (article 23). The most innovative thing remains the supple structure of both application and follow-up, since the Committee of Ministers will regularly receive "full information on the legislative and other measures taken to give effect to the principles set out in this framework Convention" (article 25) and will proceed to an "evaluation" of these measures, with the aid of an "advisory committee, the members of which shall have recognized expertise in the field of the protection of national minorities" (article 26). Third-party states might be invited to adhere to the convention framework after its entry into force, without thereby becoming members of the Council of Europe (article 29), and they would be associated with this "application mechanism," according to ways to be determined. As we see, many uncertainties remain about the practical scope and the geographic field of the Framework convention.

The last part of the Vienna compromise seemed promising a priori, in deciding "to begin work on drafting a protocol complementing the European Convention on Human Rights in the cultural field by provisions guaranteeing individual rights, in particular for persons belonging to national minorities." This was indeed an individualistic approach aimed at justifiable rights in a domain long neglected in the convention system, despite the long-standing Belgian linguistic issues.[26] Yet an equivocation in the text had to be raised: Did the summit advocate the guarantee of individual rights of any person arising from the state authorities, through precise clauses applying to all, or did it intend to mention specific rights for "persons belonging to national minorities"? The shift from a universalist conception of the convention to a category approach seems unacceptable by creating new forms of discrimination, although article 14 of the European Convention specifies that "the enjoyment of the rights and freedoms set forth in this Convention shall be secured without discrimination on any ground such as sex, race, color, language, religion, political or other opinion, national or social origin, association with a national minority, property, birth or other status." All the same, it is evident that cultural relativism cannot challenge the universalism of human rights in the name of religious or sociological considerations. With these ambivalences resolved, the protocol might have been a useful means of reconciling individual freedom and adherence to a "common patrimony of humanity," in a cultural pluralism founded on human rights. Cultural rights would no longer have been the fruit of historical determinism or nationalistic identity (born of the rejection of the other), but rather the product of the free choice of identifying oneself without exclusivity to several cultures, even several languages.[27]

Conclusion

The work of the ad hoc committee for the protection of national minorities (CAH-MIN) led to an impasse, being unable to reconcile the universalist vision of individuals' rights that lies at the heart of the ECHR of 1950 and the collective dimension founded on cultural identity conceived less as a personal choice than as historical heritage. Paradoxically, the same debates are found within the EU, now enlarged to include twenty-seven member states, which had made the protection of the rights of national minorities a key point, serving to evaluate the political maturity of candidates for membership. But the specialty of the EU is to move beyond micronationalisms toward a new European citizenship. But human rights must not be reduced to this citizenship, as with the mandate given to the first convention on fundamental rights, losing sight of the universal dimension of human rights.

Even if general commitments have been made within the United Nations, the CSCE, and the Council of Europe, or more recently the EU, the concrete means to implement these orientations in principle remain to be found. Western Europe has known for almost fifty years how to get beyond its antagonisms from above, through pushing integration in a space without internal borders and the outline of a common citizenship, but at the same time by privileging for ten years an enlargement at a forced pace to the detriment of integration. Perhaps this tension has reached a point of rupture, without being able to lastingly stabilize its frontiers. Eastern Europe seems on the contrary prey to fractioning, threatening to become a compartmentalized and rigid Europe, refusing dual nationalities or "mixed" marriages. Moreover, each new political fracture, far from solving the question of minorities, creates a chain reaction that is more and more destructive, multiplying minorities into more minorities.

It is not sure that a global legal approach can suit such different situations. The combination of a general framework and a network of bilateral treaties seems to be the best method to safeguard common principles—state sovereignty, human rights, real democracy—and to solve ordinary situations. Still, states should be modest about "teaching lessons" or offering readymade solutions. An effort at explanation is also required to reject any "bureaucratic waffle" and to accept challenges to the status quo, but without indulging in demagoguery. Also an imaginative effort to find effective mechanisms, especially about prevention, on the model of the High Commission for National Minorities of the CSCE. More than to the law, the final word here belongs to diplomacy.

Notes

1. Article 27 says that "in states where there exist ethnic, religious or linguistic minorities, persons belonging to these minorities cannot be deprived of the right to have, in common with the members of their group, their own cultural life, to profess and to practice their own religion, or to use their own language." For the debate opened in the Committee of Human Rights on this subject, cf. Emmanuel Decaux, in *L'Evénement européen* 16, 1991: 122.

2. Peremptory norms. See Emmanuel Decaux, *Droit international public*, 6° ed, Paris, Dalloz, 2008.

3. In its decision n°1 of November 29, 1991, the Arbitration Commission of the Peace Conference in Yugoslavia referred "to the principles and rules of international law" in evoking "respect for human rights and that of peoples and minorities," before specifying in decision n°2 of January 11, 1992 that "in virtue of the now imperative norms of general international law, it is up to states to assure respect for the rights of minorities." The commission did not indicate the origin or content of this new *jus cogens*. For expert commentary, see Alain Pellet, "L'activité de la Commission d'arbitrage de la Conférence pour la paix en Yougoslavie." *Annuaire français de droit international*, 1992: 220.

4. Cf. Emmanuel Decaux and Alain Pellet (dirs.) Nationalité, minorités et succession d'Etats en Europe de l'Est. *Cahiers du CEDIN* 11, Paris: Montchrétien, 1996.

5. The Act may be downloaded on the CSCE Web site at: www.osce.org/item/4046.html. For a collection of documents from the CSCE, cf. *Sécurité et coopération en Europe (1973–1992)*. Paris: La Documentation française, 1992.

6. The Charter of Paris may be downloaded at: http://www.osce.org/documents/mcs/1990/11/4045_en.pdf (accessed on April 14, 2008).

7. For an overview, Emmanuel Decaux, *La Conférence sur la sécurité et la coopération en Europe*. "Que sais-je? n°2661" Presses Universitaires de France, 1992.

8. Cf. Emmanuel Decaux, in Colloquium of the Fondation Marangopoulos pour les droits de l'Homme, *Nouvelles formes de discrimination*, Pédone, 1995.

9. Cf. the Web site of the HCMN: http://www.osce.org/hcnm/ (accessed on April 15, 2008).

10. The High Commission, instituted in 1992, has an impressive output. See the institution Web site.

11. An excellent presentation was made to the AFNU by Béatrice Le Frapper, "La protection des minorités." *Bulletin du Centre d'information des Nations Unies*, n°7–8, Paris: December 1993: 83.

12. E/CN4/1991/53: 7.

13. E/CN4/Sub,2/1995/33.

14. A/HRC/7/23/Add.2, 3 March 2008.

15. Cf. Peter Kovacs. *RGDIP* 2, 1993: 411.

16. The list of these bilateral treaties is already long, especially accords concluded by Hungary with Ukraine, Slovenia, Croatia, under negotiation with Rumania and Slovakia; or by Poland with Germany, Czechoslovakia (which now links it to the two resulting states), Ukraine, Byelorussia, Latvia, and Russia, and so on.

17. Emmanuel Decaux. "Le Pacte de stabilité en Europe, action commune ou pacte manqué?" in *Mélanges offerts à Hubert Thierry, L'évolution du droit international*, Pedone, 1998.

18. Christian Tomschat (ed.), *Kosovo and the International Community*, Nihjoff, 2002.

19. *Documents d'actualité internationale* 22, November 15, 1993: 503.

20. Text in *Revue universelle des droits de l'homme* 1991, n°5, p. 189; p. 157 for commentary by Giorgio Malinverni.

21. Parliamentary Assembly of the Council of Europe, *Worms Report*, Doc.6742 (January 19, 1993).

22. On the scope of the convention-framework, cf. my article in *Revue générale de droit international public* 3, 1984: 557.

23. The Vienna declaration of October 1993 is available online at: https://wcd.coe.int/ ViewDoc.jsp?Ref=Decl-09.10.93&Language=lanEnglish&Ver=original&Site=COE& BackColorInternet=9999CC&BackColorIntranet=FFBB55&BackColorLogged=FFAC75 (accessed on April 14, 2008).

24. Thus the reform of the 1901 law on associations that took place in 1981 suppresses any discrimination with respect to "foreign associations." Freedom of worship is exercised without discrimination in a system founded on the secularity and neutrality of the state, except for the certified exception of Alsace and the Moselle. Finally, regarding elections, we should also note progress in the regionalization and decentralization that allow all representative groups to participate in local life. Beyond constitutional controversies, the status of Corsica even calls for the first time for a régime *sui generis* for one region, with great cultural autonomy that finds its limit only in the other's freedom.

25. The Framework convention is available online at: http://www.conventions.coe.int/Treaty/ EN/Treaties/Html/157.htm (accessed on April 14, 2008).

26. European Court, July 23, 1968, decree A n°6 (bottom).

27. For a particularly stimulating perspective, cf. *Les Droits culturels. une catégorie sous-développée de droits de l'homme*, Patri Meyer-Bisch (ed.), "Human Rights Series" n°9, Editions Universitaires de Fribourg, 1993; as well as the concomitant plan submitted to the Council of Europe CAHMIN (94) 4 rev.

C H A P T E R   S E V E N

Multiculturalism and European Law

Virginie Guiraudon

To speak of a "multicultural Europe" is to venture onto a semantically slippery terrain, since the concept of multiculturalism and that of Europe have no consensual definitions. Multiculturalism has fluid meanings and serves as a mold into which new models are poured. And we could say the same about "Europe," another crucible word that everyone fills with meanings, fears, or hopes. Without neglecting these theoretical and ideological ambiguities, it is nevertheless important to hypothesize the advent of a European multiculturalism and to analyze the steps in this direction by examining existing European law.

Recent debates around the membership of Turkey in the European Union (EU) and the constitutional treaty (with countries such as Poland wishing to stress the Christian character of the European heritage) have shown that the question of culture has acquired a certain resonance in European political rhetoric. In the end, the Lisbon Treaty signed in December 2007 added the following to the Preamble of the current EU treaty: "Drawing inspiration from the cultural, religious and humanist inheritance of Europe, from which have developed the universal values of the inviolable and inalienable rights of the human person, freedom, democracy, equality and the rule of law."[1] From the cultural diversity of Europe a unity should emerge, that of the state of law as well as respect for human rights. Another reading of the sentence added to the treaty is that Europe has invented universal values. The new Union Treaty invites us to rethink the relation between multiculturalism and human rights in Europe.

One might define multiculturalism as the political accommodation of cultural differences, what Charles Taylor has called "the politics of recognition."[2] At a minimum, it requires equality or nondiscrimination on the basis of criteria such as religion or ethnicity. Indeed "misrecognition" includes having to bear the stigmatizing gaze of a culturally dominant Other and also having to face institutionalized inferiority or invisibility. Consequently, one cannot develop a positive self-image, which means enduring a lesser status.[3] To translate debates in normative political theory into legal terms, the first step toward recognition is the prohibition of direct and indirect discrimination. Further steps in the legal implementation of multiculturalism entail measures to protect cultural practices and particularities (e.g., funding minority language classes or financing the building of mosques) and to allow the presence of cultural diversity in public space (e.g., multilingual language signs and religious headdresses). An empirical manifestation of the institutionalization of difference—often to mitigate conflict—would be a consociational model of democracy with guaranteed representation for groups (as has been the case of "parity" for women or "ethnic quotas" in parliaments). One could view these steps in multiculturalism along a continuum. In fact, they each raise a different set of issues in which "identity politics" have been debated: respectively, social justice, political representation, and deliberative democracy.

I will limit my discussion to the question of immigrant communities in the regard of European law. The presence of immigrants coming from "non-European" cultures is in many respects at the center of the debate on multiculturalism in Europe today. Currently there are more than seventeen million foreigners from outside the EU who are known as "third country nationals" (TCNs) in the EU-27.[4] Thinking about multiculturalism in the European context generally presupposes the existence of an "ethnic dilemma"[5] to be managed. De facto cultural pluralism implies that the dominant universalist credo may need to be adjusted and that the problems that confront immigrants are not necessarily (or only) social and economic but may include cultural alienation and discrimination. Paradoxically, the solution that multiculturalism advocates is not one of transcending cultural or ethnic cleavages but of ensuring their durability. This may seem unrealistic in the current political context, and we will address this issue in the first section of this chapter, yet one should not underestimate the capacity of international institutions to embrace and spread ideas about minority rights and the accommodation of diversity. As Will

Kymlicka discusses in his 2007 book *Multicultural Odysseys*, the United Nations, the International Labor Organization, the World Bank, and the Council of Europe have all adopted declarations that promulgate rights for minorities. Most of the time, they have been motivated by a fear of destabilizing ethnic conflict in postcolonial and postcommunist states, yet in the case of indigenous peoples, there may have been a more positive sense of justice rather than simply a security imperative. The question is whether immigrant-origin minorities have as much of a chance as indigenous peoples and national minorities to gain protection and recognition.

In seeking to discern the role that supranational bodies might play in Europe, we must enter inside a debate within studies of immigration, over the degree of convergence of immigration-related policies in Europe and over what drives that convergence. There is no real uniformity within the EU concerning the legal guarantees enabling foreigners to express their cultures or their religions. In the early 1990s, Rogers Brubaker[6] was inclined to think that the differences among European countries that existed in the past, their ways of conceiving the nation and state-society relations, had a tendency to be reinforced in recent years, consequent upon debates on immigration. This idea was much debated,[7] for this heritage is not always completely fixed and there has been a flurry of legislative activity in the areas of immigration and citizenship in which "tradition" was amended in various ways, debates resulting in a "*bricolage*" (patchwork) of history and "integration philosophies."[8] The major 1999 reform of German nationality law also made Brubaker's argument less convincing from an empirical standpoint. In fact, he later wrote that there was convergence at the national level. He did not state that what he termed a common "return of assimilation" resulted from a top-down process.[9]

In the early 1990s, when the first comparative studies of European immigration policies were published, others took an opposite stance to Brubaker's. Yasemin Soysal in her book *The Limits of Citizenship* considers that the postwar period witnessed the emergence of norms founded on human rights that were diffused and translated by transnational actors and international institutions to guide national policies. This normative evolution displaced the source of legitimacy of rights associated with belonging to a nation-state (*state membership*), substituting the notion of person for that of national and the criterion of residence for that of nationality. According to her, the advent of what is called a "postnational model" of citizenship explains the fact that foreigners living in Europe can claim and obtain most of the rights from which nationals benefit. Soysal's argument had empirical weaknesses and the same scholars who had criticized Brubaker were also unconvinced by her account. Notwithstanding, Soysal's book invites us to examine more closely the way in which international institutions influence "from above" the principles or the practices of nation-states with respect to the treatment of migrants, in the way that international relations scholars such as Margaret Keck, Kathryn Sikkink, and Thomas Risse have done.[10]

Here I ask whether the legal norms that were produced and adopted by European institutions participate in the elaboration of a "European multiculturalism." Based on the way that we conceive of multiculturalism in this introduction, I want to know whether European law provides a minimal multicultural policy based on nondiscrimination and equality of rights, or whether it goes further and asserts the superiority of dominant national or European values. Here the European institutions to be studied are, on the one hand, the jurisdictions of the Council of Europe that interpret the European Convention on Human Rights (ECHR) (the European Court of Human Rights [ECtHR] that sits in Strasbourg) and, on the other hand, the institutions of the EU.

The chapter is divided into three parts. First, I discuss the different forms that the protection and the recognition of cultural minorities could take and which factors could impede or facilitate their adoption at the supranational (i.e., European) level. Second, I review the jurisprudence of the ECtHR and initiatives from the EU. I will try to explain their features and their limits. What can we learn from the European jurisprudence over the right of foreigners—in particular their religious and cultural rights? What was it able to bring to national jurisprudences and how was it taken into account by European nation-states? Third, I examine the evolution of EU's policy toward TCNs, integration, and antidiscrimination policies.

European Multiculturalism or Multiculturalism in Europe?

What could European multiculturalism look like? What types of modifications of European law would allow supranational institutions to enforce certain rules concerning tolerance and the treatment of other cultures, and under what conditions might these changes occur? This section offers analytical grids to categorize recent developments and posit plausible future evolutions.

It is legitimate to ask if it is at the European level that multiculturalism can and should be expressed and achieved, rather than at the national or local level. Of course, Europe is de facto multicultural; defining the basic rules for the treatment of and respect for ethnic minorities at a supranational level seems a logical stage from the moment an idea of a "Europe without borders" takes shape through agreements like that of Schengen (in effect since 1995). Setting the conditions of entry and stay of TCNs has in fact been on the agenda of the EU since the Maastricht Treaty; legislation started being passed after the Amsterdam Treaty came into force in 1999, when immigration and asylum became a matter of community policy and Schengen fell outside the remit of the EU.

Necessary Latent Conditions

Shifting competence to the European level may meet the resistance of member states due to political cost-benefit analyses made by national leaders. Are there advantages for them in seeking a European solution to their own "ethnic dilemmas?" Establishing European rules has three types of attractions for national actors, but just as many risks:

1. First, a European commitment to respect the rights of foreign minorities and the struggle against discrimination might constitute a guarantee against political fallout at the national level. This is the reasoning that Robert Badinter (then French Minister of Justice) used in the case of the death penalty in leading France to sign in 1983 protocol 6 of the ECHR. Suppose that a government meets the conditions at a given point and passes a "multiculturalist" law; it could be abrogated at the next change of legislative majority, whereas the signing of an international convention ensures greater legal durability. The origins of the European human rights regime in fact implied tying a nation's hands in the event of a resurgence of individual rights violations.[11] In the case of foreigners, this could have consequences: if public opinion is circumvented by a supranational agreement, there is a risk of aiding and abetting extremist and anti-immigrant parties, which tend also to be opposed to supranational institutions.

2. Second, relocating the legal source of the rights of foreigners (from the national to the international level) absolves national governments of a certain degree of responsibility. If groups mobilize against decisions taken to conform to an international agreement, they might say that "it's the fault of" Brussels, Luxembourg, or Strasbourg.[12] But there are caveats to this political version of "passing the hot potato." Studies of European integration stress that governments balk at delegating their authority lest they are unable to control the unforeseen effects of an international agreement and rein in supranational institutions. National governments are more ready to make concessions and compromises on the ground by authorizing cultural or religious practices (special cemeteries, ritual slaughtering, and religious festivals) and by modifying existing laws to incorporate the needs of ethnic minorities as necessary. If they want to relinquish the most controversial and politically costly aspects of policy toward ethnic minorities, national governments can also change the site of decision making from the national to the local level. In many countries, the financial and institutional means of integration policy have been decentralized. In others, instead of public authorities, "civil society" (churches and secular associations) manages the problems and demands of ethnic minorities (table 7.1).

3. Third, if debate over the cultural rights of minorities takes place within supranational institutions, this contributes to depoliticizing it at the national level. The politicization of policies toward ethnic minorities contributes to a rise in social tensions, which may give the stage to marginal or extremist actors, and divide political parties in a way that hurts in the medium term the interests of the ethnic minorities concerned.[13] As the Islamic headscarf controversy in France showed, once the debate was launched at the national level, it crystallized over issues such as *laïcité* (state neutrality toward religion) and gender equality, which proved incompatible with any effort at

Table 7.1 Internationalizing the debate about ethnic minorities

Political Objectives	*Political Risks*
Depoliticize the question at the national level over time	Provoke a short-term debate on the rightness of internationalization
Absolve national governments of responsibility	Fear of unexpected long-term effects
Avoid an eventual electoral backlash	Going against public opinion may have electoral costs

Table 7.2   Possible forms of protection of the rights of minorities

	Vague/general	*Concrete/detailed*
Recognition of differences	Declaration celebrating diversity of cultures	List of cultural minorities and their demands
Equal rights	Declaration against racism and ethnic discrimination	Catalogue of rights ("Bill of Rights"); antidiscrimination legislation

compromise. But changing the level at which political discussions take place to remove electoral pressures and local stakes cannot be done without discussion; to sign and ratify an international commitment requires public debate. The political context, the media, and the state of European public opinion all make such a debate risky. Pro-migrant associations are well aware of this: as in the case of revising the Geneva Convention, many people think that it is more prudent to consolidate what has been achieved than to put it in play—at the risk of legal regression and an agreement based on the lowest common denominator.

Form and Content

Both the form and content taken by European rules of the game regarding the rights of non-European minorities are evidently factors that will be again put into play to convince European governments that this process is desirable. This is a thorny problem. Let us consider "ideal types." From the point of view of *content*, should the accent be placed on respect for cultural particularities or on the imperative of equality of rights? Even if one might consider that these two principles constitute the two sides of the same coin and that one is nothing without the other, they are incompatible in their extreme versions. As for *form*, will the solution be a very vague and general text leaving the maximum flexibility to nation-states, but leaving a large margin of interpretation to the courts that will ensure its application? Would a very detailed and concrete list of rights and groups be preferable? Table 7.2 illustrates the different types of possible solutions in a matrix with two axes: equality/difference and vague/detailed.

Unsurprisingly, the first measures adopted at the European level were declarations of a vague or general nature. The Council of Europe and the institutions of the EU published general declarations celebrating tolerance and diversity of cultures in the 1980s and early 1990s.

Parliament, the commission, and the council of ministers of the EU in 1986 made a joint declaration on racism and xenophobia. In 1992, after the report on intercommunity relations by the Committee on Migrations of the Council of Europe, the council of ministers pronounced in favor of policies fostering equality of opportunity for immigrants, including cultural rights and the fight against xenophobia as contributing to this objective.[14]

Jurisprudence of the European Court of Human Rights on Foreigners and Its National Incorporation

Yet the above examples do not tell us which groups are to be protected by international and European law. Both international law and European law have tended to distinguish "national minorities" from other types of minorities, sometimes to exclude migrants and refugees (and sometimes the Roma/gypsies) from the remit of the law—although there are few instances of actual definitions of what a national minority is. The exception to the rule at the international level took place in 1994.[15] A cornerstone of international human rights law is the 1966 UN Covenant on Civil and Political Rights. Article 27 stipulates that "in those states in which ethnic, religious and linguistic minorities exist, persons belonging to such minorities shall not be denied the right, in community with other members of their group, to enjoy their own culture, to profess and practise their own religion, or to use their own language." In 1994, when 126 states had signed the covenant, its monitoring body, the Committee on Human Rights, published General Comment No. 23 on the definition of minorities. The committee commented on the applicability of article 27: "Just as they need not be nationals or citizens, they need not be permanent residents. Thus, migrant workers or even visitors in a State party constituting such minorities are entitled not to be denied the exercise of those rights."[16] This was clearly something unexpected and novel. A year earlier, on October 9, 1993, the heads of state of the members of the Council of Europe met in Vienna for a very important summit, where they referred to the need to protect "national minorities, which the upheavals of history have established in Europe," quite separately from migrants that were mentioned in a "Declaration and Plan of Action on combating racism, xenophobia, anti-Semitism and intolerance." In fact, while the Framework

Convention on National Minorities of the Council of Europe, opened for signature in 1995, called for a combat against discrimination in a number of precise sectors (e.g., education) concerned with migrants, it also spoke of combating "racism and xenophobia." There was in this sense no bridge built between different kinds of ethnic, cultural, and religious minorities. The question is: Did the jurisdictional system put in place within the Council of Europe framework go further than the above-mentioned framework convention in the protection of migrants and their cultural and religious specificities.

The European system of human rights protection that emerged over the ruins of World War II established the first veritable international jurisdiction endowed with the means to oversee and enforce major fundamental freedoms: the European Convention for Safeguarding Human Rights and Fundamental Liberties[17] (hereafter "the convention") went into force in 1953 and the ECtHR has sat in Strasbourg since 1959. This jurisdictional ensemble is a "test case" that allows us to study supranational norms and their influence on national laws about foreigners inside their borders. As we shall see, this influence can be only limited.

First, the convention makes a few distinctions between foreigners and nationals. For example, article 16 excludes foreigners from the enjoyment of political rights (such as the right to vote and to be a candidate in elections).[18] These "rights of the *citizen*" pertain to someone who participates fully in the polis, in contrast to fundamental liberties and certain social rights that are owed to *all persons* regardless of participation in public affairs. It is also important to stress that discrimination based on nationality is not perceived as contrary to Human Rights, as explicitly stated in the International Convention on the Elimination of All Forms of Racial Discrimination of 1966 (article 1, paragraph 2). Moreover, the reasons given as legitimate to restrain freedom, such as national security, public order, and public health, are often invoked in measures addressed to nonnationals. The same is true for labor law, inasmuch as laws protecting the national labor market are authorized. The prerogatives of nation-states to choose who enters their territory, who stays there, who can be naturalized and under what conditions, have never been questioned, as the international courts often recall in their decisions. Nation-states organize the exercise of citizenship and ensure the respect for fundamental rights.

Let us turn to the interpretation of the convention by the ECtHR. Between 1959 and 1993, while numerous immigrants were settling in

Europe, out of the 447 rulings rendered by the court, a little less than a dozen (2.5% of decisions) concerned the fundamental liberties of foreigners already resident in Europe. This chronology is explained on the one hand by the time it took for the convention and the European Court to become known and utilized as means of appeal, and on the other, for some countries such as France to authorize the right of individual petition. Yet toward the end of this period, some major case law concerning foreigners emerged that also reflected the hardening of policies to control migratory flows as well as of asylum policies. The increasing caseload of the court prompted a lengthy debate on the necessity for a reform of the convention's supervisory machinery, resulting in the adoption of Protocol No. 11 to the convention, which came into force in November 1998. The aim was to simplify the structure with a view to shortening the length of proceedings while strengthening the judicial character of the system by making it fully compulsory. Protocol No. 11 replaced the existing, part-time court and commission by a single, full-time court. Yet the number of applications continued to rise geometrically. More cases concerned persons who had migrated, but also persons from the former Soviet block, such as Russophones in the Baltic States, who had become aliens without having migrated. In brief, there has been an expansive case law on foreigners and national minorities since the early 1990s.

Most of the cases in which plaintiffs were foreigners concern expulsion orders, the refusal of a residence permit (its renewal or—in the case of family reunion—the granting of a new permit to incoming family members). The plaintiffs generally argued that the authorities dealing with their case had violated rights protected by article 3 of the convention that forbids any inhuman or degrading treatment,[19] or by article 8 that consecrates the right to have a normal private and family life.[20] Violations of article 8 were found in several cases, notably in a case where renewal of a residence permit had been denied to the divorced father of a little Dutch girl (*Berrehab v. Holland*). On other issues, the court considered that the right to lead a normal family life had been denied to members of the "second generation" under threat of expulsion due to their criminal activities because they had lived all (or almost all) their lives in their countries of settlement and had no longer any family ties to their countries of origin. In *Moustaquim v. Belgium*, a judgment rendered on March 20, 1991, the court acknowledged that states enjoy the right "as a matter of well-established international law and subject to their treaty obligations to control the entry, residence and expulsion of aliens." Yet the state right must be balanced with the fact that "everyone has the right to respect for his private and family life" (article 8 ECHR). Over the years, the court has developed a number of precise criteria to establish the proportionality of the state decision in relation to the individual freedom being violated (the "Boultif criteria" based on the *Boultif v. Switzerland* decision of August 2, 2001). In 2001, the court also answered in favor of a plaintiff invoking article 8 to request the family reunion of spouses and children living abroad (*Sen v. The Netherlands*), six years after the first landmark case in this area (the 1985 *Abdulaziz et al. v. the United Kingdom*). The jurisprudence on article 8 is a cautious case law characterized by the need to respect state rights and find coherence from case to case. It is in any event an example of an expanding and "living" case law, as new situations are examined by the court and new contexts discussed in the rulings. For our purposes, it does limit the state's room for maneuver and thus acknowledges implicitly the irreversible evolution of Europe into a "migration continent."

One interesting development in the jurisprudence on article 8 is that the court has adopted a value-laden definition of "family" that corresponds to European contemporary standards, that is, the nuclear family, in opposition to an extended view of the family that is still common in some migrants' countries of origin.[21] This has been criticized by some legal scholars as ignoring the cultural context in which plaintiffs from Asian and African backgrounds evolve, given that nuclear families are embedded in wider family networks.[22] Nevertheless it shows that there is a cultural interpretation of European human rights and an emphasis on the values of the country of destination in assessing rights violations.

There have also been cases concerning foreigners invoking violations of article 6, specifically the payment of the costs of an interpreter during a judicial procedure (*Luedicke, Belkacem & Koc v. Germany, Ozturk v. Germany, Brozinek v. Italy*). This jurisprudence deserves to be mentioned, since it suggests that for human rights to be effective, the state must take positive steps to acknowledge linguistic diversity in these cases.

One article that should be particularly relevant for migrants is article 14 of the convention. It forbids discrimination based inter alia on race, color, religion, and national origin. This article 14 must always be invoked in conjunction with another article of the convention, and this has greatly limited its impact. There was in fact a famous decision on May 28, 1985, in which the European Court ruled unanimously that one of the provisions of the 1980 British law on immigration was contrary to article 14, but this was a matter of discrimination based on sex: foreign husbands of British wives or of foreign women residing legally in the United Kingdom could not join their wives, whereas it was easy for foreign women to join their husbands in the United Kingdom (*Abdulaziz, Cabales & Balkandali v. the United Kingdom*).

One area where the European Court has been bold is with regard to social rights; in fact, there it has indeed used article 14. As Lisa Conant recently analyzed,[23] the court has rejected distinctions between social insurance and social assistance and eliminated the possibility of nationality discrimination for all legally resident foreigners. In the view of the court, resident foreigners, regardless of nationality, are entitled to noncontributory benefits, based on need, that are founded on the prohibition against national-origin discrimination under article 14 of the convention, as well as on individuals' rights to "enjoy their possessions" under article 1 of Protocol 1. Although states such as France and the United Kingdom argued that a right to property could not include noncontributory benefits, European judges declared that distinctions between contributory and noncontributory social benefits were artificial, given the complex funding of these benefits through taxation and other sources (*Koua Poirrez v. France, Stec, et. al. v. United Kingdom*).

The lawyers representing foreigners, in fact, have often wanted to prove that this article 14 has not been respected in treatment of their clients—but without convincing the judges. This confirms that the question of the burden of proof is crucial here and it is very difficult to bring forth evidence in many cases. Since the right of states to take measures to regulate entry and the conditions of stay by foreigners on its territory is guaranteed and considered as an essential element in the exercise of their sovereignty, they may "prefer" certain nationalities to others within the framework of the freedom of movement inscribed in the Treaty of Rome or in bilateral treaties, and/or make access more difficult to certain nationalities through the European Community's visa policy.

Questions linked to freedom of religious expression and cultural specificities have been the subject of controversies over immigrants and have (re)launched the debate over multiculturalism. On these questions, it seems that Strasbourg's attitude is rather reserved. This can be seen by its application and interpretation of article 9 of the convention that protects religious freedom and beliefs and includes the right "to manifest his religion or belief, in worship, teaching, practice and observance." Article 9 is a qualified right: "Freedom to manifest one's religion or beliefs shall be subject only to such limitations as are prescribed by law and are necessary in a democratic society in the interests of public safety, for the protection of public order, health or morals, or for the protection of the rights and freedoms of others." Several plaintiffs invoked violations of article 9 before the commission that decides on the admissibility of cases; only four were deemed admissible. The commission has apparently "chosen to restrict itself in the manner in which it can interpret Article 9."[24] They relied on other convention provisions to claim that they were a priori prevented from accommodating certain categories of religiously based claims for exemption from generally applicable, neutral laws. Thus Moslem litigants did not see their cases admitted. The commission avoided pronouncing on a case involving a Muslim teacher who had not been permitted to be absent to pray at a mosque on Friday afternoons (*Ahmad v. United Kingdom*).[25] It declared inadmissible the case of a Muslim who wanted to marry a girl under the age of sixteen in the United Kingdom (*Khan v. United Kingdom*)[26] and one who wanted to conduct his marriage according to a "special religious ritual" recognized by state authorities (*X v. FRG*).[27] Buddhist and Sikhs did not fare better. In their cases, the commission did not entirely "avoid the issue"[28] but stated that limitations under paragraph 2 of article 9 that "are prescribed by law and are necessary in a democratic society" did apply. According to the commission, for various health and security reasons, a Buddhist prisoner could not grow a beard that prevented his guards from identifying him,[29] nor could a high caste Sikh refuse to sweep his cell,[30] nor could a Sikh motorcyclist refuse to wear a crash helmet to keep his turban on.[31]

One recurring issue before the court involves the wearing of the veil in Turkey and affects Turkish women in their home country, rather than women migrants. In 1993, the European Commission of Human Rights declared inadmissible the request of two women who had suffered sanctions because they were wearing the headscarf and who considered that their religious freedom had been scorned. The two plaintiffs were Turks and resided in their countries of origin (one was in a military training camp and the other was studying in a secular university). The commission thought that these women had freely chosen to follow courses in a secular milieu, and they had not been prevented from practicing their religion outside these institutions.[32] In a 2005 judgment involving a Turkish medical student who had not been allowed to take her exams because she wore the veil and who then moved to Vienna (*Leyla Şahin v. Turkey*), the Grand Chamber of the ECHR further noted that "Article 9 does not protect every act motivated or inspired by a religion or belief. Moreover, in exercising his freedom to manifest his religion, an individual may need to take his specific situation into account" (application No 44774/98, November 10, 2005, para 105). The Court also found no violation of article 9 in December 2008 in the Dogru v. France and Kervanci v. France involving school girls who had refused to take off their veils during gym class.

Several national high courts have pronounced themselves in favor of a firmer protection of religious expression in public spaces, particularly in education. To cite only two examples, this was true of the French high administrative court ("*Conseil d'Etat*") in its opinion on the first headscarf affair in 1989 and of German tribunals ruling on cases dealing with the right to be exempted from physical education classes for religious reasons. Religious freedom is without doubt an illustration of what Joseph Weiler calls in this book the values constitutive of a nation-state and its "fundamental frontiers." The way in which religious tolerance is erected as a norm reflects crucial moments in the political and social history of a country. Thus Strasbourg can establish a minimum standard, but some countries in their normative production may go farther. This is one more reason not to waste the "judicial capital" of the court and commission on these questions. Still, ECHR judgments can have a legitimizing effect on national legislative developments and court decisions. In November 2004, after the French legislature had passed a law banning the wearing of the veil in schools, the French *Conseil Constitutionnel* that post facto assessed its constitutionality underlined the importance of the constitutional principle of secularism, referring expressly to the ECHR decision in *Leyla Şahin v. Turkey* (decision 2004–505 DC). Similarly, in March 2006, the ECHR jurisprudence was referred to in a high profile appeals case before the House of Lords applying article 9 ECHR via the British Human Rights Act, the *R (Begum) v. Denbigh High School* case. The girl who had appealed wanted to wear a jilbab against uniform rules but the court said that she knew the school policy and could have sought alternative modes of schooling, just as in the Turkish cases.

The National Impact of European Courts and Texts

Thus the influence of the European Court has concentrated on other aspects of foreigners' rights: (a) the right to private and family life; and (b) the interdiction against inhuman treatment and its consequences for entry and length of stay. First, there exists a certain dynamic whereby once the court has opened the way to recourse by recognizing the pertinence of an article of the convention in cases of expulsion or residence permits, lawyers and legal aid groups rush in. They try to plead other cases to consolidate this body of jurisprudence or to find other applications. This enables them to make Strasbourg jurisprudence known at the national level so that the national courts take it into account in their own judgments and/or governments will hesitate to challenge an established jurisprudence when they pass new measures. Second, a right like that of leading a normal family life (consecrated by article 8 of the convention) is not only a legal *supranational* norm, but already part of the legal norms of many countries and often inscribed in their constitutions. Moreover, this right is the subject of *national* jurisprudence that has affected the rights of foreigners; thus the court in Strasbourg strengthens or harmonizes a preexisting law more than it creates novelty by venturing onto terra incognita. In France back in 1978, the *Conseil d'Etat* in the GISTI (Groupe d'Information et de Soutien des Immigrés) case had raised it to the rank of a general principle of law and had annulled numerous regulatory provisions that aimed to suspend family reunification for immigrants. In Germany, article 6 of the Fundamental Law of 1949 on protection of the family was also taken into account to prevent the restriction on bringing together families, even before Strasbourg ruled on this subject.[33] "Legal production" at the European level is composed of recycled national materials.

To know if international jurisdiction has an impact on the legal order at the national level, you have to look for signs of institutional cooptation, that is to say, the occurrences in jurisprudence where national tribunals are incorporating the norms developed at the international level (by referring to texts or to international jurisprudence). The first decisions of the ECtHR go back to the middle of the 1980s; it is also at this time that administrative tribunals proved generally more willing to take international law and Strasbourg jurisprudence into account (the French Council of State waited longer—the 1989 Nicolo ruling—to apply article 55 of the constitution consecrating the superiority of treaties that have been signed, ratified, and published by France over domestic laws). The reactions of national jurisdictions have been very uneven, and so we are far from being able to speak of a uniform process of incorporation of legal norms. In cases concerning the status of foreigners, it seems that only the countries found guilty went on to consider the consequences of Strasbourg's decision; no transversal effect is perceived. In France and in the Netherlands, both found guilty of violating article 8, the councils of state of the two countries have clarified their positions on the interpretation of this article and a national jurisprudence has developed in internal documents, with administrations warning their civil servants of the risks of litigation.[34] In both countries, the mobilization of legal associations fighting for the right of foreigners, such as GISTI or the Dutch Working Group on Legal Aid for Immigrants, is an important factor in explaining the national incorporation of international norms. But Strasbourg jurisprudence on article 8 is largely ignored elsewhere. In Germany, for example, where the cases examined by the court concentrated on free provision of interpreters for foreigners during judicial procedures, it was on this very limited issue that the government issued clarifications, not on the ensemble of cases concerning foreigners.

This is due to the nature of legal texts and to the relative prudence with which the court has pronounced on cases whose themes— immigration, religion, culture—are emblematic of sovereignty and national identity. In cases where a dynamic of legal production is in place, half the battle has been won, and the rest depends on certain preconditions for national courts to refer to international sources of law: a direct condemnation of countries, a positive attitude by national courts to international law, compatibility between the nascent international norms and preexisting national norms, and the existence of a strategy of litigation on the part of public interest law groups.

The European Union and Third Country Nationals before Maastricht (1957–1992)

Of course, there is another important source of European legal norms: the institutions of the EU. To what extent can they affect the status of nationals from third countries? Until the Treaty of Amsterdam went into effect in 1999, there was scant European action on guaranteeing respect for cultural diversity to foreigners resident in Europe. The European treaties offered only an extremely limited legal basis for community institutions to address the rights of nationals from third countries, particularly concerning cultural policy.

Before the 1990s, the institution that undoubtedly went farthest (in word, if not action) in favor of the rights of foreigners was the European Parliament, for example pronouncing in favor of resident foreigners' right to vote in local elections, as the Vetter Report suggested. European parliamentarians are sufficiently distant from their electorates to be less tempted to exploit the question of migration in a populist manner, but on the other hand they lack the means to push progressive ideas. As for the European Commission, since the 1970s the

Directorate General for Employment and Social Affairs (DG V at the time) wanted to promote the legal status of non-community foreigners living in Europe, considering that this objective went along with its efforts to make the free movement of community nationals effective. It advanced the idea that integration of immigrants into Europe took place through the promotion of their identities of origin. In its communications, the commission also pronounced in favor of better representation of the interests of immigrants, supporting the creation of consultation committees of foreigners and support for aid associations, as in its report of 1985.

Still, in the earlier phase of European integration, the only directive adopted by the council of ministers that applied to TCNs as well as to community citizens dates from 1977 and deals with the education of immigrant workers' children.[35] In a declaration that followed its adoption, the council wished this directive to address the needs of the children of immigrants coming from third countries. It was a matter of encouraging the learning of languages of origin while improving the integration of children into the school systems of the receiving countries, at a time when some European countries were becoming aware of the poor school results of newly arrived foreign children. Later on, numerous pilot programs financed by the community included non-European children, for practical reasons of numbers and the viability of these scholastic experiments. This directive was adopted at a time when European governments believed that immigrants would repatriate to their countries of origin and hence that their children ought to be able to speak the native language. It is this ambiguity that permitted the resulting European consensus. This directive was in some ways the exception that proves the rule. Generally speaking, the primarily economic character of European integration and the fact that only Union citizens had a right of free movement both served to circumscribe the impact of European institutions on the status of non-community foreigners in member states.

The European Court of Justice (ECJ) nevertheless succeeded by detours in opening certain breaches, into which the defenders of immigrants have flooded, which enabled them to guarantee certain rights to TCNs. The major developments were:

1. The non-community family of a citizen of the Union benefited from a right *derived* from free circulation, if this citizen was going to work in a country of the Union other than his own.
2. In the Rush Portuguesa ruling of 1990, the ECJ thought that the free circulation of services and the freedom to settle presuppose

that one leaves a business enterprise with one's own employees. If the latter are not community citizens, member states cannot invoke their right to protect the national job market, for this would violate the rights of the establishment of the firm. This is also a derived right (meaning it applies only when the non-community person works for a community business functioning abroad).

3. Since 1987, the ECJ, in a few rulings (Demirel, Sevince, Kus, Kziber) addressed the direct effect of treaties of association with the EU, such as those of Turkey and North African countries, and of decisions by the Council of Association that mention free circulation. This means that citizens of countries that signed a treaty of association could claim rights (right of residence or certain social rights) by virtue of these treaties of association.

The latter two jurisprudential developments were very controversial. It seems that, as was the case in many domains, the ECJ interpreted its mandate and treaties in a very wide fashion. Nevertheless, even an activist ECJ could not go far on questions of a cultural nature. In fact, the court ruled in 1987 that there was no basis in the treaty to deal with the cultural rights of migrants at the community level, unless there were amendments to the treaty. In effect, the issue goes back to 1985, when the commission tried to establish a "procedure for notification and prior consultation" among member states, before the adoption of new measures aimed at nationals of third countries. The commission wanted to include cultural policy toward foreigners among the subjects requiring European consultation. Five member states then took the commission to the ECJ; they obtained the annulment of the European Commission's decision.[36]

After Amsterdam: Equality Policy and Integration Guidelines (1992–2007)

As for the idea of a European multiculturalism that would rely on a list of target groups (as was done in the Netherlands and in North America), there is not even one planned, and it seems quite unlikely. First of all, it seems difficult to identify a precise list, given the diversity of national situations. Moreover, this approach is increasingly criticized, since it confines groups to minority status and to reified cultural identities.

The most important advances have taken place in the domain of the struggle against ethnic and racial discrimination. In fact, these are not just declarations, but actual legislation legally based on an article of the treaty, taken up in the Charter of Fundamental Rights of the EU, which is part of the future constitution. The question of struggle against racism had appeared evident after violent xenophobic attacks at the start of the 1990s, in Germany especially. The European Council established a high-level working group that in 1995 presented recommendations to combat xenophobia and racism.[37] The Starting Line Group (SLG), a network created in 1992, which ended up including approximately three hundred nongovernmental organizations, proposed including in the treaty of the EU an article against direct and indirect discrimination. The originators of this group included the Brussels NGO Migration Policy Group, which brought logistic support and its contacts within European institutions, and a handful of academics, legal scholars, and members of paragovernmental organizations, essentially Dutch and British, like LBR (the Dutch Office of struggle against racism) and the CRE (Commission for Racial Equality in the United Kingdom). They were able to take inspiration from earlier experiences like the old article 119 (article 141) on equality between men and women, and to argue that their proposal belonged to the direct line of existing policies such as the fight against social exclusion.

At the start of the intergovernmental conference of 1996–1997, the working group on reform of the treaty set up by the European Council adopted the necessity of extending the basic principle of non-discrimination to cover gender, age, sexual orientation, handicap, and religion, and to condemn racism and xenophobia.[38] In Amsterdam in 1997, a new article was inserted into the treaty of the European Community:

> Without prejudice to the other provisions of this Treaty and within the limits of the powers conferred by it upon the Community, the Council, acting unanimously on a proposal from the Commission and after consulting the European Parliament, may take appropriate action to combat discrimination based on sex, racial or ethnic origin, religion or belief, disability, age or sexual orientation.

The members of negotiating teams suggested that member states considered the new article as a thrifty way of appearing to be "politically correct": article 13 required the council's decisions to be unanimous and did not oblige it to take measures. It was only a matter of a possibility.

In reality, in June 2000, barely a year after the treaty went into force, in record time a directive was adopted "relative to the implementation of the principle of equality of treatment between persons without distinction of race or ethnic origin" founded on article 13 of the treaty adopted in Amsterdam in 1997.[39] This directive (called the "*race directive*") that was to be ratified by member states before July 2003, was followed by another in November 2000, which bore solely on employment and work, and instituted protection against discrimination based on religion and convictions, handicap, age, and sexual orientation. The community arrangement includes an incentive, made concrete in November 2000 by the publication of a program against discrimination for the period 2001–2006.[40]

Among the reasons that explain the adoption of the directive of June 2000, the "Haïder factor" was determining. Although the fourteen other members of the Union had declared on January 31, 2000 that they would accept no official bilateral contact with Austria if its government included the FPÖ, a party of the extreme right led by Jorg Haïder, a coalition government between the conservative party and the FPÖ was formed on February 3. An informal meeting of European ministers of employment and social affairs was planned for the following week in Lisbon (February 11 and 12). The Commissioner of Social Affairs, Anna Diamantopoulou, declared there: "This is the first meeting of the Council after the Austrian elections and the coming to power of the far right... We have also seen consensus around the table that priority must be given by Council and Parliament to adoption of the anti-discrimination package proposed by the Commission last November. We now see clearly that our union is not only an economic one but a political one."[41] At the end of this summit, it was decided that more than verbal condemnations were necessary to contain xenophobic parties: they had to act.

The directive prohibiting discrimination based on race and ethnic origin is innovative in many respects. It has established a vast system of protection against direct and indirect discrimination and even allowed "positive discrimination."[42] It applies to domains where community competence did not yet exist, like housing. Finally, the transposition of the directive required numerous adaptations on the part of states where the protection system was insufficient, if not nonexistent. The diversity of national responses to the multiethnic character of society leads us to assume that no unanimous vote could be achieved in a few months. It is too early to evaluate the actual effects of the implementation of directives at the national level.[43] The EU obligation to create independent equality bodies to examine the complaints of persons claiming discrimination and to contribute to raising consciousness is an original instrument at the heart of national policies to combat discrimination.

Yet, while EU equality policy has developed, the justice and home affairs ministers of the EU member states have signed on to a soft instrument of policy cooperation on integration that shows a clear rejection of the multiculturalist experiments in some EU member states. Based on setting benchmarks and on funding information exchange about "best practices," it is an "open method of coordination," which has been a very common and legally nonbinding way of encouraging member states to converge since the Lisbon 2000 summit. Since 2004, there has been a bureaucratic process at work through a program known as INTI (integration of third country nationals) that funds initiatives related to these integration guidelines. In November 2004, the European Council adopted the Common Basic Principles for Immigrant integration Policy in the EU.[44] The project was an idea of the Netherlands when it held the presidency of the Union. It is one of the cases where policy has undergone a 180-degree change since the early 1980s when multiculturalism, along with nondiscrimination and political participation, was encouraged in Dutch minority policy. The first principle defines integration as a "two-way process of mutual accommodation," yet the document stands firm on the superiority of European values and the importance of the dominant culture and language: the second principle affirms that "integration implies respect for the basic values of the European Union."

It is noteworthy that the EU guidelines mention the importance of linguistic and civic instruction, a development that scholars associate with the return of assimilationism but also as developing a "migration-integration-citizenship nexus."[45] The fourth common basic principle states that "basic knowledge of the host society's language, history and institutions is indispensable for integration; enabling immigrants to acquire this basic knowledge is essential to successful integration." This suggests that member states should set up language and civic instruction courses to help migrants integrate. The EU framework for integration legitimates the idea of a contract between the two sides of the integration process and encourages the creation of courses that teach "EU values." In fact, eleven European countries have implemented integration courses and contracts and set up civic and citizenship tests: Sweden, Denmark, and Finland were the first, followed by the Netherlands, Austria, Belgium, France, the United Kingdom, and Estonia (although the last is mainly directed at the Russian minority, not new migrants), Germany, and Switzerland. The debate is open in Hungary and Spain.

In brief, the models that are adopted at the EU level, referring to nondiscrimination and integration policies, suggest that short of a politics of recognition, TCNs, European immigrant-origin nationals, and other visible minorities can hope at best for a *politics of non-misrecognition* in the current political context.

If we look at the treatment of one cultural and socioeconomic minority present throughout Europe, the Roma, they have faced structural discrimination in Europe and legal scholars do not believe that the ECtHR can address such issues. In fact, the European Roma Rights Centre, an NGO that uses strategic litigation, was frustrated in its efforts as procedures were long and outcomes unsatisfactory for many years, until November 14, 2007 when the Grand Chamber of the ECtHR ruled that Roma children had been segregated in Czech schools in *HD and others vs. Czech Republic* in a way that constituted a discriminatory violation of their right to education (article 14 and article 2, Protocol One ECHR). In fact, the judgment makes extensive reference to EC law and nonbinding reports and opinions on Roma education in the respondent state. This case seemed to show the emergence of a convergent and perhaps coherent attempt at redressing systematic discrimination of the Roma. Yet, the anti-Roma declarations during the Italian electoral campaign in 2008, which legitimated anti-Roma violence in the South and culminated in the recent fingerprinting of Roma populations at the initiative of the Berlusconi government tell another story. The responses of European institutions were contradictory and often meek, with the commission changing its opinion three times on whether the fingerprinting of gypsies constituted ethnic discrimination or not. We can thus conclude this chapter with a mixed message: European law has come a long way to protect minorities yet law on its own will not vanquish national populist politics and reverse some of the policies they lead to.

Notes

1. *Treaty of Lisbon amending the treaty on European Union and the treaty establishing the European community* (2007/c 306/01): 10. URL: http://eur-lex.europa.eu/JOHtml.do?uri=OJ:C:2007:30 6:SOM:en:HTML (accessed on June 12, 2008).
2. See Taylor, "The Politics of Recognition."
3. Fraser and Honneth, *Redistribution or Recognition?*
4. Source: Eurostat. See also OECD. *Trends in International Migration*, 2007.

5. Glazer, *Ethnic Dilemmas.*

6. Brubaker, *Citizenship and Nationhood in France and Germany.*

7. See Favell, *Philosophies of Integration*; Feldblum, *Reconstructing Citizenship*; Joppke, *Immigration and the Nation-state*; and Guiraudon, *Les politiques d'immigration en Europe* for nuanced rebuttals of Brubaker's book.

8. Danièle Lochak notes that the French state that had long ignored differences in its great principles has in practice been more flexible and accommodating. See Lochak, "Les minorités et le droit public français."

9. Brubaker, "Return of Assimilation," 531–548.

10. Keck and Sikkink, *Activists beyond Borders*; Risse, Kopp, and Sikkink, *The Power of Human Rights*; Checkel, "Why Comply?" 55(3), Summer 2001.

11. Moravcsik, "The Origins of Human Rights Regimes," 217–252.

12. The idea that politicians seek to shirk their share of responsibility has been theorized by Weaver, "The Politics of Blame Avoidance," 371–398, among others. According to him, it is in the interest of politicians who want to remain in power not to be blamed for unpopular policies or for bad outcomes more than they want to be praised for good outcomes. We see this in the framework of economic policy where policies of budgetary restriction are ascribed to European imperatives, globalization, and so on.

13. See Guiraudon, *Les politiques d'immigration en Europe* (2000) for an elaboration of these questions.

14. See Council of Europe, *Community and Ethnic Relations in Europe*, (1991). It was also under the aegis of the Council that the Convention on the Legal Status of Migrant Workers was elaborated. It was ratified by five countries (including France) and signed by three (including Germany).

15. General comment adopted by the Human Rights Committee on April 6, 1994. CC PR/C/21/Rev.1/Add.5. United Nations.

16. Human Rights Committee, General Comment 23, Article 27 (Fiftieth session, 1994), Compilation of General Comments and General Recommendations Adopted by Human Rights Treaty Bodies, U.N. Doc. HRI/GEN/1/Rev.1 at 38 (1994).

17. "The Convention" hereafter.

18. It corresponds to article 25 of the International Pact Relating to Civil and Political Rights of 1966.

19. Article 3 is often invoked by asylum-seekers who have been denied refugee status and who insist on the risk of inhuman treatment they would run if they were sent back to their countries of origin.

20. The court has not yet had the occasion to rule on provisions that bear specifically mention foreign migrants. Article 4 of the Fourth Protocol forbids "collective expulsions of foreigners" yet several major destination countries of immigration such as Germany or the Netherlands have yet to ratify the Protocol.

21. Thym. Respect for Private and Family Life, 87–112.

22. Van Dijk and van Hoof, *Theory and Practice of the European Convention*; Steiner and Alston, *International Human Rights in Context.*

23. Conant, "Individuals, Courts, and the Development of European Social Rights."

24. Stavros, "Freedom of religion," 615.

25. Case 8160/78 dated March 12, 1981.

26. Case 11579/85 dated July 7, 1986.

27. Case 6167/73 dated December 18, 1974.

28. Stavros, "Freedom of religion."

29. Case 1753/63 versus Austria dated February 15, 1965.

30. X versus United Kingdom. Case 8231/78 dated March 6, 1982.

31. X versus United Kingdom. Case 7992/77 dated July 12, 1978.

32. Decisions 16278/90 and 18783/91 of May 3, 1993.

33. In 1983, for example, the *Bundesverfassungsgericht* (Federal Constitutional Court) forced Bavaria and Baden-Wurtenberg to renounce establishing a waiting period of three years for the spouses of foreigners resident in Germany.
34. See Badoux, "The Netherlands," on the Netherlands.
35. Directive of July 25, 1977, *OJ* L199 of August 6, 1977.
36. See the decision of the ECJ of July 9, 1987 (Cases 281, 283–5, 287/85).
37. This commission, presided over by Jean Kahn, is called the European Council Consultative Committee on Racism and Xenophobia, *Final Report*, Ref. 6906/1/95 Rev 1 Limite RAXEN, (Brussels: General Secretariat of the Council of the European Union, 1995).
38. Working Group, *Rapport final*, Brussels, December 1995. http://europa.eu.int/en/agenda/igc-home/eu-doc/reflect/final.html
39. Directive 2000/43/CE of June 28, 2000 (OJ L 180 of July 19, 2000).
40. Directive 2000/78/CE of November 27, 2000 (OJ L 303 of December 2, 2000) and Decision of the Council of November 27, 2000 (OJ L 303/23 of December 2, 2000).
41. http://217.141.24.196/2000/03/Feature/EU0003235F.html
42. In effect, the directive stipulates that "interdiction of discrimination should be made without prejudice to the maintenance or adoption of measures designed to prevent or compensate for the disadvantages among a group of persons of one race or a given ethnic origin."
43. For a comparative account, see Guiraudon, "Equality in the Making?" October 2009.
44. Council document 16054/04.
45. Carrera, *A Typology of Different Integration Programmes in the EU*; Jacobs and Rea, *The End of National Models?*; and Guiraudon, "Integration contracts for immigrants."

Bibliography

Badoux, Ted. 1993. "The Netherlands," in Ted Badoux and Paul Gulbenkian, (eds.), *Immigration Law and Business in Europe*. Colorado Springs: John Wiley and Sons.

Berger, Vincent. 1994. *Jurisprudence de la Cour Européenne des Droits de l'Homme*. Paris: Sirey.

Brubaker, Rogers. 1992. *Citizenship and Nationhood in France and Germany*. Cambridge, MA: Harvard University Press.

———. 2001. "Return of Assimilation: Changing Perspectives on Assimilation and Its Sequels." *Ethnic and Racial Studies* 24: 531–548.

Carrera, Sergio. 2006. *A Typology of Different Integration Programmes in the EU*, briefing paper IP/C/LIBE/FWC/2005–22 submitted January 13, 2006, Immigration and Integration, DG Internal Policies of the Union, Directorate C—Citizens' rights and Constitutional Affairs. URL: http://www.libertysecurity.org/article1192.html (accessed on June 12, 2008).

Checkel, Jeffrey. 2001. "Why Comply? Social Learning and European Identity Change." *International Organization* 55(3): 553–588.

Conant, Lisa. 2006. "Individuals, Courts, and the Development of European Social Rights." *Comparative Political Studies* 39: 76–100.

Council of Europe. 1991. *Community and Ethnic Relations in Europe*. Final report of the Community Relations Project of the Council of Europe. Strasbourg: Council of Europe.

Douglas-Scott, Sionaidh. 2006. "A Tale of Two Courts: Luxembourg, Strasbourg and the Growing European Human Rights Acquis." *Common Market Law Review* 43(3): 629–665.

Favell, Adrian. 2001. *Philosophies of Integration: Immigration and the Idea of Citizenship in France and Britain*. Paperback revised edition. London: Palgrave.

Federal Government's Commissioner for Foreigners' Affairs. 1994. *Report by the Federal Government's Commissioner for Foreigners' Affairs on the Situation of Foreigners in the Federal Republic of Germany in 1993.*

Feldblum, Miriam. 1999. *Reconstructing Citizenship: The Politics of Nationality Reform and Immigration in Contemporary France.* Albany: State University of New York Press.

Fraser, Nancy and Axel Honneth. 2003. *Redistribution or Recognition? A Political-Philosophical Exchange.* New York: Verso.

Geddes, Andrew. 2003. *The Politics of Migration and Immigration in Europe.* London: Sage.

Geddes, Andrew and Virginie Guiraudon. 2004. "The Emergence of a European Union Policy Paradigm amidst Contrasting National Models: Britain, France and EU Anti-discrimination Policy." *West European Politics* 27(1): 334–335.

Glazer, Nathan. 1983. *Ethnic Dilemmas. 1964–1982.* Cambridge, MA: Harvard University Press.

Guiraudon, Virginie. 2000. *Les politiques d'immigration en Europe.* Paris: L'Harmattan.

———. 2003. "The Constitution of a European Immigration Policy Domain: A Political Sociology Approach." *Journal of European Public Policy* 10(2): 263–282.

———. 2007. "Multicultural Odysseys: The Role of International Institutions and Legal Norms." *Ethnopolitics* 6(4): 603–606.

———. 2008. "Integration Contracts for Immigrants: Common Trends and Differences amongst European Experiences." Madrid: Real Instituto Elcano. URL: http://www. realinstitutoelcano.org/wps/portal (accessed on June 12, 2008).

———. 2009. "Equality in the Making? Implementing European Antidiscrimination Law." *Citizenship Studies* 13(4) (August).

Jacobs, Dirk and Andrea Rea. 2007. *The End of National Models? Integration Courses and Citizenship Trajectories in Europe*, paper presented at the EUSA conference in Montreal, 17–19 May 2007. URL: http://www.unc.edu/euce/eusa2007/papers/jacobs-d-11i.pdf (accessed on June 12, 2008).

Joppke, Christian. 1999. Immigration and the Nation-state: The United States, Germany, and Great Britain. Oxford : Oxford University Press.

Joppke, Christian and Ewa Morawska (eds.). 2003. *Toward Assimilation and Citizenship: Immigrants in Liberal Nation-States.* New York and London: Palgrave.

Kastoryano, Riva. 2002. *Negotiating Identities: States and Immigrants in France and Germany.* Princeton, NJ: Princeton University Press.

Keck, Margaret and Kathryn Sikkink. 1998. *Activists beyond Borders: Advocacy Networks in International Politics.* Ithaca, NY: Cornell University Press.

Kymlicka, Will. 2007. *Multicultural Odysseys: Navigating the New International Politics of Diversity.* Oxford: Oxford University Press.

Krüger, Hans and Wolfgang Strasser. 1994. "Combatting Racial Discrimination: The European Convention on the Protection of Human Rights and Fundamental Freedoms," in Julie Cator and Jan Niessen (eds.). *The Use of International Conventions to Protect the Right of Migrants and Ethnic Communities.* Strasbourg: Churches' Commission for Migrants in Europe.

Lochak, Danièle. 1989. "Les minorités et le droit public français: du refus des différences à la gestion des différences," in Alain Fenet and Gérard Soulier (eds.). *Les minorités et leurs droits depuis 1789.* Paris: L'Harmattan.

Moravcsik, Andy. 2000. "The Origins of Human Rights Regimes." *International Organization* 54 (Spring): 217–252.

OECD (Organization for Economic Co-Operation and Development). 2007. *Trends in International Migration.* Paris: OECD.

Risse, Thomas, Stephen Kopp, and Kathryn Sikkink. 1999. *The Power of Human Rights International Norms and Domestic Change.* Cambridge: Cambridge University Press.

Scheeck, Laurent. 2005. The Relationship between the European Courts and Integration through Human Rights. *Heidelberg Journal of International Law* 65(4): 837–885.

Soysal, Yasemin. 1994. *Limits of Citizenship: Migrants and Postnational Membership in Europe.* Chicago: Chicago University Press.

Stavros Stephanos. 1997. "Freedom of Religion and Claims from Exemption from Generally Applicable, Neutral Laws: Lessons from Across the Pond?" *European Human Rights Law Review* 6: 607–625.

Steiner, Henry J. and Philip Alston. 2000. *International Human Rights in Context.* Second edition. Oxford: Oxford University Press.

Taylor, Charles. 1994. "The Politics of Recognition," in Amy Gutmann (ed.), *Multiculturalism: Examining the Politics of Recognition.* Princeton, NJ: Princeton University Press.

Thym, Daniel. 2008. "Respect for Private and Family Life under Article 8 ECHR in Immigration Cases: A Human Right to Regularize Illegal Stay?" *International and Comparative Law Quarterly* 57(1) (January): 87–112.

Van Dijk, Pieter and G. J. H. van Hoof. 1998. *Theory and Practice of the European Convention of Human Rights.* Third edition. The Hague: Kluwer.

Weaver, Kent. 1986 "The Politics of Blame Avoidance." *Journal of Public Policy* 6(4): 371–398.

PART 3

State, Nation, and Borders

CHAPTER EIGHT

The European State

JEAN-MARC FERRY

It is not desirable and probably not possible even to speak of a European state as one speaks of the French state or even of the American, German, or Swiss federal state. However, partisans of an integrated Europe do not seem to have their sights on any constitutional model other than the federal state. Their institutional fantasy is fixed on the "United States of Europe," envisaged along the lines of Federal Germany or the *Confédération helvétique*. It is true that Switzerland, notwithstanding its modest geographical dimensions, is a successful example of a federal state organizing peaceful coexistence and cooperative solidarity among different "nationalities" within a confederation with four official languages, of which the three principal ones even appear to represent Europe in microcosm, at least as it has been constructed. Those who demand federalism, taking inspiration from the existing national models to think of a "Constitution of Europe," do not consider a difficulty in the fact that in all these cases, the federal state that serves as implicit model is always a *national* state. Yet the trivial originality of such a European state (if for "state" we take the legal meaning) is that it would necessarily be supranational. We know no actual example of a *supranational* state, and the federal character of existing systems—for example, in Switzerland, in North America, and in Germany—does not diminish the fact that these are all national states. We might even suspect that no modern state is really possible without a national setting. There is indeed an American nation, a Swiss nation, a German nation. In Europe, empires have failed to integrate people politically, and states are no longer required except by nations (or in their name). Nevertheless there is no *one* European nation; Europe is not a nation. Why? This is a question of fact that, strictly speaking, appears to express something contingent, a situation that might evolve. Moreover, the partisans of the future supranational integration of a *European people* lean on this idea. In effect, they try to show that the goal of European construction is to socially, culturally, economically, and politically integrate communitarian Europe, such that at the end of the day European space will be as unified as the great nations that constitute it once were. We are accustomed by a rhetoric of mutual recognition and by respect for differences in the "dialogism" of a "plural Europe" to ignore counterarguments: some think it is possible to reach a situation in which united Europe would no longer have barriers between nationalities and where community bodies would have achieved the essential transfers of authority—particularly those corresponding to sovereign functions (currency, defense, diplomacy, police, justice), making the Union a state in and of itself, sovereign inside and outside. Whatever they say, this is indeed the goal pursued in Europeanist circles of conventional orientation. Nobody sees any other serious means of realizing, as they say, "a constantly closer union among the peoples" of Europe than to pursue integration down a path in many respects similar to that once followed by the great modern nations. For orthodox Europeanists, the acknowledgement that there is no *one* European nation, or even that Europe *is not* a nation, does not amount to any valid objection. On the other hand, they would be more worried by the assertion that not only Europe cannot be constituted as a nation, but that its political integration cannot be achieved in the conventional form of the state.

★ ★ ★

Why can there not be *one* European nation? It is sometimes said that this is due to one fact: the weight of past history. Those who support this point of view emphasize that the formation of European nations took more than half a thousand years to be accomplished, and that consequently the political integration of Europe is a necessarily long process, much longer than technocratic ignorance once figured. It is a matter of maturation over several centuries, which no politics, and a fortiori no European technocrat, can decree. Since it took centuries to form national public spaces acculturated to the principles of democracy and the legal state, how can one imagine that in a few years a European public space could be established—by decree? The edification of a grand European nation is a historic prospect that is much too distant and much too profound for the scope of political constructivism.[1]

Such is the substance of a critique that, under the apparent wisdom of thinking that has felt the weight of history, poorly dissimulates the prejudice it starts from: the idea that Europe is not fundamentally to be first *constructed*, but to be *formed*, as once it took a whole process of civilization to form European nations. The force of reason seems to reside wholly on the side of a critique employed to stigmatize "modern constructivist voluntarism." However, the historical argument of a process of multicentury formation might perhaps speak against a constructivist illusion of European technocratism, *if it was still* a matter of reproducing on the continental level what had previously been realized on the national level. But the formation of European nations has largely realized the very process to be accomplished, which the objection of the "long duration" seems to ignore. The formation of political cultures having integrated, each in its own manner, the normative implications of democracy and the state of law, implications sealed in national constitutions and presented in the "cosmo-political" element of human rights—*this is largely a fait accompli for Europe*. This is why the objection of history's weight is not really profound. This is what makes the substance of modern European nations; resulting indeed from a long process of formation, it offers the precise basis for constructing a European union (EU). As a power waiting to be put into action, European democracy is surely not something that has to be created ex nihilo. As for the differentiations that modernization has produced within each nation, they are clearly an achievement, "separations" that are decisive for democracies: between the religious and the political, the political and the economic, the economic and the domestic. Democracies possess a functional specialization of systems: fiscal, monetary, technical, bureaucratic, media, educational—as well as the logical autonomy of spheres of values: ethics, law, science, aesthetics. From this point of view, the national scale is only a framework for managing wider trends. At the continental level, the multicentury process by which modern European nations were formed, realizing impersonal and anonymous forms of domination, while the social and technological division of labor, the monetarization of the economy, and successive revolutions of the technological system all steered the economy toward automated production, extending de facto to the global level the effects of factual solidarity. Sustained by the fantastic extension of long-distance transportation and telecommunication networks, where we now see virtual communities deprived of any geographic and national setting, such "globalization" was accompanied by what, for its part, European construction had already achieved with respect to the suppression of barriers to communication in Ernest Gellner's sense[2]: the abolition of customs barriers, of course, but also "harmonization" of national legislation and regulation, "normalization" of manufacturing standards and commercialization for the free circulation of merchandise and then services, capital and persons. There has been a geographical adjustment at the level of "structural activities" by redistribution from one region to another, as well as transnational programs in the domains of culture, science, and the media.

Ironically, the argument of long synchronicities of maturation over centuries seems rather blind to the very history it invokes, that is to say, the fact that the history of the formation of European nations has consisted precisely of surmounting particularist obstacles—or, if one prefers, of realizing the preconditions for the formation of a great European space. This space is before our eyes; it has indeed been prepared by the centuries of history, the importance of which might have been misunderstood by the enthusiasts of European construction. But in this case, where is the "good" argument against the utopia of the supranational integration of Europe? Where is the real objection to the idea that Europe can be constituted on the image of our nation-states?

This argument surely does not consist of invoking the weight of history—the necessarily long duration of a process of *forming* modern European nations. Instead it would invoke the specificity of a logic of *constructing* these same nations. Modern nations, in effect, were *constructed* as modern by largely artificial, voluntary, and political paths that have nothing to do with the long, quasi natural, and historical path on which they could have been formed in the course of centuries, through successive moments of gentes, first, then populus and later patria,[3] then the *regnum* opposed to the imperium,[4] with all the vagaries of alliances, marriages, successions,[5] wars of conquest, epidemics, geographic situations defining axes of commerce, climates more or less propitious for agriculture and, last but not least, the horizontal (geographic) diffusion and vertical (social) diffusion of a great "civilization of writing" that carried the Enlightenment lexicon.[6] This whole process of a formation realized over the long term merits consideration if one wants to understand why, for example, France, Hungry, and England are what they are. One might also learn from this long history how to grasp what Europe is as a "spiritual principle,"[7] or how one can speak of European culture as it was awakened by Christianity,[8] then raised to modern civilization with the rise of the Enlightenment. But on the one hand, a perspective that takes the measure of the effect of European history says nothing about the pace required today to achieve an integrated constitution. On the other hand, this perspective invites us to reconstruct the formation process of European nations at the point where that construction was taken in hand by modern states, notably under pressure from the Industrial Revolution.

The *political construction* of modern European nations is articulated around a process of *historical formation*, for which the take-off of Western Christian culture is evidently decisive. Nevertheless, the logic of this political construction of modern nation-states in Europe is the only basis on which one could argue against the possibility of building a united Europe as an equivalent to a great modern nation. The logic of political construction of the nation-states of Europe can only be uneasily applied beyond the stato-national framework, despite attempts that for the most part move in the direction of a political construction that tries to replicate on the supranational level the logic of national constructions. As for the gesture, European supranationalism appears as a redoubled nationalism, where only the geopolitical scale changes, but not the philosophical principle of the nation-state.

First we must clarify this remark by explaining as succinctly as possible what the stato-national principle is, then indicate the limits to the principle being replicated by the method of the builders of the EU. Then we can analyze the reasons why such a supranationalist path would reach an impasse. This does not signify that one cannot "make Europe," but rather that the strategies to construct it politically are not suitable for integration, and at the very least there is a lack of thinking about the deep constitution of modern European states, as well as the means to develop and actualize their principles, while respecting the problematics of a truly postnational situation. The principles that express the deep constitution of European nations cannot be read in treaties or even in the planned constitution.

★ ★ ★

The logic of the political construction of great modern nations is not derived from the birth of the modern state, understood as a centre of decision making that exercises its sovereign jurisdiction over a geographically delimited territory and which refers to the passage from feudalism to absolutism.[9] It is something else to consider the emergence of modern societies: the shift from "communities" to "societies," principally marked by the birth of civil society, as Adam Ferguson has demystified it.[10] What is decisive for the political construction of modern European nations is the institution of *education* in the wide sense, including primary schools, colleges of secondary education and lycées, universities divided into faculties, the French *grandes écoles* (French Graduate schools), and higher institutes, as so many milieu organized for cultural reproduction and social integration. This voluntarist arrangement by the state is the central point for the political construction of modern nations, such that one could define the state as that ensemble of central institutions holding the "monopoly of legitimate *education*." Ernest Gellner, to whom we owe this definition paraphrasing Max Weber's famous formula, explains in detail the reasons why schooling in the wide sense must, as an "exo-educative system," take primacy for social reproduction.[11] This explanation is functionalist: faced with the challenge of the Industrial Revolution, society had to both teach individuals adapted skills and acculturate them to modern knowledge, and to suppress the "barriers to communication" by developing among taught subjects the mastery of the vehicular language, that is to say a language as formal as possible and free from presuppositions.[12] What is interesting here, even when the idea has ceased to be original, is that the constructivist strategy has consisted not simply of regulating a pseudo-natural institution (e.g., the market), but of creating a cultural medium. School for all, a scarcely "natural" institution, aimed at nothing less than to make the individual accede to consciousness, even to competence for the universal, in the sense that Hegel spoke of modern culture.[13] At the very heart of natural communities, with an energy that is more republican than liberal, state policies came long to tear from these communities the spontaneous competence to reproduce themselves culturally by means of the oral transmission of particular kinds of knowledge and to constitute *within the state* the henceforth modern medium for this reproduction. Nevertheless, the French Republic had to combat some of its own to spread this idea in the political class as well as in the social body. Jules Ferry had to argue firmly in the chamber[14] for the crucial importance of a secular school built on the principles of the republic. His political reference, the example he invoked to impress his peers as a model to follow here, was Prussia. Edified on the two pillars of compulsory education and compulsory military service, Prussia (according to Ferry) was able to realize the "alliance of light and force"—the mark of the true civilization.[15]

In conferring on schooling a functional primacy in effective social integration, political participation, and cultural reproduction, the two great European nations made the socialized individual into the true pillar of the new civilization. It was the individual who, by virtue of his *symbolic power*, was going to assure "the" civilization faced with the rest of the world. It was not banking or industrial giants buoyed up by a communication system disseminating the mass symbols to an audience of "receivers"—who would eventually be summoned to inform themselves à la carte in a cyberspace bourgeoning with information. No. In the (vanished) era of the great modern nations, industrial societies were trying to concentrate within *public education* all their potentialities and their symbolic results, to assure a humanist basis for civilization, the only one that appeared sure and effective.

This orientation has been largely renounced by postindustrial societies. We understand that the principle—properly political—of constructing modern nations intervened upstream from civil society, understood as the sphere of economic exchanges. For in conferring on education the functional primacy in the organization of industrial societies, national states would guarantee to their society (and singularly to industrial enterprises) all the input of expertise, skills, culture, competences, symbolic structuring, as well as the ethical and motivational dispositions able to assure their dynamism. It is the state that produced the spiritual energy the civil society needed for its material reproduction; and it is only on the basis of the cultural capital thus formed by the state among its national citizens that economic capital could really be made profitable. We see why colonial imperialism—the state's attempt (sometimes materially more disinterested than one could imagine)[16] to initiate industrial and (more widely) civilizing development overseas that was comparable to the West's—was often a failure. Lacking were the heavy investments in education comparable to what national states were able to realize in the metropolis. At the same time, by this path of educational investment, the state secured a good return on the investments made by bourgeois society for reasons of material growth, not limited to fostering outlets for individuals in business and to enterprises among well-trained producer-consumers. The state also offered numerous careers in public services, within various ministries and foreign services at home and abroad, as well as new kinds of jobs, in particular corps of engineers, the liberal professions (physicians and lawyers, notably), thereby constituting local elites, a middle and upper-middle class capable of managing the new civilization and assuring an income allowing individuals to contribute efficiently to internal demand.

This incomparable dynamic of development occurred under the impetus of national states, at the same time as they developed their own bureaucracy. We might say that any positive phase, punctuated by the great industrial wars of nationalisms, could last as long as the state was producing growing returns for civil society; in other words, as long as the balance of domestic exchange between the state and its society remained positive for the latter.

It is presumed—and many are convinced—that this dynamic has been recently reversed; that the balance of accounts between national states and national societies has become a deficit for the latter or at least society has ceased to be the clear beneficiary. And so the welfare state is accused of having become not only *tutelary,* but also *parasitic,* of costing society and its businesses more than the advantages it procures. This is essentially a utilitarian calculation of costs and benefit that is today one of the common reasons for fighting for the "conservative revolution," with its procession of privatization, deregulation, flexibility. This same utilitarianism also demands an energetic reorientation of *public education* policies toward *professional training,* with a valorization of the said "technical culture" as the new principle of selection designed to recruit the light infantry of the "intelligence revolution." The state must stop increasing its bureaucracy and become "lean," less openly so than private enterprise, of course, by counting more on retirements and reducing its expenditures, lightening infrastructural costs, and developing professional training schemes that are relatively brief and on-the-job; by better adapting the structural resources to manpower or employment needs; by making social security payments more drastically contingent on the "assisted" concretely demonstrating their desire to work; by controlling the rates of the monetary and financial markets; by making scientific research dynamic by distributing it toward the private sector by removing social protection against lay-offs. These are the postulated demands by the "civil society" directed against the state. It is intensely reliant on bodies of the European Community, resulting in the widespread conviction that national states have become positive obstacles to the foreseeable developments of a postnational society that is also imagined to be postindustrial.

Two reasons (or two orders of reason) may be prima facie invoked to explain this phenomenon of inverting the positive dynamic of modern industrial nations, or even to explain the destruction of the synergy previously realized between national states and national societies. First, the public service has entered into phase with the diminishing returns *for private enterprise.* Its marginal cost seems to have overtaken its marginal utility. Social security contributions, fiscal, social, and parafiscal taxes appear to have outstripped the advantages whose costs they serve to finance. It is estimated that the major enterprises of economic infrastructure (transport, energy, telecommunications) might be advantageously privatized now that the public monopoly has sufficiently guaranteed their power. The fixed perspective of the short term market does not allow the admission that health and education services might be really profitable on an economic level, for such profitability is so invisible and immaterial that it seems to be part of the air one breathes. Regarding education, the strategically central point, the *cultural* training traditionally provided by the school is largely uncoupled from technical training, on the one hand, and from narrowly scientific on the other. This specialization entails three easily perceptible consequences that cumulatively act in a negative way. First, technical specialization is only profitable in the short term, in such a way that the school loses long-term and strong profitability. Second, scientific specialization accelerates the tendency (always present and indispensable) to technological innovation, which modifies the structure of need for qualifications, but also induces undeniable gains in efficiency, dispensing with large and massive recourse to a workforce that is more or less qualified. Third, this dual call to abandon a "generalist" cultural formation results in suppressing certain symbolic, moral, and intellectual resources, whose utility has been tragically underestimated by scientism, technicism, instrumentalism, and the pragmatism that all constitute the common ideological funds of working societies. All that is not immediately and visibly effective, functional, operational, and profit-making is thrown out, in the cause of rationalization; and there is the question of what should be done with students in history, philosophy, or literature, anybody educated in humanist culture and motivated by it, practiced in reflexivity, judgment, and in general the essential dispositions of the type of civilization industrial society stemmed from and the resources by which it was almost entirely fed. This is fundamentally because industrialism, whether capitalist or socialist, thought that humanism was a *luxury*; the civilizational principle of modern nations today is tending to crumble. All our conventional mediums of social integration, whether traditional ones such as family, church, and army, or else modern ones such as school, university, and business *from the point of view of social integration* are losing power. And we are almost desperately in search of replacement mediums to assure the development (or even simple maintenance) of what for us is civilization.

★   ★   ★

Europe—not the historical Europe of nations, but the political Europe of their integration—is aware of this situation. But it is aware in its own manner. Perhaps Europeanist milieu that are called upon to train the new political class do suspect that it would be problematic to liquidate the nations by "accompanying" with too much hast the rampant abolition of their sovereignty, for this would risk increasing the isolation of the regulatory power and the disconnection of the European political system from the lively forces of the great civil society that is supposedly in formation. Perhaps there is a wealth of bad conscience in the current dynamics of integration. One does not want to remain deaf to appeals for prudence and reason from intellectuals concerned with heritage.[17] I suspect though that this bad conscience is really a false consciousness. It is not because we have blown up "obstacles" like national sovereignty, customs barriers, national currencies and regulations, or have created competences both shared and not in common, competing and nonexclusive, that we risk destroying a civilizational substance that is impalpable but essential. If someone says "Careful! Do not destroy nations, for you may throw the baby out with the bathwater by diluting the substance of European civilization like that"—but it is a facile refrain. The decline of nations is problematic only because as a symptom it reveals the loss of the power of the principal mediums of socialization the modern nations were able to stress. On the European continent, there is no doubt that the French state and the Prussian state (now gone) did indeed have a *civilizational project*, and that they largely realized this project by the most energetic organization of the cultural reproduction of their respective national societies. These states incarnated in their social institutions what Hegel called the "national spirit," that is to say, the spiritual principle in which a people discover and objectively exhibit their conception of freedom through the edifice of an extended state, a veritable constitution of the society as a whole, of the national community allying the state and civil society. And no doubt political Europe would also like to have a civilizational project like certain great nations once did. But it cannot simply recompose the social as radically as some nation-states did, often by authoritarian or semi-authoritarian means, and so it must trust the *superficial principle of civil society*: the laws of the free market.

Political Europe cannot act in the manner of a state *constructing its nation* because it cannot act at the heart of the principle of organization. On the one hand, the conventional integrating mediums are losing power and are only illusorily reactivated as effective mediums of socialization. On the other hand, what spirit might Europe have, what supranational principle, to give it the remarkable energy of creating new powerful and effective mediums for widescale social integration, political participation, and cultural reproduction? There lie the limits of a European political integration comparable to what it once was at the level of nation-states, that is to say, a *vertical* political integration resting on *obligations* (school, army, taxation). For the EU, political integration can now only be horizontal, that is to say, engaged in exercising *soft power* in relation to civil society, where the state acts more like an initiator of consensus and a pronouncer of rules. Still, community bodies are on the lookout for ways of arousing and supervising the emergence and take-off of mediums of social integration.

Thus they are betting on small and medium businesses that do furnish, it is true, almost three-quarters of the employment in the Union; and they are wagering on the development of the so-called information society, aiming perhaps at Europeanization of a media system strong in satellite technologies, fiber optics, the Internet, cable, and digitalization—the functional equivalent of what, mutatis mutandis, the school system represented for the construction of modern nations. But unlike the nationalist principle centered on Gellner's exo-educative system, the new public space fantasized for Europe[18] cannot act in a constructive and planned way on the basic cultural formation of individuals, that is to say, *upstream from civil society* or else between the family and society. Television, the Internet, the home computer, and any innovation expected from an integration of "multimedia" based on new information technologies for home use cannot be the functional equivalent of a classroom. Similarly, professional mediators like journalists, hosts and presenters, program producers and schedulers, will never be possible substitutes for teachers. The media system resembles the educational system only by the formal possibility it offers to transmit symbolic contents to an audience. But the media diffusion of these contents does not follow procedures of pedagogic and supervised inculcation that are adjusted to the students' pace and combined with sanctions aimed at progress through courses that take account of what has been learned. The diffusion of messages to segmented audiences is merely rather superficial cultural scanning. We would have to mobilize a science developed differently from semiotics and rhetoric that would be up to elaborating media packages for the *education* of individuals.

It is around *information* that community bodies are working, particularly the information offered to the principal economic agents and to small and medium businesses so they may better integrate the manufacturing and organizational norms that make them competitive in the market.

If those responsible for community integration had aspired to a real *civilizational project* that could be compared to what was borne a century ago by the French Republic or the Prussian monarchy, they would probably have targeted their strategy quite differently. They would not have reasoned only in liberal-democratic fashion (by favoring all sorts of free circulation) or in liberal-technocratic fashion (by harmonizing the tiniest regulations of economic activity). They would not have simply assumed that a *European civil society* would already be in formation and in sight as soon as the conditions of the Common Market were assembled, so that there was nothing to do to make this civil society emerge, except to liberate all the potentialities supposedly locked (incarcerated) in the fetters of national states, a creative potential that only needs to be actualized in the full light of community law! No. Rather than wanting to remove obstacles to the free circulation of persons, merchandise, services, and capital, while creating uniform rules of play in line with international commercial agreements, against the backdrop of monetarist discipline, the politicians of European construction could have given priority to the political and social anchoring of at least one medium suitable for forming the future European citizen.

We should not misunderstand the implications of this expression. "Forming the future European citizen" does not mean giving children and adolescents a modernized civic education under the auspices of right-thinking Europeanist doctrine—a democratic and European equivalent of the French song "Maréchal [Pétain], nous voilà !" ("Maréchal, here we come")—with all the nonsense that passes for political education when it pursues the edification of correct thinking, whatever the content. Forming the future European citizen would mean an original pedagogic project of universal culture, proceeding from a philosophically intelligent critique of the national educational systems currently existing in the Union.

This would break with the routine of the scholastic curriculum, revising the selection of knowledge to be inculcated on the basis of a few fundamental questions: What type of individual do we want for civilization? What kinds of knowledge should be acquired to understand and orient this civilization, as it is now and could be later? What sciences should be favored in the curriculum that are now simply ignored by national teaching? How can you communicate really current knowledge so as to overcome complexity without erasing it? Community bodies are largely uninterested in an educational project of this kind, that is to say, one that has the ambition to respond to calls for understanding and explanation from civilization in its current state of complexity and opacity. Intergovernmental and community authorities have thought that member states were big enough to manage an educational project well, whereas in fact they often—invariably—fail to reform education, resigned to "nonadaptation" or worse, to imagining that this nonadaptation is primarily measured by the needs of the economic market. But what market could measure the vital needs linked to the very fate of a civilization whose destiny is to constantly develop or else collapse?

In line with the utilitarian spirit dominant in the domain of school and university policies,[19] community bodies are especially concerned to convince states that are a little too humanist to form young people with a view to the needs of skilled labor, the key word being *adaptation.*[20] They are occupied with recruitment of their own functionaries, thanks to higher institutes specialized in "European studies," in the essentially legal and economic subjects that concern the Union. But among the educational institutions bearing the European label, none seriously express the originality of a civilizational project of great scale.[21] This today is a defect of educational systems in general, and the originality of a European pedagogic project would not be a "philosophy of education" that is made positivistic as educational science in psychology and sociology. What would justify such a project for the education of a European citizen is rather a *philosophy of civilization.* Reflection about teaching techniques and "tools" is relatively sterile. Pretensions to reform that think more substantially about the "purposes" of schooling lead to little more than chitchat. In any case, it matters little to society whether the European Community takes close or distant charge of the training of civil servants, whether they are jurists or engineers, bureaucrats or business people. National states have been effectively occupied with professional training for the needs of industrial societies, and so-called multinational groups might take charge of training in the private sector. In short, it is not a supplementary version of a formation linked to so-called European studies that in the current situation would distinguish a community project from existing national routines.

The originality of a European project that might be illuminated by a *philosophy of civilization with didactic orientation* would be to aim at the properly humanist and actualized objective, putting the future European citizen in a situation to understand in *ordinary language* what contemporary science conceals in specialized languages. An "ethics of the scientific age"[22] that assumes the competence to respond practically to all cognitive domains, would bring within everyone's scope the great stakes of humankind and the natural environment, between other people and himself as an individual. We are astonished that university doctors can say almost nothing sound about natural systems "as explained to children" from a global standpoint. This is especially the case with biology and ecology, understood at the level of elementary definitions concerning, for example, what separates and links together the mineral, vegetable, and animal kingdoms. There is also a need to dissipate the dramatic ignorance afflicting even PhDs concerning the technological environment: people do not know what our technological civilization is about, at least since the second industrial revolution, and especially about the functioning of distance communications, even when the appliances are domestic: telephone, radio, television, modems, GPS, DVD, I-pod. A plan to educate that is informed by a philosophy of civilization does not try to train engineers capable of advancing the technology of integrated circuits, but trains a citizen capable of explaining to his or her children the forces that compose our natural environment and out day-to-day civilization.

The "man of breeding" today does not exist, even at the level of a rudimentary cognitive competence able to assign the things that surround us a scientifically pertinent concept without ceasing to be intelligible to everyone. Such a demand is not original in itself. But teaching it would presuppose an unprecedented and salutary performance with rich philosophical implications: appropriating in ordinary language the contents of knowledge concealed in the languages of experts and communicating them as translated into the daily world of experience.[23] This is the new *culture*, if one means the competence that results from a reflexive appropriation of the contents incorporated in the objective realizations of *civilization*, whether of techniques or institutions, or even the symbolic edifices of formalized knowledge.

One cannot overestimate the civilizational scope and philosophical implication of a pedagogic enterprise of this type, which would establish on a major level—that of the enlarged EU—universal teaching procedures and protocols enabling everyone, each future citizen of the Union, to respond to a civilization on the move—which today, thanks to exclusive specialization, only a few very rare individuals know how to do, even when children are supposed to be capable of it. Only then might we envisage the emergence of a *European state*, with a power capable of carrying its political will, not over trivial technical regulations, but about the saving of a civilization whose real abstractions, formed by the great currency and banking systems of industry and commerce, of civilian and military technology, of bureaucracy and the media all demote human beings—whom they almost don't need to reproduce. Then we might understand the negative phantasms of *critical theory*[24]; only a few specialists in artificial languages will remain attached to social utility as appreciated by the system—for example the posthuman language of monetary signs and even legal rules, all this artificial semiosis in which are enunciated the codes of circulation and transformation of grandeur on automatic pilot to prevent dysfunction and to advance organizational concepts. Meanwhile stockholders, citizens of yesteryear, stripped of even their traditional function of producers, have no more honor than proletarians for selling their labor on the market, happy to be still regarded as consumers.

For having refused to find a philosophical dimension for a civilizational project (understood in a way remaining to be explained), intergovernmental and community bodies strictly speaking (essentially, the council and commission) are losing their political energy in a weak regulatory power, without being able to put in place the powerful mediums for forming European citizens. It goes without saying that, lacking these citizens, Europe will not exist, either as a political Union or a fortiori as a state.

★ ★ ★

This is why a voluntarist orientation (along the path to a European state worthy of the name) is *necessarily* unrealistic: not because political will is still lacking among "Eurocrats" for such a humanist project (this would underestimate the fervor, generosity, and imagination that animate many agents of European construction), but because the conditions of social reproduction apparently no longer lend themselves to it. "Apparently" because they are today dominated by a restrictive and quasi-monopolistic definition of social utility.[25] European bodies do not pose as a state but rather as a political and administrative system that does not espouse, even in constitutional appearance, the classical form of a legal state. Unlike a state whose perfect formula is found in Hegelian philosophy, a *politico-administrative system* cannot be ethically formative. It is at best a producer of intelligibility and complexity at the same time.[26] On one hand, it raises interactions that it judges socially pertinent to the intelligibility of legal rules that one might call "constitutive"[27]; and then as a function of these prior definitions, it prescribes to actors social behaviors that conform to the "rules of the game," whereas these prescriptions would normally be combined with sanctions. Thus the whole legal arrangement, from legislation to jurisdiction via regulation, contributes, according to bureaucratic style, to the "cold" intelligibility and norms of the social world. On the other hand, the politico-administrative system puts in place rules that ramify considerably in the social landscape of licit procedures. In pursuing communitarian integration essentially along this path of intensive legal codification, the bodies responsible for European law are confronted with a specific problem that has little to do with the elaboration of a civilizational project; it is essentially about integrating new norms of community law: decisions, directives, and regulations. For setting rules does not suffice; the rules must be followed. For that, the tool of sanction represented by the tribunals attached to the cause of integration, starting with the European Court of Justice in Luxembourg, risk being rapidly overwhelmed by the task of making the new laws respected. Moreover, it is not *ex post* that the rules must be validated as obligatory, but preferably *ex ante*, so that these rules of the game effectively govern the target interactions of member societies of the Union. This is why the political path chosen essentially by the commission is not only the partner of national administrations[28] but also the "lively forces" of these societies. These are neo-corporatist representations of diverse syndicalist, professional, and associative activities. Hence the importance of *lobbies*, or interest groups and pressure groups[29] whose proliferation in proximity to decision making has been encouraged, so the decision process might be valuably informed and accepted by interested parties. Thus these decisions, regulations, and directives become accepted as norms. The rules of community law may be followed since they have become known and recognized beforehand in the semiprivate space of preparatory decisions.

Once the rules have been endorsed by *soft power* legitimation, they become in principle applicable to everyone, and they must be taken into account, even when people are most immediately focused on rules of national origin. The new law must be universally known across the territory of the Union by the economic agents concerned for it to be recognized and followed. This partly explains why the strategic tool, the substantial lever of community integration, is not formation but *information*; why community's medium of the future is not the university but the media,[30] and especially the vast complex composed of satellite, television, computer, and telephone, with the new technologies of information and communication (NTIC), such as fiber optics and digital compression: the *multimedia complex*. At the same time as multimedia appear as a privileged medium of integration, Europe is also seeing in the new technologies serving the advent of the "information society" unexpected chances for a new economic boom propelled by the "intelligence revolution." Social actors, households, banks, and businesses can be persuaded of the resources offered and prospects opened by the setting up of interconnected networks, a great encyclopedia containing all the knowledge of our time in multiple domains. This great book of open civilization, made transparent thanks to new technologies for transmitting information, is represented online by data banks accessible through networks, and off line by printing content in hypertext on CD-ROM's available in stores and utilizable on home computers.

Can the social fabric be recreated and revitalized in the cabled materialization of telecommunication networks replacing the concrete sites of business and the school by telecommuting and distance-learning? This would imply a great deal of flexibility in the use of time, the economy of transportation, the decongestion of cities, more personal autonomy—but also isolation and perhaps desolation. Would the contacts thus freed from spatial and bodily constraints then liberate transnational solidarities by a protean community of global communication? We easily fantasize about such a community—informal, moving, overarching, and uncensorable—that would be capable of discouraging policing, mobilizing world opinion for the causes of peace and ecology, the struggle against famine and disease, world solidarity with those suffering from natural or political disasters, or realizing the unexploited treasures of knowledge held by individuals at the other ends of the earth—dynamizing the unprecedented power of communication without borders to achieve the real formation of a planetary person. At this stage of our technological utopia, the "information society," directly or by the intermediary of operators, does intensify communication among people, but will it become a medium of formation, better adapted to the desires and dispositions of young "audiences" than the traditional and severe medium of teaching: the school in the widest sense?

Technically, the interconnected networks of the "information superhighway," the great universal medium called upon to serve the transnational integration of the European continent and beyond, the transcontinental integration of the planet,[31] relates politically to both the paradigm of the school, medium of education, and the paradigm of the market, medium of exchange. The education promoted by the school, like the exchange performed by the market, may be subsumed under categories of communication. In fact, this objectified communication of network technology may perform the *transmission of knowledge*, by analogy with the school, as well as the *circulation of ideas*, by analogy with the market. It seems that, independently of the technological innovations profiling the "information society," the acquisition of knowledge increasingly takes place along the path of mutually intensified information. Being educated tends to signify in practice that you are informed about what is done somewhere. It means communicating, or rather obtaining the results of reflection or research. This is true for scientific research or for the logic presiding over the growth in scientific knowledge; this logic is much less than that of discoveries manifested by the great systematic theories, than exploration that might turn up intersecting facts; that which can be transmitted in the informational mode, while the dissemination of a grand systematic theory in the scientific community presupposes the mediation of books and articles in the form of lessons corresponding to a whole course cycle. But this is true more generally, including for the education of children by other means than the traditional didactic ones. That teaching is, or wants to be, more "interactive" does not signify only that the student dialogues more with the teacher, but that the student can free his curiosity and follow his caprice by posing questions that come to his mind. The pedagogic body would try to furnish answers with a degree of depth corresponding to the evolution of each individual demand.

Many illustrations might converge in this direction to give credit to the thesis that information is presented much more than previously as a legitimate procedure of formation. It is almost a new culture, even a culture of the future, whether it is acquired pragmatically thanks to exchanges of information, by the circulation of messages, or more or less informal communications whose principal motor is a sort of anecdotal (possibly fleeting) curiosity. One gleans information and thus acquires an intuitive basis of knowledge that it would then be possible, but by no means indispensable, to broaden more systematically, methodically, academically. The essential thing is that everyone's mind remains in contact with news contained virtually in the minds of others, so that instead of each person being seated at a school desk to compete for the best grades by hiding his writing from the neighbor's gaze, one asks open questions all over the place, and each person answers as he can.

It is as if the living tradition, the traditional mode of cultural reproduction by oral transmission today might (but in a different form) reassume its rights by virtue of the preference granted to the informal flexibility of cognitive exchanges that, direct or mediated, are realized on the most liberal principle of information-on-demand. This would have the consequence of subverting the renovated humanist (almost heroic) ideal of an educational project supposing the translation of very elaborate scientific content into the natural language of the world. Here a tension between theory and practice, between the specialized language of science and the natural language of life, ceases to be a problem. What matters is not to understand well in one's own language what was taught otherwise in science, but to transmit what each person draws in his own way from the practical and sensory fallout of civilization, whether the fruit of individual experiences or by virtue of contacts with persons presumed competent in their particular domain. One does not count, as formerly, on the intellectual performance of each individual to draw from schoolbooks the substance of scholarly culture. One counts much more on the communicational competence of everybody to propagate and to coconstruct *social knowledge* that, unlike the content of the sciences, will be to a great extent offered freely, like the air one breathes.

The argument made by enthusiasts of postindustrial society is "why want lift the person of the street to the level of educated elites?" since the latter assure their reproduction by lineages of directors of studies, teachers, researchers, professors, graduate assistants—in short, the whole system allowing the intergenerational continuity of scholarly research? Why continue to award selective degrees, sanctioned by the criteria of universities and *grandes écoles*, instead of clearly acknowledging their elitist character? For those concerned with equality, the harm only persists as long as perceptions of social legitimacy remain fixed on a hierarchy of diplomas, as long as it still governs the hierarchy of the three orders: money, power, and prestige.

With the objective social demand now massively affects not up-to-date knowledge, but (as sooner or later will have to be recognized) the socially positive externalities of communicational skills of everybody in daily life, then there will be no need to organize a race to diplomas each year, while remaining impotent about the social consequences of failure. For the stakes of success will be redeployed on terrains that instead value the almost natural ability to live in society, foremost the expressive abilities, it becomes so clear that the best resource results from the socialization of individuals.

★　★　★

Let us now go back to the more ambitious "humanist" project of making universally accessible the products of civilization, as explained by science. This project of renovated education proceeds on the dominant model of (intelligent) *information*, too, even it does not necessarily contain a real discipline of *formation*, and therefore would not pull Europe up to the stature of a state. A European state presupposes the formation of a European people. It does not mean contrasting the unity of the European people with the plurality of the nations that compose it, which would have the effect of posing a contradiction between a European state and the member states of the Union, while aiming to suppress the latter. Supranationalism is not only contradictory in itself, but is what it pretends to overcome: a nationalism moreover blind to this contradiction and stubbornly pursuing its simple work of devastation. No. In speaking of a European people, one is not aiming to suppress national differences, but to form a common spirit. Consciousness of the community that the nations of Europe could form when gathered in a single people is still an ethnic consciousness, understood in the wider (apparently inoffensive) sense of a consciously shared cultural identity (demarcated, e.g., as Nipponese, Arab, or even American identity). The idea of a European people must be situated beyond culturalist or identitarian oppositions; it can only result from an awareness of the universal, a consciousness that would have to be formed. The content is not the universal as it is usually presented in the instituted forms of modern civilization, whether in the economy or law, science, or philosophy. Rather it would be the universal of humanity as its spirit is formed in the fundamental experiences of living, depending on cultures: experiences of *play, love, dealing*, also of the *reflection* developed secondarily *about* these experiences linked to forms of ludic, erotic, and pragmatic existence, and which itself arises from a form that could be called "philosophical."

Of course, this does not mean teaching the proper fundamental experiences linked to the aforementioned forms of existence (ludic, erotic, pragmatic, philosophic—the last of which would be closely identified with the pedagogic project), but rather putting into language or verbalizing how young Europeans might by intuition realize these experiences, while seeing it as the medium of intercultural understanding. This presupposes, for example, that the game is taken sufficiently seriously to be developed practically as a formative activity, that is to say, as a schematized experience susceptible to reflective elaboration (which is again a discipline linked to formation and education). The same for *love*, sentimental relations and everything that touches emotional life, as well for fusion and separation, the giving of self and the possession of the other, discord and reconciliation, conflict and gratitude. *Dealing* in the widest sense, the *pragmata* that touch any activity governed by public norms puts into play the habitual rules of civility and the interiorized principles of civics.

Such an in-depth education presupposes intelligent information on the state of knowledge incorporated into institutions and technologies, for it aims to elaborate lived experience starting from universal fundamental experiences under the governing idea of a *secular science of experience*. Although it can represent only the plinth of humanist information, it would permit situating the ambition of the pedagogic project at the loftiness of a civilizational project. On this base a European state might then be envisaged. But still it would not suffice that Europeans be conscious of being a people, or even for them to take up the task of being a politically united community; public education would have to be anchored in the same system of sociopolitical references.

To be vibrant, the reality of the state must accord with the concept of it.[32] This is why the unity of a European people, working with the plurality of nations through the formation of the future citizen, would not be the answer—unless the EU managed to assure the objective basis for this unity at the levels of (1) the system if economic needs, and (2) the system of political justice.

Currently the formation of young Europeans, so they constitute a people, can scarcely use the disciplinary form of pedagogic constraint, unless public schooling gives up its conventional forms of school organization. It would probably cost too much for the school to create among future citizens the abilities analogous to those once formed by nation-states at their apogee. In the new context, many more sacrifices may be required, in scholastic subjects as well as by public agents. The school should "open onto life" is the awkward slogan used for a correct intuition of the necessary *secularization of public education* (postnational). This corresponds with current customs and necessities of social life; the educational system is diluted in a vast ensemble where the media system predominates. This *new* public space, whatever its faults, at present signals itself as the rising medium apparently able to take over from the

educational system. But it will not be effective for the political unification of the European people unless it can produce something new in
ethical life. From this standpoint, minors do not have to know about
civil law and the organization of the state; what is important to their
ethical formation relates to politics in a larger sense. Their intelligence
penetrates more easily and willingly into the forms of prepolitical life,
structured around the categories of (first) play and (then) love; to a
lesser extent it is applied spontaneously to matters arising from civil
society.

The openness of the school to life on the street probably means
investing public space with formative missions, but the specifically
political space is the affair of adult citizens of different nationalities.
Without ceasing to be multicultural, such a space might still form some
common sense about the highest forms of rationality as incarnated in
political institutions and in public law. Everything that touches the
system of social life, whether the system of needs or of justice, can be
rethought from the perspective of a confrontation among national traditions; but why presuppose that a deepening of the universal would
result? One might imagine that the particular convictions represented
in national traditions confront reason because it is experienced quite
negatively as objective resistance to juridical reality as structured by
legal interpretations of this reality. In fact, competing interpretations
are offered by diverse cultures and national sensibilities. In a European
legal space that wants to be shared by different cultures, it is clear that
the meaning of community norms is strongly underdetermined, since a
shared political culture has not arisen among member states. This culture is also elaborated in the shock of competing interpretations over
the same principles, even the same legal rules. It is not a bad thing if
conflicts over interpretations are then resolved in the process of public
debates.[33] The idea of public law might be revivified and rejuvenated
if the rising criticism perceived that the contemporary evolution in the
law, quite visible at the community level, largely amounts to legaliz-
ing the particularity inherent in civil society. Otherwise the *principle of
legality* risks being no more than a formal and regulatory supervision of
procedures valid for negotiations over contracts, understandings, and
agreements between social partners. To this extent, it no longer relates
to the state understood as a real public force, a power for justice or a
power for the universal that is indifferent to particularity. Here again
appears something the EU lacks to be a state; community institutions,
even strengthened in relation to nation-states in their effective or normative power, only in *appearance* form a state that is simply animated by

negative compulsion. There is a tendency to weaken public authority in general, by seeing nation-states as so many adversaries or obstacles and substituting the force of private interests. The latter are elevated to a high degree of generalization, but the generalization of private interests is not the universalization of what public character is, which traditionally only the state, as distinct from society, can guarantee.

★　★　★

Might the *principle of publicity* give to the principle of legality the universal substance diluted in the semipublic procedures of administrative regulation? The publicity principle appears to be external to the state, possibly a force opposed to it, a force of criticism, by which the spirit and the body of the state are dissociated, as we think about things concerning death. This public spirit that cannot be found either on the side of the socioeconomic system (that is to say what used to be civil society) or on the side of the politico-administrative system (that is to say what used to be the state) takes refuge ideally in a site that we can call "culture," and which one imagines as the resource from which a public space might draw. This vision combines an idea of Kant's, when he saluted the "Enlightenment era" as what would permit a public *to enlighten itself,* to *educate itself,* as a consequence.[34]

Kant supposed that, lacking financial resources, nation-states, exhausted by public debt, might one day be unable to guarantee the public education essential to the maintenance of power.[35] He saw in culture more than a simple civility: a morality resulting from a process of formation in which individuals interiorize the norms of public life and may thus elevate civility to the civic. Implicitly at least, the public space might offer a substitute for civic education in the formation of citizens, an ethical purpose that, for his part, Hegel assigned to the state. There the state takes on the significance of a public authority, but in another sense than previously. In effect, public reason may also be manifest elsewhere than in the state constituted, so to speak, in its native condition, in a space of public discussion taking place against the background of the cultural resources of meaning.

This presupposes a morality proper to culture. According to Hegel, this means the "subjective freedom we call liberty in the European sense of the word."[36] "The cultured self-defining man desires that he himself be in everything which he does."[37] This morality demands the autonomy of the human subject and brings the citizen not just to require that public norms gain his assent, but also to demand that the

overall system of organizations, the environment that he himself has
helped produce as a member of society, does not remain something
foreign to him. This liberty in the European sense of the word cannot
be satisfied completely with what he would feel in experiences of gifts,
desires, fusion, and separation, excluding the less burning experiences
born of social and political confrontation. Liberty in the European
sense could not be substantially nourished by the affective resources of
love or friendship; someone looking in these warm values for resources
of meaning able to offer an advantageous substitute for the cold issues
posed by the organization of collective life and the state in general,
would renounce quite gladly the essence of his liberty. The moral
necessity that seems thus opposed to the European citizen is justified
not because it belongs to duty, but because it refers back to the essence
of this liberty that Europe was able to invent as a concept and to realize
in institutions and laws. Nevertheless, nothing says that the Europeans
of today are still attached to it in a vital enough fashion to take pains
to realize it in the constitution of a united people and a politically integrated community.[38]
    Whatever the case, Europe has been asked to invent an original
method to erect its political unity, as soon as the discussion of the advantages and disadvantages of the constructivist–statist model (which was
presumed to found the national principle) is over. There is a temptation to transpose that principle onto the supranational scale. If cultural
homogenization may be judged positively, to the extent it suppresses
barriers to communication, the imposition of *global lifestyles*, or generalized standards of living, carries the risk of arousing reactionary and
particularist formations: regionalisms, nationalisms, fundamentalisms,
culturalisms.[39] The political unity obtained by conventional state paths
apparently prevents any explosion and assures the Union's functional
coherence. But the formation of a supranational state carries the risk
of disconnecting community power from national public opinion (a
crisis of legitimacy) and from economic and social actors (a crisis of
regulation). Consequently, a supranational transposition of the national
principle would not be agreed in the historical situation in which
the important phase of construction of a European political union is
engaged. In light of the risks just mentioned, a different path than that
of state constructivism is desirable.
    Political unity must be combined with national plurality, the univer-
sality of the legal framework with the singularity of cultural identities.
One simple solution is the adherence of member states and (virtual) citizens to a common constitution. Then the political identity of citizens

of the EU could be expected to stabilize around a constitutional patriotism. This solution sometimes runs up against objections of formalism and abstract universalism. People deplore a lack of flesh and substance, or else visible defects in the plan. Objections of this kind are ambiguous for they conceal the trap of being too concrete, while leaving the truth pierced by a dilemma. On one hand, formalism and universalism represent the necessary conditions for peaceful coexistence and for mutual recognition of different nationalities within the same political community; on the other, the assumption of formalism of rules and universalism of principles should not imply a political void. How then can we provide substance to European policy? This is not exactly the same thing as elaborating a concrete mobilizing project, which might address social Europe, for example. But to respond to the former is to worry about the formation of a shared political culture. The postnational substance[40] of European politics lies there, like the indispensable mediation among the cultural identities of member nations, on one side, and the political and legal framework on the other. This condition itself presupposes openness and structuring of a European public space.

From the principle of civility to the principle of publicity. The initial dynamic of a shared political culture within the community has a plausible scenario. We note that the intra-community relations formed by representatives of the member states do not obey the schema of ordinary international relations, always well marked by the state of nature. Intra-community relations appear to be a civilized mode of international relations. Historically, the principle of civility, elaborated in the culture of the first modern humanism, in the century of Erasmus, played a decisive role, first to form at the town level (in the face of the peasantry and aristocracy) the class identity of the nascent bourgeoisie; then to constitute at the level of nations civil societies that were autonomous through the gradual insertion of social activates into the market economy; and finally, to integrate regions to the scale of continents into the networks of world commerce contributing to realize a global civilization. The latter risks turning against its initial principle, by consecrating a disconnection of the economy from societies, with all the cortege of "incivilities" this generates and will continue to generate as long as the crisis lasts.

Beyond a simple bourgeoisie politeness as distinct from aristocratic courtesy, civility possesses an eminent political value. As a function of civility, crude conflicts of interest in intra-community relations may be sublimated into the civilized register of conflicts of legal interpretation. The latter may be resolved or realized in the process of public argumentation. The principle of civility is politically elaborated in a principle of discussion, at the same time as it turns to a principle of publicity.

There resides the condition of a public space that is properly European. Its presupposition is still only achieved on paper. Are people pleased to harp on the fact that European public space does not exist, only national public spaces? Still, we can at least count on the power represented by three principles: civility, legality, and publicity. They are the patrimony of European civilization. *Legality* conditions the possible openness of such a space, or if you prefer, its basic structure, by guaranteeing formally the liberty of citizens against arbitrary use of power, while *civility* assures the continuity of the concrete exercise of daily practices of cooperation, whose results are made opposable to concerned parties by the *publicity* of debates, by virtue of the force of non-violent constraint represented by the third party: public opinion. As regarding the link between the openness of a European public space and the formation of a cultural base of community law, the dynamic of formation of a shared political culture within the Union can only be deployed in the movement of confrontation among different national traditions. As I mentioned earlier, this confrontation of culturally anchored traditions coincides with the style of conflicts of legal interpretation. The rules and principles offer, in effect, contentious matter that is particularly productive. The conflicting interpretations, or at the very least, competing ones, about community law, are not flat bearers of pragmatic stakes: they call for contradictory arguments that are fed by different national sensibilities. Thus through legal contention is played out the confrontation of national political cultures, a confrontation whose many occurrences leave traces that elaborate the first *topoï* of a common political culture, the rudiments of a common politico-legal sense acquired by the partners of the European Community due to their active participation in the discussion process.

To declare that a political culture shared by members of the Union "cannot be decreed" is a rather trivial and narrow objection if it is seen as an argument against the optimism of those who seek to glimpse it as a real scenario. More productive is the hypothesis that, given the potential offered by the very heritage of the nations of Europe, a common political culture should now be able to be formed in legal, public, and civilized practices, whose substantial procedure would fundamentally be the discourse itself, carried on in successive registers, where argumentation and reconstruction would manage to resolve contentions that narration and interpretation had previously made explicit.

This scenario puts at the center the procedures in four registers[41] of the discourse conducted under the auspices of three principles. Of course, the contractual condition of membership of member states and their nationals can easily be linked to constitutional principles of the political community of reference (which as regards the EU would need to be systematized). Nevertheless, it differs substantially from the classic version of constitutional patriotism far beyond consensus on the fundamental principles of democracy and the legal state, it profiles the advent of a common sense that is politically operational, which is not the case with even authentic) consensus over the assorted fundamental principles of universalist values.

It is the *idea of politics as culture*. Since Alexis de Tocqueville, we know that democracy is not founded solely on a legal mode; it is also and primarily formed in discursive, cooperative, and deliberative practices. This is why the openness to a democratic European public space as the milieu required for the formation of a shared political culture is more essential strategically for the rise of European politics than the elaboration of a state along legal avenues of an organization of the Union's public authority. That does not mean that the community must not also develop the principle of legality.

But the principle of civility as well as the principle of publicity, which was decisive for the civilization of Enlightenment Europe, seems to take over, among strategic considerations for the blueprint of a properly European political substance. Principles of discussion and of publicity are elements that citizenship evidently demands. We can add the principle of civility that codifies or formalizes respect for differences in individual sensibility, allowing individuals to be safe in society. These principles themselves conceal rules of procedure. Still, it is interiorization, the appropriation of these rules by individuals, which forms them in a culture of citizenship. As long as the rules of civility and publicity are not appropriated, as long as they are lived as constraints, then they arise from what the *Aufklärer* called "external culture," distinguishing it from true culture, closer in their eyes to morality, just as the civic is distinct from simple civility. Overall, civility, legality, and publicity are principles constitutive of our democratic spaces or rather their normative ideal. But putting these principles to work in the practices of discussions and decisions manifests the effectivity of democracy. The latter is impossible without a culture of citizenship, which proceeds from an appropriation by individual citizens of the procedures required to put these principles into effect. Alexis de Tocqueville thought there was no liberty and no citizenship outside such procedural and cooperative practices, which have been so well interiorized that they have become for citizens like second nature, a veritable culture.

Politics as culture is therefore the formation that results from learning the procedures inherent in civility, legality, and publicity understood in the noble sense of a public usage of ideas and arguments. This implies a strongly reflexive identity, if it is true that politics does not become culture simply by the obstinate engagement in a militant cause but rather by virtue of the decentering demanded by the need to consider a great plurality of interests, opinions, and viewpoint—and also of cultures. Politics as culture is also the capacity of different cultural identities to communicate. From the perspective of European construction, and considering the risks of failure, I would like to relate this problem directly to the question of the importance of procedures and citizens' learning them. What does a citizen learn about procedures linked to the three principles of civility, legality, and publicity?

He learns not only to respect, but also to adopt norms that may even contradict his initial interests or convictions. For learning practically that he is not alone is to learn to accept the norms that cannot be deduced from his chosen values, but which take into account other interests or convictions than his own. For that, it is necessary to enter into procedures of civility, legality, and publicity that respectively codify the recognition of sensibilities, interests, and arguments of others. But it is also necessary to accept formal regulations, decisions that even if they perchance shock our spontaneous convictions (e.g., by contradicting our values), seem acceptable to us, nevertheless, because the procedure in which they were taken would be correct in the sense of being as fair as possible to all viewpoints, interests, or convictions.[42] In reality, there is a sort of fetishism of democratic procedures, notably those that consecrate majority rule. There is a tendency to accept a decision made in procedures presumed democratic, but little serious speculation about why such procedures may be considered as valid in reason. For example, is a decision by vote, even with universal suffrage, a law of reason? Why not instead the law of numbers, "a law of lively strength," (*"une loi de vive force"*) as Joseph Proudhon wrote of it, a reason for which he shamelessly refuted democracy? (Not because this conclusion was reasonable, but he was right to wonder about the basis of the validity of decision-making procedures.) Already people feel the results of a vote as a sort of violence when it is resorted to in brutal fashion. This is why electoral campaigns are democratically important, despite the excesses and upsets of which we know. In effect they are useful not only to candidates; they are useful in principle to the whole conventional democratic ritual, that of electoral voting, so that not only can citizens vote in knowledge of the issues, at least ideally, but also for each person to be able to have an approximate idea of the reasons for the result of the vote as they reside in the opinions of citizens. Each person, in effect, needs not only to know for whom "we" have voted, but also to feel at least why we have voted in this way rather than another. And if the democratic mechanism is somehow cut off from this basic intuition, then it becomes violent, as impeccable as it may be formally conducted. On this subject, let us imagine what the electoral mechanism, the pivot of our democratic systems, would mean if we did not have access to the public opinion that animates the political will expressed in voting; and if moreover we did not have the slightest notion of the common sense that underpins this public opinion. We would be quite alienated from the diktat of the polling booths or the norms that result, and we would be dispossessed of the sentiment of participation in political will, as well as the sentiment of belonging to the corresponding political community. For it is only to the extent that democratic procedure stays articulated with political substance (shifts of opinion felt around him) that this procedure keeps its meaning for the citizen, and thereby has value. If the procedure is disconnected from substance, it makes the democratic system a cold monster, where the political cannot be invested as a culture; it would be regarded as a machine and treated as such.

This problem of disconnection arises particularly sharply at the level of the EU. One can increase mechanisms of consultation and codecision at the level of community bodies (commission, council, parliament), but that will not fundamentally change the nature of the problem, since political substance is lacking at this level. What counts for democracy is that the European citizen understands the pertinence of community decisions. Before sketching the equivalent of a federal European state by elaborating a conventional constitution organizing public powers around a precise sharing of authority combined with a clear hierarchy of norms, it is important to reflect on the conditions for a civil society to emerge that would not be a great market. It must then become a political society, that is to say a milieu where interests and political passions confront (and thereby recognize) each other. Let me gather together the simple terms in which the current problematic of European construction is formulated: just as the political unity we need must be able to be reconciled with the plurality of national cultures, so it would be fatal for Europe to make a blank slate of the identities that compose it. One wonders how, lacking a supranational state, can realize the political integration of the Union along the path to a shared political culture, without regard for national cultures and languages as so many obstacles to communication.

Of course we in Western Europe share almost the same fundamental political values. We roughly adhere to the same principles of representative democracy, the legal state, and human rights. But this adherence, which merely outlines the contours of a constitutional patriotism, grounds only a soft consensus with no great practical value. We think of attempts by theologians to ground a global ethics on values common to all cultures or civilizations. The search for a greater common denominator in this domain, leads to results so banal (e.g., recognition of the value of innocent human life) that what one gains in consensus one loses in effectivity. To adhere to very universal values, like subscribing to very formal procedures, is worth practically nothing unless the framework thus defined is not devoid of elements to interpret it according to situations and in light of different traditions. But let us not assume this is about developing a demagogy. A framework of universal values and formal principles are superfluous; the constitutional framework enunciates the limit-values of a political community. It represents the element of a European social contract, and it is thus the symbolic reference without which any concrete practice might become dubious. Yet community political decisions must be articulated with public opinions, themselves structured by cultural traditions and sensibilities that are just starting to be open to each other. The European public space has not yet taken shape. Therefore there is not yet a communicational basis for a political culture shared among member states, as well as among citizens of the Union. Missing also is a glimpse of these citizens in communication flows, which constitute what Hannah Arendt called a "power," in contrast to "violence," and which is then channeled into procedures of political participation. If we accept decisions on condition they are taken according to democratic procedures (like the results of general elections), it is not because we are followers of procedural formalism (which still remains the domain of professional deformation in legal circles); rather it is to the extent that we are in the situation of saying, in the end, that "we" are the ones who have decided X or Y. But to be able to say that, we need to know that the procedure followed was formally fair. We need to be able to refer the result of the vote intuitively to a political will, that political will to public opinion, and that public opinion to a common sense. We need, in other words, to understand what was thus willed to be able to say that "we" wanted it. If not, it is not legitimate. And to be able to say that "we" wanted

it, we have to know how and why. For that, we have to be put into
contact with opinions, which presupposes a public space. And we feel
all the more integrated into this "us" of political will if we ourselves
have counted among the authors of this opinion as author-actors, participants in the discussion. At the national level, such contact exists at
least as an "intuition" of public opinion, an intuition that the media
contribute to forming and distorting. But the European level lacks the
elements that would allow us to understand what would justify the
result of a vote as the expression of "our" will. The decision appears to
fall from the sky.

This drastically marks the limits (both historical and systematic)
imposed on the edification of a political Europe. It is impossible to
develop it in the direction of a federal supranational state without being
careful to anchor it in a public political space, which is currently lacking. European politics, so to speak, has no choice: either it is a culture
or else it is an imposture. And if it is a culture, this shared political culture is formed, shaped in the practices of confrontation and dialogue.
Is it realistic to envisage that for Europe? This amounts to asking if and
how a culture of European citizenship is possible concretely. Prudence
obliges optimism to moderate itself by envisaging three progressive
degrees.

The first degree is modest, for essentially it is intergovernmental
(but there are also the political formations of the European Parliament):
conflicts of interests occur on the civilized register of conflicts of legal
interpretation when it comes to elaborating and applying common
norms. These conflicts of legal interpretation mobilize (unconsciously)
national traditions and make them enter into discursive confrontation
insofar as they are able to be untangled in the process of public argumentation. I should note that civility is not lacking at this level. But
what is deficient is the publicity that is the prime medium of the political inclusion of citizens.

The second degree is hypothetical: European political society (not a
European state), as well as public democratic space would improve by
being initially structured not so much by the mass media as by communication—horizontal and vertical—among the national (even regional)
parliaments of the Union, presented by the European Parliament as the
body of synthesis for proposals to the council. It is the idea of a system
of parliaments that would activate representative democracy within the
Union, much more seriously and surely than a conventional reinforcement of the powers of the European Parliament (legislation, censorship,
oversight, investiture). This goes along with a structuring of a public

space that is not merely about the media as an audiovisual space, but also and firstly democratic as a parliamentary space.

The third degree is more prospective, for it would approach basic European politics and would authorize the emergence of a culture of citizenship: establishing procedures aiming to associate categories of interests with decision-making processes—this is of course already done in the economic and social committee as well as in the commission—but in the spirit of a parliamentarization of interest groups in line with the principle of publicity. This would presuppose a second kind of parliamentary representation, not political but socioeconomic, whose members would be confronted not only with a state or its equivalent, but before that, with each other, interprofessionally, on an interregional and international (intra-community) scale.

In these visions of political representation and of socioeconomic representation, the parliamentarization of interests ought to be combined with communication among numerous bodies that represent them across the whole territory of the Union. To activate the channels designed to irrigate European society politically through networks of representations, the arsenal of new technologies of information and communication has an obvious function. This function would even be of prime political necessity. But the prerequisites are not simply technical; they are fundamentally ethical and cultural. Thus, it is clear that politics, especially at the supranational level today in Western Europe, calls on the citizen to develop a culture of decentering, to consent consequently to very wide-ranging solidarity that is not "warm," not being sustained emotionally by proximity or kinship. The functional necessity of a shared political culture within the Union requires national public spaces that are open to each other by mobilizing the frontline resources of civility and publicity. Such a requisite does not matter unless people are resolved to forsake the national principle, tacitly transposable to the supranational level, without renouncing the political integration of European space, that is to say a political union. In this case, public space is destined to offer the milieu where, following differentiated discursive procedures, a common political culture would form (without the prejudices of the cultural differences that are historically anchored between the national traditions composing the community); this public space should necessarily be pluralist. This engages a concept of freedom of communication. This renovated concept would be critical of the one that is judicially dominant in Strasbourg, Luxembourg, and Brussels.[43] Among other things, it would be able to ground a law of the media adjusted not only to the reality of public audiovisual space, but also to the satisfaction of normative criteria, including the principle of pluralism in the idea of mandates for cultural (education) and civic (information) responsibility on the part of the great broadcasting media.[44]

Notes

1. Wolton, *La dernière utopie.*
2. Gellner, *Nations and Nationalism.* Gellner explains statist construction of modern nations by the suppression of "communication barriers" which for him presupposes fundamentally that human language, beyond the diversity of patois and dialects, conceals the "vehicular" potential of a formal language free of contextual presuppositions.
3. Hewig Wolfram. *Geschichte der Goten.* Munich: Beck, 1979; Wolfram, *History of the Goths.* This is true for the establishment of "barbarian" peoples in the declining Roman Empire.
4. Pomian. *L'Europe et ses nations.*
5. Elias. *The Civilizing Process.* The reference model here is the small duchy of the Île-de-France, which would later become the kingdom of France.
6. Chaunu, *La Civilisation de l'Europe des Lumières.* Chaunu speaks of a "cultural voyage of Europe."
7. "Spiritual principle" is the expression that Ernest Renan used to characterize the nation. It seems to echo the Hegelian category of *Volksgeist,* and we know that Hegel saw no higher form of identity that realized in the national state. This should not discourage us from envisaging that Europe might realize an identity representing a spiritual principle in the world.
8. Wolff. *Histoire de la pensée européenne.*
9. Anderson. *Lineages of the Absolutist State*; see also, Pomian, *L'Europe et ses nations.*
10. Ferguson. *An Essay on the History of Civil Society.*
11. Gellner. *Nations and Nationalism.*
12. Pierre Bourdieu and Jean-Charles Passeron grasped in their way this deep functionality of education, as well as the central importance of "scholastic" mastery of language, while they centered the social critique strategically on the school and not, for example, on the market and capitalist enterprise, or else on the state and techno structures. Bourdieu and Passeron, *Reproduction in Education, Society & Culture.*
13. See Bodei. *Le Prix de la liberté*; M. Theunissen. *Réalisation de soi et universalité,* trans. Hervé Pourtois. Paris: Le Cerf, 1997.
14. Ferry. "Quel patriotisme au-delà des nationalismes?"
15. Jules Ferry was deferring to Victor Cousin. The citation he gave is as follows: "In Prussia, the duty of parents to send their children to primary schools is so national and rooted in the country's legal and moral habits that it is consecrated in a single word, *Schulpflichtigkeit;* it corresponds in the intellectual order to military service, *Dienstpflichtigkeit.* These two words are Prussia as a whole; they contain the secret of its originality as a nation, of its power as a state, and the seed of its future; they express, for my taste, the two bases of true civilization, which is composed of both enlightenment and force […]. I am convinced that a time will come when popular education will be recognized as a social duty imposed on all in the general interest […]."
16. French colonization does not have the same significance as British colonization and did not obey the same rationales. Unlike England's motives, which with a few rare exceptions were openly economic, the motives of France were only apparently so. The diffusion of the French cultural model counted for more than the prospects of material profitability, even though the latter were eagerly advanced in public argument. The economic arguments

raised publicly (they were seriously debated in the Chamber of Deputies) therefore appear as a rationalization of more spiritual interests! The Germans, with all their prejudices of the time about France, were scarcely mistaken when they saw in French colonialism an additional sign of the vanity of their neighbors.

17. Paul Thibaud. "L'Europe par ses nations et réciproquement," in Jean-Marc Ferry and Paul Thibaud. *Discussion sur l'Europe*. Paris: Calmann-Lévy, 1992.
18. See the ridiculous utopia in the Bangemann Report on the information society.
19. See the interesting study by Renaut, *Les revolutions de l'université.*
20. The White Paper *"Growth, Competitiveness, Employment"* of the European Economic Commission presents its seven priorities "communally accepted for the adaptation to industrial change and the struggle against unemployment":

    1. Improve systems of education and professional training, especially continuing education; businesses to increase their flexibility
    2. Encourage businesses to increase their flexibility faced with the realties of the job market;
    3. Reorganize the means of production of goods and services of enterprises;
    4. Reduce the costs of salaries;
    5. Utilize more effectively the public funds designed to fight against unemployment;
    6. Adopt specific measures in favor of untrained youth;
    7. Conduct active policies of job creation;

    The expression "active policies of job creation" should be interpreted as: (a) flexible payment and work time; (b) retraining in the interests of greater professional mobility; (c) continuing education; and (d) harsher conditions for social security and unemployment benefits.

    Like that White Paper, the ADAPT initiative has priorities as follows:
    1. Accelerate the adaptation of man power to industrial change;
    2. Increase the competitiveness of industry, services, and commerce;
    3. Prevent unemployment by improving the workforce's qualifications, by developing its internal and external flexibility and by guaranteeing greater professional mobility;
    4. Anticipate and accelerate the development of new jobs and new activates, in particular of work intensity.
21. The higher institutes of European studies, a sort of *grandes écoles* for European civil servants, are neither European schools nor European universities. They are not institutes of European culture, although such an expression might produce a "Euro nationalist" misunderstanding. "European" schools or *lycées* in existence can often boast a high level of teaching and a high quality of education. But this is hardly more than an elitist characteristic in relation to ordinary schools and *lycées*. So-called European universities cannot yet pretend to rival the great traditional universities.
22. Apel. *L'éthique à l'âge de la science.* Apel does not go into pedagogic considerations.
23. Jean-Marc Ferry. "Raison scientifique, décision politique et opinion publique," in *La civilisation tributaire du bien-être.* Brussels: Éditions Entre-vues & Labor, 1997.
24. Horkheimer. *Critical Theory: Selected Essays.*
25. Ferry. *L'allocation universelle.* See also my article "Revenu de citoyenneté, droit au travail, intégration sociale." *La Revue du MAUSS,* 7, first semester 1996; my interview with Olivier Mongin, "Pour une autre valorisation du travail. Défense et illustration du secteur quaternaire," *Esprit,* July 1997.
26. Luhmann. *Rechtssoziologie.* This is an ambivalent function, since the politico-administrative system in a sense reduces complexity. The law regulates interactions and stabilizes behavioral expectations by performing selections, otherwise contingent, in an environment in itself undetermined. For Luhmann, the shift from the old law to a modern law that is positivized, formalized, and differentiated can be analyzed as the shift from a simple, nonelastic, reduction to a complex, elastic, and conditional reduction of complexity. See Jean Clam,

"Phénoménologie et droit chez Niklas Luhmann." *Archives de philosophie du droit*, 39, (1995): 335–375.

27. This notion, initially due to Ludwig Wittgenstein, has been extended by John Searle to language acts. Paul Ricoeur offers the following definition: "By constitutive rule is meant those precepts whose sole function is to rule that, for instance, a given gesture of shifting the position of a pawn on the chessboard 'counts as' a move in a game of chess. The move would not exist, with the signification and the effect it has in the game, without the rule that 'constitutes' the move as a step in the chess game [...]." Paul Ricoeur. *Oneself as Another.* (sixth study: "The Self and Narrative Identity," 154). I have suggested an application to the question of law in Jean-Marc Ferry. "Une approche philosophique de la rationalité juridique." *Droits. Revue française de théorie juridique.*

28. E. Gonzales Sanchez. "La négociation des décisions communautaires par les fonctionnaires nationaux: les groupes de travail du Conseil." *Revue française d'administration publique* 63, 1992. See also C. Hausschild and H. Siedentopf. "Europäische Integration und die öffentlichen Verwaltungen der Mitgliedstaaten." *Die öffentliche Verwaltung* 11, 1990.

29. We prefer to reserve the term *lobbies* for the North American institution of pressure groups acting directly and very openly on legislators. The European practice and concept are different: European interest groups intervene higher up in the decision-making process and address more the "executive" than the "legislative" branch (although these expressions no longer make sense as concerns the organization of Community powers). Whatever the case, European pressure groups are invited by the great public administration that is the commission to collaborate with the formation of compromises by helping inform normative proposals that are generally raised by the intergovernmental body that is the Council of the Union, but before the decision-making process properly speaking, which may involve European parliamentarians.

30. For a balanced discussion on the strategic use of the media for European integration, see André Lange. "Descartes, c'est la Hollande. La Communauté européenne: culture et audiovisuel." *Quaderni* 19, Winter 1993: 99–104. For a critique of the difficulties, see Pierre Musso. "Audiovisuel et télécommunications en Europe: quelles recompositions?" *Quaderni* 19, 1993. A synthesis offered by J. McLeod and Daniel McDonald. "Beyond Simple Exposure: Media Orientations and Their Impact on Political Process." *Communication Research* 12, 1985: 3–33 and by Franklin Dehousse. "La politique européenne des télécommunications." *Courrier hebdomadaire du CRISP*, 1493–1494, 1995.

31. Castel. *La révolution communicationnelle* and especially in *Réseaux*, dossiers on: "Télécommunications: d'une organisation à l'autre," CNET 56, November–December 1992; "Droit et communication," CNET 59, May–June 1993; "L'économie des télécommunications," CNET 72–73, 1995. Also, *Rapport sur le développement mondial des télécommunications* 1994, UIT (Union internationale des télécommunications), 1994; Harmeet Sawhney. "Universal Service: Prosaic Motives and Great Ideals." *Journal of Broadcasting and Electronic Media*, Autumn 1994: 375–395; Jean-François Tétu and Françoise Renzetti. "Internet: évolution d'un projet d'espace public de recherche." TIS (Technologie de l'information et société) 7(2), 1995; "Vers la convergence des systèmes de communication," *TIS (Technologie de l'information et société)*, 1995, 7(2).

32. Hegel, *Hegel's Science of Logic*, v. two, section three: "The Idea." In the English translation by A. V. Miller. Atlantic, NJ: Humanities Press International, 1989: XXX, Hegel says "That actual things are not congruous with the Idea is the side of their finitude and untruth, and in accordance with this side they are objects, determined in accordance with their various spheres [...] But, if an object, for example the state, did not correspond at all to its Idea, that is, if in fact it was but the Idea of the state at all, if its reality, which is the self-conscious individuals, did not correspond at all to the Notion, its soul and its body would have parted; the former would have broken up into the solitary regions of thought, the latter would have broken up into the single individualities. But because the Notion of the state so essentially

constitutes the nature of these individualities, it is present in them as an urge so powerful that they are impelled to translate it into reality, be it only in the form of exterior purposiveness, or to put up with it as it is, or else they must needs perish."

33. Jean-Marc Ferry. "Pour une 'philosophie' de la Communauté," in Jean-Marc Ferry, Paul Thibaud. *Discussion sur l'Europe* also, "Culture et citoyenneté dans l'Union européenne." *Cahiers internationaux du symbolisme*, 80–82, 1995; "Pour une démocratie participative." *Temps européens. La Revue du Centre européen de la culture.* Geneva: Spring 1997.

34. Immanuel Kant. "What is Enlightenment?" in Kant. *The Philosophy of History*, trans. Lewis White Beck. New York: Bobbs Merrill, 1963: 4: "[...] There are few who have succeeded, by their own exercise of minds both in freeing themselves from incompetence and in achieving a steady pace. But that the public should enlighten itself is more possible; indeed if only freedom is granted, enlightenment is almost sure to follow."

35. Immanuel Kant. "Idea for a Universal History from a Cosmopolitan Point of View" (1784), trans. Lewis White Beck, *The Philosophy of History*, Eighth Thesis: 22–23: "Enlightenment comes gradually, with intermittent folly and caprice, as a great good which must finally save men from the selfish aggrandizement of their masters, always assuming that the latter know their own interest. [...] Although, for instance, our world rulers at present have no money left over for public education and for anything that concerns what is best in the world, since all they have is already committed to future wars, they will still find it to their own interest at least not to hinder the weak and slow, independent effort of their peoples in this work."

36. G. W. F. Hegel. *Encyclopedia*, § 503, Remark. Hegel goes on as follows: "By virtue of the right this freedom has, man must in a general manner possess a knowledge of the difference between good and evil. Moral and religious commandments should not only require of him that he conform as to laws prescribed by an external authority, but it is in his heart, his conviction, his conscience, his way of seeing that they should be approved, recognized, and even grounded. The subjectivity of the will is in man the final goal, an absolutely essential moment."

37. G. W. F. Hegel, "Principles of the Philosophy of Right," § 107, in *The Philosophy of Hegel*, ed. Carl Friedrich, New York: The Modern Library: 254.

38. On this subject, it must be said that a remarkable strategy of Community bodies until recently consisted of allying the aim of ideological propaganda with the style of commercial advertising. This is an alliance able to destroy the principle of publicity from within. By addressing the European citizen by means of stimuli, the lowest part of his conviction, they are underestimating the risk of what on the political level is morally repugnant, and sooner or later proves tactically maladroit. Manipulation is rarely skillful enough for the effects not to boomerang back on the authors. At the very least it produces after a while only indifference and contempt among those it is aimed at. But abuse of rhetoric may entail discredit for the European project itself. Instead of addressing the moral substance of citizens, the subjective freedom in the European sense of the word, it calls in communication consultants who know how to treat citizens as consumers; they excel at reducing the freedom of subjects to the rank of a simple object. This is an attack on the public spirit that betrays the fact that power is essentially lacking to bodies that want to be superior to nation-states and to take their place. On the other hand, recent initiatives like the "Citizens of Europe" (informing them of their rights and paying attention to their difficulties), appear positive for the formation of a European civic space.

39. Naisbitt and Aburdene. *Megatrends 2000.*

40. See Destatte, *Nationalisme et postnationalisme.* Also Jacques Lenoble, Nicoles Dewandre (ed.). *L'Europe au soir du siècle: Identité et démocratie.* Paris: Éditions Esprit, 1992.

41. Ferry. *Les puissances de l'expérience*, 1, Le Sujet et le Verbe, II, 1, 2, 3, 4: 103–160.

42. Jean-Marc Ferry. "De l'élection de valeurs à l'adoption de normes" in S. Mesure (ed.), *La rationalité des valeurs*. Paris: PUF, 1998.

43. The editors of the Green Book of December 23, 1992 on pluralism and media concentration considered explicitly that the principle of pluralism intervenes as a limitation on freedom of communication. The commission remarks that "the Community right to competition is not an instrument adapted to the maintenance of pluralism [even if it can contribute to it]," [p. 91]. Nevertheless, the same Green Book recalled [p. 16] that "the European Court of Human Rights considers that pluralism is an exception to the principle of freedom of expression having the goal of protecting the rights of *others*." [art. 10, § 2]. It noted in this respect [p. 15] that "the legal analysis of the European Convention of Human Rights, as interpreted by the European Court of Human Rights and by national legislation, still allows two common characteristics to be noted:

the concept of pluralism has the function of limiting the scope of the principle of freedom of expression;

the object of this limitation is to guarantee to the public the diversity of information."

44. Jean-Marc Ferry. "Sur la liberté de communication dans l'espace européen," in G. Harrscher and B. Libois (eds.). *Mutations de la démocratie représentative*. Brussels: Éditions de l'Université libre de Bruxelles, 1997: 81–101.

Bibliography

Anderson, Perry. 1979. *Lineages of the Absolutist State*. London: Verso.

Apel, Karl-Otto. 1987. *L'éthique à l'âge de la science. La priori de la communauté communicationnelle et les fondements de l'éthique*. Translated by Raphaël Lellouche. Lille: Presses universitaires de Lille.

Birnbaum, Pierre (ed.). 1997. *Sociologie des nationalismes*. Paris: PUF.

Bodei, Remo. 1995. *Le Prix de la liberté. Aux origines de la hiérarchie sociale chez Hegel*. Translated by Nicola Giovannini. Paris: Le Cerf.

Bourdieu, Pierre and Jean-Charles Passeron. 1990. *Reproduction in Education, Society & Culture*. Translated by Richard Nice. London: Sage.

Castel F. (du). 1995. *La révolution communicationnelle*. Paris: L'Harmattan.

Chaunu, Pierre. 1982. *La Civilisation de l'Europe des Lumières*. Paris: Flammarion.

Destatte, Philippe (ed.). 1995. *Nationalisme et postnationalisme*. Namur: Presses universitaires de Namur.

Elias, Norbert. 1994. *The Civilizing Process*. Translated by Edmund Jephcott. Oxford: Blackwell.

Ferguson, Adam. 1988. *An Essay on the History of Civil Society*. New Brunswick, NJ: Transaction.

Ferry, Jean-Marc. 1991. *Les puissances de l'expérience: Essai sur l'identité contemporaine*. Paris: Le Cerf.

———. 1995. *L'allocation universelle. Pour un revenu de citoyenneté*. Paris: Le Cerf.

———. 1997. *La civilisation tributaire du bien-être*. Brussels: Éditions Entre-vues & Labor.

Ferry, Jean-Marc and Paul Thibaud. 1992. *Discussion sur l'Europe*. Paris: Calmann-Lévy.

Gellner, Ernest. 1983. *Nations and Nationalism*. Ithaca, NY: Cornell University Press.

Hegel. 1989. *Hegel's Science of Logic*. Translated by A. V. Miller. Atlantic, NJ: Humanities Press International.

Horkheimer, Max. 1972. *Critical Theory: Selected Essays*. Translated by Matthew O'Connell. New York: Herder and Herder.

Kant. 1963. *The Philosophy of History*. Translated by Lewis White Beck. New York: Bobbs Merrill.

Luhmann, Niklas. 1987. *Rechtssoziologie*. Opladen: Westdeutscher Verlag (3rd ed).

Naisbitt, John and Patricia Aburdene. 1990. *Megatrends 2000: Ten New Directions for the 1990s:* New York: William Morrow.

Philippe Wolff. 1968. *Histoire de la pensée européenne*, vol. 1, *L'éveil intellectuel de l'Europe*, Paris: Seuil, 1971. Translated as *The Awakening of Europe* by Anne Carter. Baltimore: Penguin.

Pomian, Kryztof. 1990. *L'Europe et ses nations*. Paris: Gallimard.

Renaut, Alain. 1995. *Les revolutions de l'université*. Paris: Calmann-Lévy.

Ricoeur, Paul. 1992. *Oneself as Another*. Translated by Kathleen Blamey. Chicago: Chicago University Press.

Wolfram, Hewig. 1988. *History of the Goths*. Translated by Thomas Dunlap. Berkeley: University of California Press.

Wolton, Dominique. 1992. *La dernière utopie*. Paris: Flammarion.

CHAPTER NINE

Nation, Democracy, and Identities in Europe

DIDIER LAPEYRONNIE

The question of multiculturalism and national identities all over Europe is the subject of a large debate, nourished by wars following from the crumbling of the Soviet Empire and by the controversies raised by the Maastricht Treaty. This "return" of identity and national issues takes place in a paradoxical and complex way. To the East of the continent, the countries released from Communism have been, or still are, the theater of a "nationalist" fever that recalls the worst periods of European history. States have seemed powerless to curb national and popular movements, when they do not feed them directly, accentuating or using their force of fragmentation and disintegration. The "return" of nationalisms thus proceeds at the cost of their political instrumentalization by former apparatchiks: total nationalism is the ultimate stage of Communism, as Edgar Morin puts it.

In the West, these national popular movements are also increasingly visible due to a growing xenophobia, the emergence and installation in the political landscape of parties of the extreme right, as in France, in Belgium or in Austria. But in this part of the continent, states are participating in a European construction that appears to strip them of some prerogatives and to weaken their capacity for integration. Europe is perceived by some as the principal agent of "globalization" and of a destructive free-market logic, which only recourse to the national state can stop, or at least brake, to avoid excessive deregulation. The appeal to the nation-state as a space of integration is thus at the root of other nationalist (hence political) movements, whose opposition to European construction and rejection of multiculturalism are their central characteristics.

But these same nation–states are also confronted by an internal rise in minoritarian cultural, ethnic, and regional assertions that oppose both a Europe considered no longer as liberal but as technocratic and unifying, and well as states judged to be centralizing, both of which are equally ignorant of the specificities of such groups. Beyond local particularisms, states seem to find it increasingly difficult to contain the demands from national minorities that are already long-standing, like Corsicans, Catalans, and Basques, or even directly threatened with explosion, as in Belgium. But they also have to face a much wider multicultural demand, including numerous groups affirming their specificity: immigrants, ethnic, and sexual minorities.

National popular movements, nationalist assertions, and multicultural demands are the three principal forms of the "identity" question on the European continent today. The European Union (EU) has some-times been accused of putting a brake on them, sometimes of encour-aging them. Revolts against free-market globalization, resistance to a homogenizing modernity—any attempt at interpretation that is too hasty or too global is likely to be stunningly disproved by a historical counterexample. It suffices to think of nationalisms undetermined on the political level, always heteronymous and dependent on the ide-ologies and movements with which they are associated: here "factors of war," there "factors of peace," here factors of disintegration, there factors of integration.[1] The diversity of situations a priori prevents any generalization. What relation is there between the Irish question, the separation of Czechs and Slovaks, the National Front in France, con-flicts between Hungarians and Rumanians over Transylvania, the war in Bosnia, the impetus of racism and xenophobia, the autonomy of the Catalans, the status of the city of Brussels torn between Walloons and Flemish, German reunification, the status of minorities, and immi-gration policies? Each confrontation, each demand, is by definition particular and belongs to a specific history. In Europe, the nation has been the theater of integration and political management of very het-erogeneous populations and territories. All these conflicts, in the East as in the West, oblige us to speculate about the nation and the national idea, which have apparently become incapable of facing the diversity of identities and offering an integrated site for constructing the future. With the nation weakening and the demands from identities surging, in what space can a new democratic articulation of differences take place?

Might the EU be this site—or must we remain attached to preserving nations?

The Language of Nationhood?

Even if the word was not used for it, the idea of nation was born in Holland at the same time as modernity, forged at the end of the sixteenth century by the collective consciousness acquired in the struggle against the Spanish occupiers, the construction of political unity and the development of a common culture. Founded on affirmation of Dutch exceptionalism and the conviction of its divine mission, the idea of nation was a powerful factor of political integration in a country divided and weakened by its diverse religions and multiple languages, a country that would invent itself and construct an urban culture, cement of a unity based on economic power, rootedness in a biblical tradition, and civil bourgeoisie modernity.[2] Later, the idea of nation would influence the construction of modern states, sovereign and independent, in Great-Britain, France, and the United States, essentially in the eighteenth century. The political idea of nation is associated with modernity, sovereignty, and citizenship.

Reason, Will, and Justice

From the start, three grand dimensions appear in the idea of nationhood and in the national political discourse: reason, will, and justice.[3] In the eighteenth century, these three dimensions structured Enlightenment political thought. They would constitute autonomous languages, experienced as competing and contradictory discourses. Their sole link was criticism of royal power. The first half of the nineteenth century, after the French Revolution saw nationalist movements that integrated the three into the same language: reason, will, and justice were henceforth strongly linked to each other by national mobilizations and they would allow the political construction of nations. It was around these dimensions that modern democracies were built. The invention of the language of nationhood thus allowed the formation of a space of action and of meaning in which these discourses acquired a "symbolic coherence and a political force."[4]

As Ernest Gellner has shown, nations were invented by nationalisms and by modernizing states. Modern nations integrating reason, will, and justice, were formed in Europe and the United States in the nineteenth century. They were built by the creative national mobilizations of modern societies, forcing a deep rupture with the past, with the traditional communities and hierarchical orders of the *Ancien Régime*, and economic, political, and cultural unification around shared institutions. Made necessary by industrial economies in full development, national integration appeared as the political societal form best adapted to modernity. It was in this framework that the modern democracies were born and that citizenship found full expansion. Thus nationalism was linked to a political project of constructing an independent state associated with a movement of cultural and economic modernization and with a process of social unification.[5] This conjunction between reason as carried by modernization, justice as founded on affirmation of a shared popular identity, and the will as incarnated by mobilization and construction of an independent state would allow nations and democracy to integrate spaces that were sharply diversified and multicultural. Nationalism permitted overcoming local and particular identities and thus opened the space to processes of individual emancipation, foundation of democracy. The nation is a new form of unified political language offering a new way of organizing action and giving it meaning. From this standpoint, it is not "national reality" that is invested with political authority, but it is the language itself, with individual and collective existence being founded within the space of the nation's language.[6]

Modern nations are foremost the product of a movement of rationalization. At the end of the nineteenth century, the nation as a statist and political organization appears as a sort of natural response to the upheavals introduced by the industrial and individualist revolutions. The old world of communities has disappeared, incessant change and industrialization threaten social stability, individualism blights solidarity. Modernization and industrialization of the economy have destroyed ancient communities, too reduced to contain their development. Industry necessitates bigger markets and spaces of communication that outstrip peasant communities. Nation permits the creation of territories controlled politically by the state and integrated by the diffusion of a "high secularized culture" by means of unified education systems. Subject to the same rules, individuals are capable of communicating and exchanging.[7] This process of rationalization also affects the organization of the modern national state, built around an administration or a bureaucracy structured by impersonal rules. The nation is thus conceived as the product, inside a particular territory, of the relations among an economy, a culture, and a state all dominated by principles of instrumental rationality. Henceforth, the nation substitutes for communities, organic solidarity replaces mechanical solidarity, inherited status cedes to acquired status, modernity effaces tradition. The language of the nation permits a construction of the past as a time that is gone (the *Ancien Régime*) and distance it to orient itself to the future. Nations are constructed by a strongly integrating and industrial economy, a modern secularized culture constituted of interchangeable individuals, and a bureaucratized state, an integration enabled by the rupture with the past that they contribute to inventing.

But domination by the principles of reason in all domains of collective life risks weakening the nation's political capacity. Of course, instrumental reason is necessary for the construction of a state and a society that are united and powerful. Nevertheless, the autonomy of mechanisms of economic calculation, the abstract principles of bureaucratic regulation, and the general mediatization of human relations all may deprive the nation of any capacity for historical action. Bureaucratic routine, the market, and utilitarianism of individual behavior lead to withdrawal and to the neglect of public affairs. This is why the nation should also be a political will.

From this point of view, the nation is foremost the product of the collective determination of the individuals that compose it. It is a choice, a decision not only to live together, but also to develop, to face adversaries and the difficulties of international competition. The nation is elective. But this dimension is not as clear as it appears. Certainly the general will is the common will, collective choice, but will is often exercised either by charismatic leaders or incarnated by historical figures convened by circumstance, or else, more frequently, by the state that assures its continuity. This is because national will would have no meaning unless it was not also already present in the nation's history, like the nationalism that reconstructs it. Each nation is invested with a "divine" or "civilizing" mission, it is "elected" by Providence, and it has a "political destiny." Ypsilanti, Herder, and Mazzini, like Renan, have affirmed the original vocations of their respective nations.[8] Will is often found in the exaltation of the "national character," which is always only the obstinate pursuit of a political unification necessary in the same state, for it is inscribed in the historical reality by the members of the nation, either collectively or else behind a leader. Thus, it is at the moment when nations are constructed as modern realities that they invent a past and traditions.

The nation is will to the extent that this will is inherent in its history. It is the product of a choice made by necessity, a sort of historic duty. Contrary to the discourse of rationality, the discourse of the will makes a bridge between the past and the future through the present. Will is thus the capacity and the duty to enter into history, to make it and be an actor in it. It presupposes independence and mobilization. The nation, through political and state mechanisms, is identified with the collective will of the individuals who compose it, in that they make profound tendencies occur in its history. Will is also a sort of mission. The charismatic leader or providential personality, just like the state, by identifying with national values, incarnates this link between heritage and the active collective will, and it has the capacity to mobilize the members of the nation for its defense, its grandeur, or its continuity.

Reason and will construct nationalism from above by exalting the universe of action, which is opposed to that of tradition. Reason and will would be only an ideology of modernizing economic, cultural, and state elites if a final dimension was not integrated into the national idea: justice. Justice gives its whole legitimacy to the will and to modernization. The national discourse is doubly a discourse of justice. First, it is a matter of "equality of conditions," in Tocqueville's expression. The affirmation of the nation creates a membership that transcends all others and that effaces the inequalities of heritage or even of wealth. Once a member of the national community, the individual is equal to all the other members. The nation institutes civil equality, an equality of everyone before the law. Membership in the nation and in the national community are therefore both fully modern: on them are founded individualism and democratic equality—in short, they are the conditions for real citizenship.

This equality means not only recognizing the individual as a moral person and citizen. It is also associated with affirming an identity and with shared belonging. This is why national identity is more "pure" in working-class categories, among whom it is not perverted by money or cosmopolitanism, as it is in higher and urban social groups. The "truth" of the nation is thus in the people and individuals who compose it, who incarnate most perfectly the "national spirit." From this point of view, the idea of nation carries inside it the condemnation of overly strong social and cultural inequalities. Too much wealth and overeducation distances someone from the nation's deep identity, inviting treachery. The nation cannot tolerate too many gaps; it must also be unified socially. The establishment of a certain social justice is the logical consequence of national construction. Therefore justice presupposes a unification of the nation, first civil, then political, and finally social, according to the theory of T. H. Marshall; it permits the gradual incorporation of social groups in the political space, beyond differences and inequalities.[9]

Justice has a second meaning here. The nation is endowed with a certain number of rights that are its due: its integrity, its territory, its independence. Justice implies recognition of the "grandeur" of the people and of the particularity of its identity. The nation makes it a "great people" sovereign and necessarily respected, a "morally and socially achieved" unity, fully developed on the political and cultural level, at least an equal among other nations. In other words, the discourse of justice rests on the affirmation of continuity between past, present, and future.

The State, the People, and the Civil Society

National language associates the three discourses of modernizing reason, mobilizing will, and equal justice. Modernizing reason on its own risks provoking tensions over identity and forms of rejection, if it is not accompanied by membership and justice. Similarly, the mobilizing will presupposes being associated with reason and justice not to result in a simple construction of a dictatorial and repressive state without a real social basis. Finally, justice would be difficult to realize if it were not relayed by will and reason, which must apply it and protect it. Yet this association of three discourses may take different concrete and historical forms as a function of the priorities given to them by one or another principle. From this standpoint, we cannot indulge in the overly commodious and frequent—and especially overly ideological—opposition made between the "nation-contract" and the "nation-genius," an opposition that harmfully confuses the idea of a civil contract, that is to say the identification of the nation with democratic space and the political contract with the meaning of the state. Within the language of the nation, we may distinguish three sets of interlinked national theories: republican, civil, and popular.

The first theory associates will with reason, mobilization with modernization. It leads to a statist conception of the nation, for they give a central role to the state as incarnating will and reason, the state identified with universal values, confronted by a society that has remained largely traditional. In this *republican* vision, the nation is simultaneously elective, carried by a strong collective will, and the incarnation of

Reason. Justice is a consequence of national construction. Democracy is subordinated to the affirmation of the state-bearing nation. For the individual, belonging to the nation is synonymous with belonging to the state. His citizenship cannot be dissociated from his nationality. His rights flow from those of the nation-state.

The second theory associates reason with justice, modernization with the equalization of conditions. This is a contractual vision of the nation, with a central role given to civil society, and consequently a more modest role to the state. The nation is carried by a representative system founded on legal equality among citizens. Parliament expresses its unity (justice) as well as its diversity (reason). This is a conception of the nation as a *"civil* contract." The contract between free individuals incarnates universal values and must be protected against encroachments by the state. Will is here a consequence of national construction. For the individual, belonging to the nation occurs by means of citizenship. The nation's rights flow from those of the citizen and are subordinated to them.

The third theory associates will with justice, mobilization with equalization. This is a vision of the identity and unity of the nation, with a central role given to people and a more modest role to modernization. The nation would be borne more by culture and shared values, by a spirit or character. It is incarnated not only in the popular spirit, but also sometimes in leaders who know how to absorb its charisma and manifest its will. This is a conception of the nation as a common cultural and *popular* identity, from which flow the identity and psychology of the individual in the form of his "social habitus."[10] Belonging to the nation is a birthright; it is one's "emotional community"; it is inherited. The individual's identity flows from the national identity.

These three forms of national discourse are not absolute. They are tonalities or priorities given to some perspectives without excluding others. Modern nations are constructed by the partial and fragile association of these three orientations that in many aspects are three contradictory and complementary paths of entry into modernity. We may represent them as shown in figure 9.1.

If we want to identify empirically these various conceptions, we find a "French" conception in which priority is given to the association of reason and will and in which the state[11] is the central element; by contrast, the "German" conception gives priority to the association of will and justice and in which the people is central. But we may observe that these two conceptions are not completely opposed in that they grant a major place to the principle of will. Finally, in a third "Anglo-Saxon"

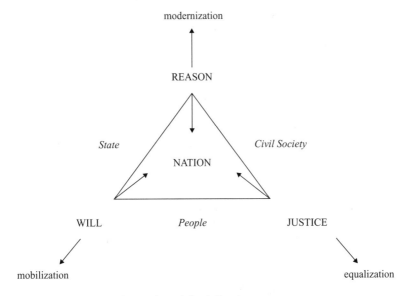

modernization

REASON

State   Civil Society

NATION

WILL   *People*   JUSTICE

mobilization   equalization

Figure 9.1   The state, the people, and the civil society

conception, priority goes to the combination of reason and justice, and civil society and democracy are central, a conception that is opposed to the French conception of the role of justice, and to the German conception of the role of reason. But it is true that the idea of nation rests concretely on the close association of the three complementary—though mutually opposed—elements, in other words, to a state, a people, and a civil society. Nation is in some way a reconstruction of the world that heralds their unity as founded on some reconciliation of justice, will, and reason. Nationhood is foremost a relationship between time and history. The national language both opens and orients the historical space of action. Present society is not completely what it should be as a function of its past, or of the unified future inscribed in this past and which it must "actively" bring about. The nation is always only the *promise* of the nation.

The national discourse is a supple and plastic political language that allows a specific collectivity to integrate modernity. It links disparate elements essentially on the symbolic mode and thus traces a unitary space of political action. This is why there can exist no conceptual or empirical definition of nation: neither language nor history nor state nor ethnicity can define it. The nation is not a fact; it is always just a projection, a symbolic creation, a language. It is a play of signs without referents that enables us to see it as evident and natural, "indisputable." The nation is neither an ideology nor the point of view of an actor. It is precisely a language erected into a political myth,[12] or as Benedict Anderson puts it, "an imaginary and imagined political community (to which must be added spoken and written) as intrinsically limited and sovereign."[13] From this standpoint, the nation is constantly produced by spoken and written "locutory acts" that make it exist through discourse, books, and studies devoted to it that unendingly redesign it and trace the symbolic space in which actions—past, present, future—are endowed with meaning. Thus the nation may harbor competing, sometimes contradictory, definitions that it connects in the same ensemble: France can be just as well the country of Renan, of Ferry, and other republicans, as of Michelet, Barrès, Drumont, and Maurras—or even Guizot and Tocqueville. The nation integrates them into a single ensemble with reference to time and a sense of history.

Beyond the National Synthesis

By its plasticity and mythic nature, the language of the nation allows a political synthesis of the contradictory orientations of modernization. It assures the political unity of societies constituted of isolated individuals, it promises justice despite the rationalization of the economy, and it guarantees identity despite change. The language of the nation offers the moral and political framework necessary for the functioning of democracy. Modern democracy is deeply tied to it since national myth has associated the individual's independence with collective membership, the freedom of Moderns with that of Ancients, popular sovereignty with the rights of the citizen. National institutions have integrated everyone's motivations with affirmation of a common norm, diversity of interests with respect for collective values, which allows democracy to develop.

But today the language of the nation seem out of breath and no longer able to unite the discourses of will, justice, and reason. Once again, the world appears irreconcilable, constructed of realities, values, and languages that compete with and contradict each other. More than the fragility of European construction, the explanation of this evolution should be sought inside the logics of national societies, in the conjunction of two series of phenomena that reinforce each other: social rupture of the national pact and the exhaustion of the language of the nation as history's language of reference. Their consequence is a profound crisis of democracy.

Breaking the National Pact

The language of nation had found its mobilizing force in the gradual realization of the promise of nationhood. National integration advanced along with the standard of living. Despite its costs, modernization would mean the construction of more rational, more just, and more active societies. But for more than twenty years, the link between progress and national integration has been broken.

In the West of the continent, on the economic and social level, the long postwar period was marked by a prodigious "self-centered" development in which reduction in inequality, construction of social protection systems, and the economic impetus of the state have played a central role. Since the mid-1970s, this model has been exhausted: economic integration is practically achieved on national territories; already largely open, economies "turned" toward the outside. Decided and applied at the start of the 1950s, European integration has progressed and the interdependence among countries has also sharply increased.[14] Populations find themselves increasingly divided as a function of the level of their incorporation into foreign activities, making cleavages and conflicting interests among "competitive," "protected," and "exposed" workers.[15] These transformations are also accompanied by technological and industrial mutations, increasing the demand for skilled labor, for "symbol manipulators" and "service providers" to the detriment of unskilled workers.[16] This crisis of the welfare state and increasing public deficits are the direct consequences. States have been subject to double constraints—the renovation of social protection and the search for "economic attractiveness"—which do not diminish their role, quite the contrary, but induce a reorientation of their objectives manifested by a wave of privatization, by reduction in public spending, and disengagement. States have become less *dirigist* (statist) and interventionist and are more preoccupied with creating social conditions favorable to growth.[17] Increasingly organized by criteria of efficiency and rationality, the economy becomes autonomous in relation to policy, whose function is less to mobilize the population than to intervene to guarantee the maintenance of the kind of equality necessary for the social stability of the territories.

The first result of these mutations is growth in unemployment, a rise in the number of people excluded, and the appearance of an underclass, as well as the growing difficulties in "integrating" immigrant populations and workers who are disorganized and restless. The second consequence is the weakening of the middle class notably that linked to activities of integration, whose symbolic status is frail and increasingly subject to labor mobility and job precariousness. The social categories that had been at the heart of the industrial nation found themselves enfeebled and felt threatened—essentially the working class, victims of industrial restructuring, and middle classes linked to the civil service and public enterprises. Henceforth for these social groups, the logic of economic development seems contrary to the traditional logic of solidarity and to the social and national unity guaranteed by the state. Moreover, in weakened populations, the replacement of institutional mechanisms of integration by the market and the economy's openness engender a feeling of change imposed from outside, as a destructive constraint, accompanies an economic unification that seems to threaten the very existence of the local and national cultures and identities of which they thought they were bearers. At the same time, this counterlogic is fed by more dynamic and attractive regions that have asserted their will to disengage from the constraints of unproductive redistribution, if not from national solidarity, like Flanders in Belgium vis-à-vis Wallonia, northern Italy vis-à-vis southern, or Catalonia vis-à-vis the rest of Spain, taking nations into a sort of vice that crushes them and leaves them no more space. Nation-states experience a growing tension between their internal logic (of national integration) and their external logic (of power).

To the East of the continent, the crumbling of Communism has created problems of incomparable scope that arose from the same logic, however different the scale. These countries have been confronted with the necessity of building an economy and thus the obligation to roll back state regulation and institute privatizations, to reconstruct social assistance programs, and finally, to abandon costly and unproductive industries. The rise in unemployment in the working class and the weakening of the middle classes employed by the state or the party were the first direct consequences. The retreat of the Communist state was accompanied by an explosion in inequality and in many places a vertiginous fall in the standard of living for the victims of these changes. Similarly, tensions increased between rich zones and poor zones, between those who already knew how to engage in the real economy and those who were strictly tied to state power, engendering oppositions between Transylvania and Walachia in Rumania, the break between the Czech Republic and Slovakia, and more seriously, wars between Slovenia and Croatia on one side and Serbia on the other.

On the whole continent, for the territories and social groups most directly touched by these mutations, social and historical changes do not appear to have any other meaning than an increase in political instability and an internationalization of the economy, with the concomitant weakening of the state, deregulation, the polarization of societies, and the development of social exclusion—in short, the social and cultural tearing apart of nations. Modernization and economic development are no longer factors of progress and integration. On the contrary, they create inequality. Only the "elites" of dominant nations seem to have kept the capacity to produce a synthesis and to trace the future while protecting and defending their own identity. Other social groups and "peripheral" territories are subject to a fearsome dialectic: integrating into the flux of the world economy by accepting its constraints, at the cost of their social and cultural identity, or else maintaining this identity at the cost of marginalization and of rapid and fatal impoverishment.

Thus in the countries of the European periphery we observe a clear split between concern for development and concern for the nation. In Romania, for example, the issue is posed practically in mutually exclusive terms: either remain Rumanian and strengthen identity, but by accepting to remain the poor relations of Europe, or else to enter fully fledged into the modernity of Western Europe, but by forsaking its soul and sacrificing its identity. This dilemma constantly comes back to political discourses, often oscillating from one extreme to another, from pure neoliberalism to a strict defense of identity.[18] In other countries of the East, more brutally entering the market economy of European space, this either/or dilemma is expressed by reactions hostile to "Westernization" denounced as devastating for collective identity and the rise in a powerful feeling of being the victim of a sort of colonization.[19]

In the West of the continent, among the social categories that are victims of restructuring or worried about losing their jobs, the "future" is rejected and denounced as an extension of capitalism of "Americanization," and the process of cultural unification by the market is accompanied in classic fashion by the growing marginalization of spaces and populations that cannot enter. And so they oppose a modernity that excludes them and whose principles appear destructive to them. In their eyes, there is little difference between "internal" and "external" margins of the EU. In every case, people feel relegated and maintained in a sort of ghetto outside the rich, developed, and democratic zones to which they cannot accede.

All these socioeconomic transformations provoke strong social tensions within nations: social groups are animated by more divergent—even irreconcilable—interests. Amelioration of the situation of some seems to occur to the detriment of others. Formerly founded on the shared sentiment of being a collectivity working for progress to benefit the whole population, the national pact is now broken. The future of countries does not seem to move toward more integration, but on the contrary toward a growing gap between social classes and hence toward disintegration and irreconcilable futures. The language of the nation is directly affected.

The Exhaustion of Nationhood

Social transformations and European integration are inseparable from the rupture of national pacts and various forms of withdrawal into belonging, notably into popular identity and national traditions. The state, the people, communitarian, religious, or ethnic identity appear for many as the only really stable frameworks, the only way to preserve and even resist phenomena of "globalization." The old theme of "blood against money" dear to Spengler, or "civilization against cosmopolitan barbarism," has thus gained a major part of the political formations of Western countries as much as in the East, on the left as on the right. These themes generate two types of sociopolitical movements.

In the middle classes, a nationalist discourse of attachment to the "threatened" nation-state and the opposition between a "nation-centered logic" and a "logic of a destructive European neo-liberalism" serve as ideological cement for the defense of social status guaranteed by the state and the denunciation of the treachery of "cosmopolitan elites."[20] The language of nation becomes a language of last refuge, translating the degradation of a modernizing and mobilizing state into a defensive and corporatist state.

In the working class, the consequence of breaking the national pact is a strong comeback of what Eric Hobsbawm calls "popular proto-nationalism": movements that activate popular feelings of belonging (religious, ethnic, linguistic, identitarian, and exclusivist) to oppose modernization.[21] They cannot lead to the political formation of a modern nation. They are even these days one of the major obstacles to the formation of a national political consciousness in Eastern countries and they actively participate in the destruction of this consciousness in Western countries. In opposing history and modernization in the name of the defense of exclusive identities, they accelerate the processes of fragmentation of political spaces and prevent any synthesis of reason, will, and justice.

In Eastern countries, Communism was experienced as the imposition of a dictatorship of reason and history that destroyed popular national identities. The shock of its collapse sometimes enabled the political fusion of proto-nationalism and defense of the corporative state by former nomenclature and gave it a major destructive force. In Romania, for example, the long maintenance in power of former apparatchiks rested on an alliance with "nationalist" political parties of the extreme right. This was accompanied by official exaltation of the definition of national popular identity by associating "Latinity" with orthodoxy, thus forbidding any development of a positive political definition of the nation that would be capable of including minorities and going down the path of modernization. Paradoxically, this Romanian consciousness seems more present among those who are not "true Romanians" within minorities who defend a more modern and civic conception of nationality.[22] More generally in the Balkans, the struggle of former Communist *nomenklatura* to keep power goes hand in hand with the obsession with "nation" in the sense of exclusive ethnic, linguistic, and religious identity. It is indeed this fusion between proto-nationalism and corporative nationalism that appears as the principal obstacle to the formation of modern nation and to the development of democracy, and it is also one of the explanations that might be advanced concerning the conflicts in the former Yugoslavia and more particularly in Bosnia.[23]

From this standpoint, the difficulties encountered in certain Eastern European countries, submerged by the alliance between proto-nationalism and corporative nationalism, derived essentially from a deficit of national awareness—not the opposite. The inability to construct a national political awareness and to develop a national discourse of synthesis seems indeed to be one of the major obstacles to development, the source of interethnic tensions, and one of the central elements in triggering conflicts.[24]

In Western Europe, the language of nation appeared more commonly as an ideology of "middle classes" who were seeking a guarantee of their status and protection by the state, faced with exogenous modernization. But the difficulties of nation-states entail the affirmation of proto-nationalist movements, which appear in the form of groups of the extreme right that are very xenophobic and antidemocratic, of the National Front type in France, in Austria, or in Belgium, or in the form of populist ideologies marked by hostility to Europe and not only to "globalization," but also to "parliamentarianism" and to democracy. Proto-nationalism is asserted with all the more force when the language of the nation is no longer capable of taking charge of it or even contributes to nourishing it. But because the middle classes know how to protect themselves, the political link with corporative nationalism has not (yet?) taken place, thus limiting their influence.

All these movements are very directly linked to the weakening and degradation of the language of the nation that results from the rupture of the national pact. In a certain way, the promise of the nation has not been kept. The future is a refutation of the nation. The language of the nation can no longer rely on the association among justice, reason, and will, with reference to time and a sense of history. Henceforth, this language loses all capacity to integrate. It is less and less capable of giving meaning and of tracing a space for action. On the contrary, it undergoes a sort of inversion. It focuses on the present and consists of rejecting the future in the name of a more or less mythical past. Deprived of "transcendence," it risks being appropriated by particular social categories; it may become degraded into a simple ideology.

The Crisis of Democracy

The language of nation is also torn between logics (1) of European integration and transformation that invalidate it, (2) its inversion into an ideology of the corporative state, and (3) proto-national movements that contest it very directly. Also, the national myth gradually fades, with the elements that it had combined rediscovering their autonomy, separating and becoming contradictory again, as in the eighteenth century: the discourse of reason is opposed very directly to the people and to discourses of the will (in the name of the emancipation of the economy) and of justice (in the name of efficacy). The discourse of justice is opposed to the state and to discourses of reason (in the name of social equality) and of the will (in the name of respect for diverse identities). The discourse of the will is opposed to that of civil society and to discourses of justice (in the name of "necessity" to change) and of reason (in the name of the necessary mastery of this change). The logics of the people, civil society, and the state all push "national societies" in contradictory directions and empty politics of any capacity of intervention and regulation. Reason, will, and justice appear more and more irreconcilable.

With the national reference weakening, no other political institution appears able to regulate change and to offer the symbolic space necessary for the construction of a democratic and integrated life. European construction is quite far from being able to offer a language of alternative reference capable of operating a synthesis.

The EU is today too weak to master changes. Like political ectoplasm, it proved its impotence over Bosnia. For social categories that are victims of social transformations, it seems bent on applying the single "free market" logic of "deregulation" with no counterpart. The EU no longer "protects"—or at least appears on the political and economic levels, to bring no guarantee. Hence the disappointment, distrust, and worries about it. Moreover, too distant from people, it offers neither the possibility of defining a positive political consciousness nor a fortiori the institutions necessary to construct democratic life. In the face of the political inability of the EU to reformulate another level of national synthesis in all European societies, the problem is now to reconstruct a new articulation between identities, democracy, and national unity. European societies are increasingly pursuing three divergent paths toward three contradictory images of Europe.

In some societies, the external orientation of the economy rests on acceptance of a "disarticulation" of the society and the search for cultural homogeneity so as to foster the mobilization of resources for international competition. Thus another image of the nation appears, closely associating the strengthening of national identity with economic and political activity directed toward inclusion in regional and international commerce, marginalizing a portion of the population. The role of the state is reinforced, but democratic space must be reduced to a minimum in favor of a capacity for mobilization for the profit of national interests. It is a first idea of Europe: space of wealth in which nation-states representing "homogeneous cultural identities" try to insert themselves. From this standpoint, there is no opposition between unification of Europe by the market on one hand, and on the other the reinforcement of states and the affectivity of identities and "nations." On the contrary, there is great complementarity—to the detriment of democracy. Politically, this idea takes the form of the association between an antipopular policy, economic neoliberalism, and conservative "cultural" activity designed to defend and even to reinforce national specificities. Minorities no longer have a place in national spaces that want to be

homogeneous. Any form of democracy or multiculturalism is an obstacle in this process of mobilization. In analytical terms, the priority is
given to the association of rational action and the will, to the detriment
of justice. It is a matter of being inserted into the world market, even
at the price of social rupture. Identity is instrumentalized: it is a means
of ecocultural mobilization. It is the "people" identified with the state
that is mobilized to produce wealth, and no longer the nation-state that
mobilizes society to better integrate it.

On the other hand, in those spaces left out, an inverse process tends
to occur. Identity appears threatened by a modernization that remains
external, experienced doubly as a cultural invasion and as economic
hardship. Another image of Europe, complementary to the first,
arises: a two-speed Europe that imposes its globalizing rationality on
national spaces that are weak and impoverished. Here appears a split
between the global and the particular, development and identity, the
market and the people. Politically, this image takes the form of a close
association between populist movements and nationalist ideologies
(often expressed by *déclassé*/downwardly mobile intellectuals) that are
violently anti-European and antidemocratic and try to restore or to
reconstruct national, political, and cultural specificities, erected as an
absolute. Minorities no longer have a place, either, for they are considered as one of the vectors of the destruction of national identities and
one of the agents of modernity. In general terms, exclusive priority
is given to justice and will, to the detriment of rational action. It is a
matter of preserving national and popular identity, equality and justice between members of the community, and thus expelling foreign
elements and refusing modernity. The popular community mobilizes
to defend national identity—and no longer to better modernize and
develop itself.

Finally, in central and developed spaces that take full part in modernity, the generalized market and weak social integration mechanisms
give civil society a growing autonomy. This leads to the development
of multicultural movements that oppose any form of national or statist
unification in the name of individual rights and the necessary respect
for diversity of identities. So a third image of Europe appears, that
of regulated free exchange, allowing each community and group,
like each individual, to assert its specificity in the face of necessarily
homogenizing others. Europe here is at best a vast civil society, a federal world freed from state bureaucracy and protecting the diversity of
its minorities. Here cities and great regions, like Catalonia, Piedmont,
and Provence, play a central role. In analytical terms, it is a matter

of the combination of justice and reason against will. Civil society is affirmed absolutely by rejecting any institutional pretension to unity. Democracy finds itself directly weakened and challenged, since absolute identities are no longer negotiable, and the idea of constructing shared collective will or a representative system is necessarily rejected because it implies an alteration of these identities. The call for a pure multicultural society and the rejection of any form of central political regulation, of any idea of values and shared membership, leads to the juxtaposition of market and ghettos.

Today we are witnessing the emergence of these three antidemocratic models, to the East as to the West of the continent. (One thinks, e.g., of the North/South opposition in Italy, or Basque and Catalan nationalisms in Spain, or the opposition between Flemish and Walloons, but also the multicultural demands in Great Britain or in France, or even the various forms of nationalism in the former Yugoslavia.) Their sole link is negative. They all mark a deep rupture with the language of nationhood: they are a refusal of history, the mark of a desire to get out of it, and a rejection of nation as a unified historical actor. They are three paths for exiting from the world of modernizing and mobilizing nations. The idea of common political action designed to mobilize society to bring about the nation appears as an obstacle to adaptation to external constraints, as a negation of the heterogeneity of individuals and groups, or even as a promise of modernity that is destructive of peoples' fundamental identities. The nation as a symbolic space capable of giving a shared and recognized meaning to past, present, and future actions seems no longer able to supply the language of reference that underpins democracy.

We may resketch our initial diagram as in figure 9.2.

We are experiencing the crisis of the language of nationhood and the separation of reason, will, and justice. Deprived of reference to history, the language of nationhood is no long strong enough to link these three dimensions, and the EU is proving incapable of offering a new synthesis. The consequence is a deep crisis in democracy. On one side is the space of rational action, economic development, and markets that corresponds for the citizen to participation, and on the other side, the space of cultural integration and collective identity that corresponds to the citizen's membership. But the link between participation and membership is gone—hence the current trends—withdrawal into identity politics, the emergence of multicultural demands that are increasingly absolute, and more or less authoritarian forms of antipopular mobilization—all of which are fatal for democratic life.

From the Mobilized Nation to the Multicultural Nation?

Socioeconomic transformations and the rejection by European societies of a burdensome history have led to rupture of the national pact and exhaustion of the language of nation. Europe does not have the capacity to offer the space of political and social unity and to promote an alternative language of reference. Each element of the national synthesis has become autonomous and appears contradictory with, rather then complementing, the two others. The state promotes economic mobilization at the expense of justice. Popular national identity is asserted by rejection of reason. Civil society and multiculturalism develop in opposition to will. These three evolutions will eventually spell the death of a democracy that can no longer found itself on a shared language of reference. The problem is then to know how to combine anew justice, reason, and will in a way to make democracy live. In other words, in the East as in the West of Europe, the challenge is to reconstitute "political units able to sustain the exercise of democracy," therefore founded on respect for heterogeneous social and cultural situations.[25] The weakness of the EU and the permanence of "national attachment" demonstrates for the time being that there is no other solution than that of national political and social space. Citizenship and democracy only exist within this space. This is one of the reasons that explains the hostility of the most developed and richest societies to any European construction that challenges the functioning of national democratic institutions.

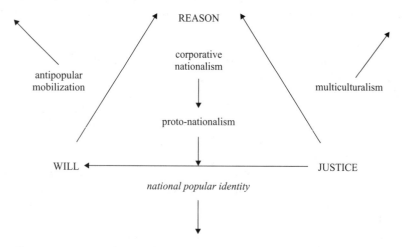

Figure 9.2   Antipopular mobilization, national popular identity, and multiculturalism

But this solution presupposes a reorientation of the language of nationhood, which to remain a language of reference must continue to integrate the three dimensions of political modernity—reason, will, and justice—without which there is no democracy possible. Today in Europe the question is no longer located between past and future, or part of history. It is not a matter of tearing away from a past of underdevelopment and becoming an actor in history. If nineteenth- and early twentieth-century Europe "divinized history,"[26] the end of the millennium was marked by the refusal of the language of history in all European societies. The national synthesis cannot be made by reference to time. Once entry into modernity is achieved, the question becomes much more synchronic. It is about the management of the diversity of identities, of territories, and modes of action and organization.

In societies that reject any mobilization in the name of history but that still continue to refer to justice, reason, and will, the language of nation must redefine itself in a relation to diversity, not time. The nation can no longer be conceived as a product or promise of history; it must be understood as a production of democracy, as the "political good" of an ensemble of individual that gives them a "shared understanding of social goods" and the reconstruction of their national pact.[27] It constitutes a "community of language and mutual discourse," product of the democratic space where the diversity of belongingness and modernity may be combined; the necessary respect for identities, whether national or minoritarian, combined with economic and political unity; the reason that engenders diversity, the justice that presupposes the equality, and the will that produces unity are all mixed together.

In other words, the language of nation must be "turned around" to become the symbolic space of reference offering the guarantee of respect and of development of individual and collective identities in the face of a homogenizing modernity. Thus we must pass from a "mobilized nation" to a "multicultural nation." The nation is the site of protection for diversity and heterogeneity of groups and lands in a Europe whose logic is growing unification and economic and political integration, consequently making the continent uniform. Within the EU, the nation must become the site of the "politics of recognition" of which Charles Taylor speaks and thus remain the space of democratic life for multicultural societies.[28]

The language of nation can no longer be the principle of entry into history and the realization of nationhood. It must become the language of the "(political) community of citizens," the unified foundation of democratic life, the language of political and symbolic reference of an ensemble of individuals and groups defined by their diversity.[29] It will thus be able to avoid a fatal crystallization of the three tendencies we have observed, each as dangerous as the other for minorities and especially for democracy. The language of nationhood must be identified with democratic debate on the very nature of national unity, a debate coinciding with the terms of our initial sketch since it contrasts the "institutional" republican conception that combines will and reason, the liberal conception that mixes reason and justice, and the "populist" conception that unites justice and will.[30] National unity, then, is uniting the terms of this debate in positions that are theoretically contradictory but complementary in practice.

The "solution" to the problem of the deterioration of the old language of nation certainly does not lie in sterile and false oppositions between affectivity and rationality, between a multicultural model and a republican model, between the national state and Europe, or even between multiculturalism and national unity. It lies inside the EU, in constructing national policies of "recognition" and formation of systems of democratic mediation that foster the emergence of real sociocultural actors who have the practical capacity to link reason, will, and justice. In other words, the solution lies in the patient and difficult (re)construction of real "national" consciousness within Europe, of a reoriented language of nation that enables a democratic (not just historic) synthesis of the contradictory elements of our modernity.

Notes

1. As Bernard Michel notes, the nineteenth century, the century of nationalities, was "relatively" peaceful. Bernard Michel. *Nations et nationalismes en Europe centrale, XIXe-XXe siècle.* Paris: Aubier, 1995. In an article devoted to ethnic conflicts, the historian Eric Hobsbawm presented Mexico as a good example of a country having overcome its ethnic divisions. At the moment of its publication the revolt by Indians of Chiapas burst out. Eric Hobsbawm. "Qu'est-ce qu'un conflit ethnique?" *Actes de la recherche en sciences sociales* 100, December 1993.
2. Simon Schama. *An Embarrassment of Riches: An Interpretation of Dutch Culture in the Golden Age.* New York: Knopf, 1987.
3. Keith Michael Baker. *Inventing the French Revolution. Essays on French Political Culture in the Eighteenth Century.* Cambridge: Cambridge University Press, 1990. For a discussion of Baker's theses, see Robert Darnton. *The Forbidden Best-Sellers of Pre-Revolutionary France.* New York: W. W. Norton, 1995: 175 and following.
4. Baker. *Inventing the French Revolution.*
5. Ernest Gellner. *Nations and Nationalisms.* Ithaca, NY: Cornell University Press, 1983.
6. Baker, *Inventing the French Revolution.*
7. Benedict Anderson. *Imagined Communities: Reflections on the Origin and Spread of Nationalism.* London: Verso, 1983.

8. Peter Alter. *Nationalism*. London: Edward Arnold, 1985.
9. T. H. Marshall. *Class, Citizenship and Social Development*. Chicago: Chicago University Press, 1977.
10. Norbert Elias. *The Society of Individuals* (edited by Michael Schroter, trans. Edmund Jephcott). New York: Continuum, 2001.
11. Translator's note: State is always capitalized in French.
12. Roland Barthes. *Mythologies* (trans. Annette Lavers). London: Vintage 1993.
13. Anderson. *Imagined Communities*: 15.
14. For a discussion of the themes of "globalization" and *mondialisation*, see Elie Cohen. *La tentation hexagonale: La souveraineté à l'épreuve de la mondialisation*. Paris: Fayard, 1996.
15. Pierre-Noël Giraud. *L'inégalité du monde: Économie du monde contemporain*. Paris: Gallimard, 1996.
16. Robert Reich. *The Work of Nations: Preparing Ourselves for 21st Century Capitalism*. New York: Knopf, 1991. Many studies conclude about a tripartite division of the world of work, by crossing the nature of occupations and the status of the job occupied, as for example, the opposition among Internet workers, flex timers, and the jobless described by Manuel Castells, *The Rise of the Network Society*. Cambridge: Blackwell, 1996. In all cases, the "middle class" is weakened to the benefit of superior and inferior groups.
17. On the French case, see Vivien A. Schmidt. *From State to Market? The Transformation of French Business and Government*. Cambridge: Cambridge University Press, 1996.
18. Catherine Durandin. *Histoire des Roumains*. Paris: Fayard, 1995.
19. Marcin Frybès and Patrick Michel. *Après le Communisme: Mythes et légendes de la Pologne contemporaine*. Paris: Bayard, 1996.
20. Christopher Lasch. *The Revolt of the Elites and the Betrayal of Democracy*. New York: Norton, 1995.
21. Eric Hobsbawm. *Nations and Nationalism Since 1780: Programme, Myth, Reality*. Cambridge: Cambridge University Press, 1990.
22. Nadia Badrus. "La société roumaine à la recherche de la normalité." *Cahiers internationaux de sociologie* 95, 1993.
23. Paul Garde. *Vie et mort de la Yougoslavie*. Paris: Fayard, 1992; Paul Garde. *Les Balkans*. Paris: Flammarion, 1994.
24. On the case of Ukraine, cf. Charles A. Kupchan (ed.). *Nationalism and Nationalities in the New Europe*. Ithaca, NY: Cornell University Press, 1995.
25. Guy Hermet. *Histoire des nations et du nationalisme en Europe*. Paris: Le Seuil, 1996.
26. "It was in the nineteenth century that history replaced God's omnipotent role in man's destiny, but only in the twentieth that the political follies born of that substitution would emerge," wrote François Furet in *The Past of an Illusion: The Idea of Communism in the Twentieth Century,* trans. Deborah Furet. Chicago: Chicago University Press, 1999: 30.
27. Michael Walzer. *Thick and Thin: Moral Argument at Home and Abroad*. Notre Dame: Notre Dame University Press, 1994.
28. Charles Taylor. *Multiculturalism and the "Politics of Recognition": An Essay*. Princeton, NJ: Princeton University Press, 1992.
29. The work of Dominique Schnapper might be interpreted in this way. See Dominique Schnapper. *La Communauté des citoyens*. Paris: Gallimard, 1994.
30. For a rehabilitation of the populist political tradition in relation to liberalism and republicanism, see Christopher Lasch. *The True and Only Heaven: Progress and Its Critics*. New York: Norton, 1991.

CHAPTER TEN

Space, Culture, and Boundary: Projecting Europe Abroad

RÉMY LEVEAU

The inability of Europe to construct a military force or a common foreign policy contrasts with the dominant vision it produces. The European Union does not have to defend its borders, NATO is in charge of that, and one of the principal powers, Germany, was long since deprived by its constitution of any possibility of participating in foreign military action. Only France and Great Britain possess credible means of intervention, but in the case of the Gulf War of 1991 or the crises in Bosnia and Afghanistan, their mobilization could only be envisaged in conjunction with the United States. European space is scarcely unified except by its fears, about drugs, terrorism, or illegal immigration. This leads the Union to organize itself internally and therefore offers the outside world the image of a rational edifice that rejects anything that is foreign to it. This approach based on collective fear leads to structuring monitoring activity, already now largely transferred beyond its borders for reasons that are both internal and external. The imposition of visas granted in advance (and parsimoniously) transfers the restrictions to the offices of diplomatic services and especially to airline counters. The effect this projects onto the societies surrounding Europe is very strong and contributes to constructing an image in the Other's eyes that does not correspond to a voluntarist politics. Influence is now exercised by Europe's image, by ideas and the lifestyles associated with them, and perception of them is undoubtedly the most important element in its involuntary projection of itself.

Refusal of Empire

This situation has complex effects. Europe does not want to be construed as an empire gradually extending its boundaries to populations with diverse cultures and ethnicities. It aims instead at a certain cultural and political unity and asserts itself more by the defensive refusals with which it confronts those who want to enter it than by any desire for conquest. Entry is selective and conditional. The admission of southern European countries made the countries of Eastern Europe after the fall of the Berlin Wall dream of the same fortune, an identical recognition that would mean both the benefit of a new Marshall Plan and their democratic choices taking root. But their integration already posed the problem of reconstructing the mechanisms of the Union's functioning to conserve a power of decision making that is concentrated for the benefit of a central kernel. This core will accept paying the price for its power by the partial renunciation by member states of the fiction of their autonomy. But the builders of Europe are now wondering about the sense of its extension to Turkey and the Balkans.[1] Several of these countries have expressed—some for a long time—the desire to join the community space. Some, like Turkey, have made this attempt the central axis of their domestic and foreign policies for decades already.

These neighboring countries have also furnished, at various times and under variable conditions, important groups of migrants who established themselves in European space without any idea of returning. The rejection of their country of origin by Europe prevents them from hoping to accede to equality other than by the individual routes prescribed by states. This condemns those who refuse this path to becoming a sort of communitarian cyst within receiving countries if they do not want their culture to disappear. In return, since the fall of the Berlin Wall and the 1991 Gulf War, Europe has made use of the fear of an imaginary Islamic peril that would ally the minorities already established with Muslims kept outside its boundary to construct mechanisms for the authoritarian monitoring of the space unified under the Schengen agreements. Lacking the ability to make states and public opinion accept the principle of a central kernel of strong federal power under the control of democratic procedures, the civil servants who construct this unified space were going to use (only at first?) collective fears to weave their technocratic networks.

To manage the free circulation of persons and goods, Europe needs a minimal power that must be capable of both keeping outside those populations and states that it does not admit, and neutralizing their nuisance capacity without resorting to American help. Belonging to the United Nations and refusing to transfer to the European Union the elements of sovereignty and power that would make it an autonomous power do persist in various European countries, particularly in France.

To safeguard what has been achieved in common without running up against governments and public opinion, the temptation is great to play on collective fears. The anticipatory establishment of centralized and restrictive structures is taking place partly through the mobilization of fears that foreign Islam incarnates, with its extension into its own populations "at risk" due to an amalgam running from clandestine immigration to drugs and to terrorism. Thereafter one will be able to justify (if necessary) a multilateral abandonment of sovereignty that will go much farther than any supranational institution would be able to do for a long time. But this seems the price to pay for community construction to progress: by means that have nothing much to do with the principles of legitimacy Europe has proclaimed.

Behind this approach lies neither plots nor clandestine orchestrators, but a sort of collective logic and networks of bureaucrats who are less located in Brussels' offices than in various sovereign state administrations (interior, justice, and defense). Each will secrete at its own level the means of collectively managing the restrictions of a unified space: by anticipating the fears born of this novel situation and by creating over time the technical conditions and political motivations that might result in a transfer of sovereignty to a federal level. Presented as such today, this proposal would have no chance of succeeding. Yet its insidious insertion into the practices of collective regulation will later govern the evolution of the system.

From Constructing Fear of the Other to the Call to Empire

Europe projects abroad an image that attracts individuals—and makes it desirable to transgress the rules that it imposes to keep them outside. This attraction is not the consequence of a deliberate policy of influence, as *francophonie* is for France. It results more from the effects of televised images, and models of behavior transmitted by emigrants, as well as the deterioration of their own societies. A rapid shift from rural to urban, where the threshold of 50 percent (rising sometimes to 70 percent) of urban population is attained in one generation, is one of the causes. A significant mass of young people, often unemployed, agglutinate on the peripheries of cities, touched by an educational system without being able to draw much practical benefit from it. They are waiting for the "elsewhere" they dream about. Still attached to the values and behavior of a peasant society and to familial solidarity, they are incapable of really integrating into the city.[2] They are a natural clientele for images transmitted by satellites and television stations from nearby Europe (French, Spanish, Italian channels) that symbolize this projection that is unintended but valorized by the expectations and frustrations of North African societies.

They know intimately about life in European societies, thanks to constantly illuminated screens. They also participate in their political lives, electoral debates, sports, and legal scandals—all of which are fields of reactions and analysis in relation to lived experience. The desire to see them is exasperated by the impossibility of going there and managing to participate in this feast of modernity, perceived as an injustice that contributes to the depreciation of one's own society.[3] The gap grows during major events like the fall of the Berlin Wall, which suddenly shows how much Europe feels close to those newly arrived on the scene—and all the more distant from those in countries of the South who are hardly more poor, but of a different culture. At the time of the Gulf War in 1991, the projection of an aggressive Europe that refuted its tradition of solidarity and openness to the South that had accompanied the conflicts of decolonization, especially in France, took on disproportionate significance because of the effects of satellite televisions that mobilized the masses. The Maghreb elites feel themselves betrayed and powerless to avoid submitting to the image of their own decay. Whether Arab or Islamic nationalism, collective reactions are joined in a fascination with, and a rejection of, European models—which are exposed in conducts where neglect of Arab reactions—that domineering indifference that characterizes Europe—is considered more wounding than the aggression against Iraq. The end of a crisis does not make this troubled relation—a mixture of fascination, attraction, and rejection—disappear, however. It contributes to the South's construction of an image of a strong Europe, of a united European space with a much more coherent functioning of its institutions than is really the case. In turn, this image entails reactions of rejection that are going to be translated into an Islamicist discourse that takes over from Arab nationalism in its contesting the West. This results on the other side of the Mediterranean in a recuperation of this threat to build the beginnings of potency that these southern collective emotions thought they were already opposing.

Curiously, the commercial policy of Europe, which on the one hand is open to reciprocal trade and on the other applies tariff barriers or places quotas on southern products, is ignored by the masses and spared criticism from the elites; the policy is totally confined to exchanges among technocrats.

Construction of the "Islamic Threat"

With a large historic dimension, Islam occupies a unique place in the European imagination. The memory of the Crusades or the siege of Vienna can play a role in these perceptions, but in the more recent past it is colonization and decolonization that create traumatizing images. This analysis applies especially to France, where the civil war in Algeria was experienced as a new stage in decolonization.[4] But in various ways Great Britain, Italy, and Spain share this memory.

It is the settlement of large groups of migrants of Muslim culture originating from the Maghreb, Turkey, and the Indian subcontinent that revives these traumatizing reactions. The problem was first posed in 1974, the symbolic date of the decree on immigration and the shift from a system of coming-and-going with the countries of origin to a system of residential settlement. Since then the problem has been implicitly posed in the collectively imaginary by the acceptance of an ethnic minority of Muslim culture. The rational response of the political leaders of the European countries as a whole has been positive—on condition that the migrants and their descendants accept conforming individually to the norms and values of the groups who settled in ancient times. On this level, the unified European space offers a spectrum between models of French-style secularism (*laïcité*) and a codified pluralism inherited from the Augsburg tradition.

In this process of random settlement, Islam has become a symbolic stake, as much for the minorities that want to establish themselves without overly abandoning their particularism, as for the majority populations of the receiving countries, who often express, in reactions comparable to those of threatened *minorities*, their difficulties in situating themselves in relation to the new groups they fear losing their identity in a multicultural society. This symbolic conflict is often superimposed on very real economic difficulties for both parties, and it is one of the major stakes in the construction of European space.

These conflicting perceptions reflect the attitudes among groups and are revealed in opinion surveys performed in France or Great

Britain, particularly when a crisis situation arises (the Rushdie Affair, the crisis over the headscarf, the Gulf War). The desire for visibility by the peoples of Muslim culture, even if associated with a feeling of loyalty to the symbols of the state, entails a strong reaction of refusal and suspicion on the part of the long-resident groups. Consequently, politicians and opinion leaders (Valéry Giscard d'Estaing, Jordi Pujol, John Paul II) express this diffuse sentiment by speaking of "invasion" with regard to immigration, declaring that Islam cannot be assimilated or insisting on the Christian cultural foundations of Europe. While the majority of politicians who exercise (or have the vocation to exercise) government responsibilities have stuck to a prudent attitude that does not challenge the right to a peaceful and legitimate stay by peoples of Muslim culture, the problem has been much more brutally raised from time to time, notably by the parties of the extreme right. We find a characteristic expression during the French presidential campaign of 1995 in statements from Jean-Marie Le Pen, who declared in his platform[5] that he intended to inscribe in the constitution the principle of "national preference" and to stigmatize the presence inside the national territory of "foreign populations that cannot be assimilated," arguing they were potential allies of countries to the South. To counter this danger, he proposed converting the military apparatus to create a National Guard to fight against "the domestic insecurity created by the presence of foreign elements," this term being understood in a wider sense, since he envisaged reexamining the conditions for having granted French nationality to 2.5 million foreigners and naturalized immigrants since 1974. There exists a current of opinion in various European countries (ranging from 5 to 20 percent) among voters who are ready to challenge the existing composition of their societies and to chase out the most recently settled by stigmatizing their cultural membership.

This extreme position, openly situated in the lineage of measures undermining citizenship that were adopted by the Vichy regime with respect to Jews during World War II, influences the political debate to the extent that certain actors from parties in government, not wanting to leave the field free to the National Front (or at least wanting to recuperate a portion of the current of protest that it represents), exploit in a minor key the themes Le Pen supported. Similar currents are found today in the European political field from Austria to southern Europe. Their nationalist objective is not extension or conquest but rather to preserve group identity, in a national framework now and eventually in a European framework.

Situating themselves like this, they contribute to redefining both an internal and an external border that is supposedly impassable for cultural reasons, while those who want to cross this border do so as a function of an individual desire to integrate into the European space, thanks notably to the economic and cultural image that it projects abroad.

The political controversy would be indirectly fed by a scientific debate on the nature of conflicts after the fall of the Soviet system and after the Gulf War. The wider debate around the theses of Samuel Huntington reflected the stakes in this debate. According to him, the fundamental source of future conflicts would no longer be ideological or economic, but cultural: "The fault lines between civilizations are becoming the central lines of conflict in global politics." Then, relying on M. J. Akbar, he stated: "It is in the sweep of the Islamic nations from the Maghreb to Pakistan that the struggle for a new world order will begin." Finally, taking up Bernard Lewis, "This is no less than a clash of civilizations—that perhaps irrational but surely historic reaction of an ancient rival against our Judeo-Christian heritage, our secular present, and the worldwide expansion of both."[6] These theses, widely taken up and discussed both by the press and by political actors, theorized at the level of the West as a whole certain ideas that dominated the issue of redefining space, especially the real and potential *conflicts of interests* between Europe and its proximate environment. It is astonishing to see to what extent the conflict has been expressed in a defensive attitude that mixes the internal and external, feeding on neighboring instability to reinforce its position. This has also permitted other political and administrative actors to translate this climate of a crisis in domestic and foreign security into a European legal construction.

The European Security Response

The setting up of a European security policy began long before the great debates accompanying the fall of the Berlin Wall and the 1991 Gulf Crisis.[7] At first it was a matter of monitoring migratory flows and populations "at risk," giving rise to multilateral negotiations that preceded and accompanied the signing of the 1985 Schengen accords on the free circulation of peoples. As a counterpart to the opening of European space, bureaucratic networks belonging to various ministries (interior, justice, finance, defense) and to national departments whose existing rationale and functioning were challenged by the suppression of national border controls (customs, police) gathered together to anticipate the nuisance effects that might be created (and by the same token, to define new missions for themselves). The goal was to work for the implementation of the agreement and its extension to other countries, while assuring the optimal security conditions of the unified new space. The logic of community construction would have wanted the policy to be developed at the level of the Union, involving a partial abandonment of the power of individual states. But this solution was excluded, as much for practical reasons as out of principle. The community before the ratification of the Maastricht Treaty did not have authority over migration, drugs, or security. Member-nations choosing openness (except for Great Britain) preferred to remain within a multi-bilateral framework that did not call for definitive relinquishing of sovereignty. In 1985–1986, the approach by specialists in security problems was justified by terrorist attacks, the taking of hostages, the fight against drugs, and against the criminal financing linked to these activities. The transnationality of policies of coordination was intended to respond to the transnationality of the aggression coming from the Middle East.

It is also necessary to consider the fact that the departments moving in this direction are looking for a new definition of their own authority and mission. The opening of borders challenges their traditional tasks of inspection linked to precise notions of the role of the state, of the territory subject to their jurisdiction, and of boundaries. Taking advantage of the new situation to survive and if possible to increase their authority in relation to competing departments, they contribute to fostering the construction of a new space of European security. This change will in time produce progress toward regulation by an authority that can only operate at the quasi-federal level, with a share of democratic oversight. Lacking this framework from the start, they use myths that are the product of contemporary anxieties. Thus collective fears and received ideas about the existence of an Islamic peril, which might upset Western Europe by drawing on new and dangerous segments of the population, become instrumentalized.

Networks of bureaucrats are skillful enough to take advantage of mental schemas of perceived political violence in such a way as to organize internally and within intergovernmental frameworks those responses that will make themselves indispensable. Thus the compensatory measures foreseen under the Schengen accords are being organized in a collective way that is very restrictive, to the point that the implementation of provisions will be delayed by several years. In effect, it is a matter of harmonizing the practices of different states regarding the monitoring of common borders, the granting of visas, foreigners' right to stay, and the right to asylum. Since the approach aims to limit as much as possible access to community territory, the concerns and expertise of police bureaucrats largely trump those of specialists in international relations (who are indirectly dispossessed of their previous authority). To deal with the practical question of regulating the flows of people, the fight against clandestine immigration, and regulating the right to asylum, they demonstrate a concern for any technical efficiency that is superior to their rivals. They make themselves the spokesmen of a social demand that tends to dissuade or push the foreigner back outside the space of the agreements. They do not hesitate to engage the responsibility of transporters in that monitoring to externalize it more and create a sort of security amalgam associating illegal immigration, drug trafficking, terrorism, and abuse of the right to asylum. Setting up identity files covering suspect persons in various categories strengthens the official scope for action. This approach (via the security techniques of centralized information systems) leads them to demand the transfer to their own agents of the attribution of visas in consular services.

Gradually the logic of "Europe for Europeans" wins over the traditional approach that aimed to facilitate freedom of circulation while moderately supervising any perverse effects that might result on the domestic level. The construction of an imaginary threat about Islam makes these situations intolerable in public opinion. Police personnel appear able to recuperate the perceived fears as objectively validated to internationalize their field of action and increase their "share of the market" in European construction. They compete with both neighboring services (the *gendarmerie*) and with those civil servants traditionally concerned with what is international (Foreign Affairs).

In this upheaval, borders lose their territorial sense. Monitoring transnational flows presupposes on the one hand a projection onto the outside, and on the other surveillance of so-called risky groups who have settled inside European space. The definition of the risk tends to vary and shifts from security problems to questions of national identity.

By abolishing internal borders, Europe raises with new urgency the question of its identity and a new positioning between "Us" and "Others." Like the majority of major European issues, this essential debate has been steered by a transnational network of specialists, whose role has been perceived belatedly because they do not belong to the Brussels administrative apparatus. Associated with a process of establishing European citizenship, they have helped create a "Europe of the polices" (*Europe des polices*) that in some respects advances better than monetary Europe. Their approach is rarely questioned because it remains within a multilateral state framework that is sometimes in conflict with community institutions. But it involves a questioning of European identity and its relations both outside and even inside European space, particularly relations with social groups situated outside the dominant culture. It relies on traditional state practices that adjust poorly to forming a common identity.

When European political or religious actors refer to the sources of this European culture, they usually mention a "Biblical and Christian" tradition that constitutes its unifying principle.[8] From this perspective, Muslims may be those who are accepted but are never part of the central kernel. On a similar basis, other less generous actors might challenge their very right to remain. The rise of the extreme right in various European countries means that these themes are not merely topics for school essays. It is hard to imagine the repetition in a nation-state today of the practices of expulsion or marginalization that accompanied the formation of nation-states over the centuries. If the inhibiting factors still exist in historical memory, starting with the memory of the extermination of Jews during World War II, one may believe that the European cultural and political space would stay on the alert for such tendencies that might appear here and there.

Nevertheless, in constructing a Europe made of polices and in using the fear of Islam, the risk is run of stigmatizing social groups who are judged incapable of integrating. Thereby are redefined the boundaries between internal and external, as well as the identity of the dominant group. Unlike the nationalist tendencies that accompany political changes and which, in the early twentieth century, incorporated peasants, the middle class, and the working class into state political systems, perhaps European construction will find the counterweights to changes that affect both its space and its identity. This evolution will only take place by institutionalizing a large part of the informal networks that were established around this construction and by ensuring procedures for democratic control that are currently absent.

The changes in perspective introduced by the attacks of September 11, 2001 and the interventions that followed in Afghanistan and then in Iraq have only accentuated these tendencies. On the one hand, the call of empire symbolized by the enlargement of the European Union, the creation of a common currency, and debates over institutionalization have only accentuated the differences between the stable zone of calm and prosperity, and a conflictual and uncertain surrounding environment. After the integration of the Eastern countries into the Union, the Balkans appeared to stabilize in the hope of integrating in their turn into an empire that builds its attraction upon the conditions that it sets as a condition for entry.

But at the same time, internal evolution is going to increase tensions with minorities stigmatized by a double belonging that is most often only cobbled together (*bricolé*) from the culture of origin. Europe is poorly managing the inevitable reopening of migration flows imposed on it by the constraints of its demography. It also risks compromising its relations with its immediate environments to the East and South. The debate has become dramatic in France, notably with the opening of negotiations over the membership of Turkey in the Union. The elites' acceptance of this perspective is accompanied by an ambiguous debate and by the resurrection of old fears. If these fears are overcome, the Union will manage a dynamic of openness whose resulting diversity will increase its capacity for influence and attraction. If on the contrary it opts for a blanket rejection of external Islam, the consequences of this choice will be difficult to measure on its domestic equilibrium and on the positions taken by established Muslim minorities. And Europe will have to mobilize itself to face new rogue states—for it will not have the leisure to dictate the future behavior of those whom it is rejecting.

Notes

1. Zaki Laïdi. *Un Monde privé de sens*. Paris: Fayard, 1994.
2. Mounia Bennani-Chraibi. *Soumis et rebelles: Les jeunes au Maroc*. Paris: Editions du CNRS, 1994; Mustapha Belbah. *Les nouveaux immigrés*, (PhD, Sciences Po Paris), 1989.
3. Susan Ossman. *Picturing Casablanca: Portraits of Power in a Modern City*. Berkeley: University of California Press, 1995, especially Chapter 2 "Television as Borders": 63–79.
4. Rémy Leveau (ed.). 1995. *L'Algérie en guerre*. Brussels: Complexe.
5. *Le Monde*, April 6, 1995.
6. Samuel Huntington. *The Clash of Civilization and the Re-making of the World Order*. New York: Norton, 1996, quotations 125, 212.
7. This section leans on the work of Didier Bigo on European police cooperation. See Didier Bigo. *Police en réseaux*. Paris: Presses de Sciences Po, 1996.
8. Speech by Cardinal Lustiger in Berlin on May 3, 1995; *Le Monde* May 10, 1995.

CONCLUSION

"Multiculturalism" and Democracy in Europe?

Guy Hermet

To try to conclude this volume would amount to impoverishing the many avenues of reflection that it has suggested. Consequently, I will try to add a few more points of discussion to the debate by starting from a single realization. As the fundamental element of what might become a new social pact, multiculturalism is undoubtedly running counter to the historical principle as well as to the actual practice of European democracy. This must be stated from the start. But we must quickly add that this incompatibility is not necessarily something to be regretted, or that people can still affirm themselves as democrats without referring to the quite republican logic of representative classical regimes. However, the old European democracies (apart from the Swiss exception) at the level of their values of reference as of their political instrumentation are based on a unitary vision in perfect contradiction with the praise of difference that governs multicultural ideology.

This postulate of a unity (either already acquired or else to be constructed) rests on three interdependent considerations. First, on the conviction that there exists for each people a general interest that can be objectified; second, on the idea that the sentiment of the majority expressed by this people defines this interest; and finally, on the third idea that makes this "sovereign" people accept that they ought to be circumscribed in the limits of a political community, which at the start is that of a nation-state in gestation (itself the direct heir of monarchical states). We see that the first principle of a moral nature goes hand in hand with a second element of quite another order since it remains purely procedural and contingent. Ultimately this results in a paradox that hinders at its very root the effectiveness of a popular sovereignty, always subject to unchanging obedience to the essential thing: the identification of the governed with the governors.

This explains why the two terms of citizenship and nationality are impossible to separate in Western Europe. Currently, one cannot be a full citizen within a political community without being at the same time a national of a state that arrogates to itself alone the right to define this community. In this logic of nonchoice, the first term "citizenship" refers to notions of law and allegiance, whereas the second, "nationality," suggests rather the protection received in a situation of dependence associated with a feeling of belonging that grounds national solidarity (solidarity understood as an expectation of reciprocity on the part of members of the political community), and interpreted as a condition of good "governance" by those who hold power. To this is added a repressive trait deplored by Jürgen Habermas: that which requires of a good "national citizen" that he make of this generally native and independent quality of his will, the almost unique element of his public identity, that he give it priority over all other, more intimate traits (or on the contrary, the least localist ones of his overall personality). At the end of the day, the universality so demanded from the model offered by the old national democracies resides only in the universal vocation it lends to this type of soft incarceration. Narrow particularism—subnational—as well as cosmopolitanism were the enemies of European democracies when they were born. And Europe caught them quite off guard.

But do we really have to make multiculturalism one of the principal challenges posed to the hypothetical European democracy of the future? Riva Kastoryano perceives the problem from the first pages of this book, when she distinguishes rightly the diversity of Europeans from that of non-Europeans, those *strangers* in the ancient sense who have come from elsewhere. Still, we must go beyond this simple warning, courageous in a context where certain intellectuals blur the reasoning by resorting to debatable amalgams. To apply the same concept of multiculturalism in cases of the nationals of European democracies as well as relatively recent immigrants from outside Europe in fact only contributes to obscuring the reality. Let us give an example: how can we in the name of blissful multiculturalism apprehend in the same way the recent establishment of a Muslim colony in Tourcoing (a city in northern France) and the close historical proximity of this town to the Belgian city of Mouscron (located exactly on the border with France). Better to consider that the establishment in Tourcoing or elsewhere of immigrant groups for only two or three decades does relate to the multicultural-ist problematic, but on the other hand, the juxtaposition in Europe of human and political ensembles that clearly have been territorialized for centuries must be envisaged in light of another frame of analysis, which should also be called something else—"pluriculturalism"?—to avoid confusion. Therefore, multiculturalism concerns a portion of the new populations dispersed and still mobile across all of Europe, as well as the rare sites of secular coexistence between distinct linguistic groups in Brussels, Bienne, and Fribourg in Switzerland or Barcelona in par-ticular, or else in Alsace, Wales, Friesland, southern Tyrol, and the Val d'Aosta. But "pluriculturalism,"[1] on the other hand, regards the dom-inant fact, and especially the major question to be resolved from the perspective of a European democracy that can only be founded on a reconciliation between old national identities and a new public or civic identity—destined perhaps to outstrip them in time. It would probably be simpler to call this kind of identity "confederal," if this adjective was not unwelcome among those who contemplate with apprehen-sion a citizenship exceeding the frontiers of the country in which they learned to be politicians or opinion leaders.

If it is born, the sovereign people of Europe will not be multicultural for one precise reason: it will not define itself primarily as a function of the policies to integrate the extra-European immigrants coming to join it. It will be pluricultural: linguistically, culturally, and politically composite, without becoming mixed or crossbred, fashioned less by the widespread but unpredictable internal migratory movements than by the persistence of its "ethnic" borders in the weak sense. These frontiers often precede the development of nation-states, and it will remain sta-ble despite the hierarchical relegation that separated them on maps, as well as the gradual enlargement of the mental horizons of Europeans. Imagining that it is now conceivable to assign a directive value to the plural political community that they would form, I agree with Riva Kastoryano in thinking that this value could belong to nothing but the sublimated realization of this diversity, combined with a parallel shift from a democracy of national unity to a democracy of tolerance and difference.

That could be the nature of the political community to which these still rather imaginary Europeans might rally. As with multiculturalism, it appears once again that there are community and communities: one, public or civic, of future confederated people who will not have changed place essentially, and the other, a private although not very individu-alistic community, issuing from the mobility of members of groups of extra-European origin who claim a right to difference that is somehow transversal and a-territorial. The former is the classic community of the governed such as Hobbes understood it in the seventeenth century in his *Leviathan*, rather abstract or legal, but also irrevocable from the moment when a new social pact—European in this case—is concluded.[2] On the other hand, communities of the second type have nothing in common with this pact. Deriving in theory from the distinction between community and society made by Ferdinand Tönnies, they rest on the attachment to particularisms that engender, practically on their own, the identities of their members and that ignore both territorial attachments and the irrevocability of a political allegiance.

These purely intellectual reflections still leave aside most concrete aspects of a European project of democratic construction. It is important now to match them with the possible avenues this might take. Everybody agrees that putting this project into operation presupposes quite especially that a European public space worthy of the name is configured in advance; in other words, the public debate within the community closely concerns hundreds of millions of persons. On this level, it would be an illusion to count too much on the edifying speeches from the preachers of Brussels or elsewhere, and scarcely more, especially for minorities, on awareness of the tangible stakes contained in EU policies regarding agriculture, protection of the environment, or even immigration.

Still, an optimistic conjecture is counterbalanced by other observations that are much more ambiguous. The most general relates to the globalization of a market logic that seems to render the future European sovereignty as obsolete as the existing states even before it has actually come into being. The result for some is a reaction of withdrawal into national enclaves, and for others, especially in Great Britain, very clear skepticism about the rationale of the European process. Moreover, several challenges internal to Europe are intimidating. Chief among them is the problem posed by the territorialization of its various linguistic and cultural identities. Will Europe become a vast Belgium, tense with antagonisms along almost every meter, where one's place of residence removes any faculty for the individual to choose an identity? Or else will it borrow some elements of the dream among Austro-Marxists like Karl Renner before 1914, preoccupied with inventing a new Austro-Hungarian Empire where shared citizenship would not prevent anyone from enjoying wherever he lived all the educational and other facilities conforming to his freely determined membership (membership called nationality)? The first hypothesis is unfortunately the most probable, inasmuch as the treatment reserved for minorities of extra-European origin is grafted onto this question.

These minorities that already constitute a subject of discord in every country have entailed supplementary discord at the European level. In tackling the problem positively, they possess all the advantages able to make Europeans the most advanced, as long as they are not hampered by the national attachments of indigenous populations, or where cross-border networks encourage minorities to go from one country to another.[3] But handling the affair negatively, this advance might provoke jealousy and increased rejection on the part of most of the population, while feeding, as in Canada with respect to Québec, conflicts between member-countries of the Union, particularly in cases where groups of extra-European origin privilege one or two languages or cultures of preference over others. In that event, the conflict might go to the extreme of a frontal clash between two conceptions of European democracy, one pluricultural and transnational in the perspective sketched here, and the other cosmopolitan and postnational in the manner of Yasemin Soysal.[4]

Even if the triumph of the first conception seems the most plausible, its probability does not exhaust the debate. If it manages one day to assume substance, "Euroculture" has strong chances of overturning the recognized reciprocal order of public identity and private identities. In the republican model in particular, the common identity of citizen is placed in the front rank, consequently above the multiples private identities considered as subaltern and destined to bend, in the name of civics, to the general will. It is a wager if this precedence can be maintained within a framework where private identities would always include the sentiment of national membership not only to a country, but also to a specific culture that previously remained unperceived. Quite inversely, private identities and national memberships boosted by this cultural fortifier could tend to triumph rather widely over a European civic identity reduced to a simple allegiance of convenience to a central "service government." Then there would be only one means of compensating for this kind of deterioration: one that on the Swiss pattern would lead the nationals of the European Union to consider themselves no longer as the grateful beneficiaries of political and social rights conceded by a benevolent state, but as the proprietors of their citizenship as individuals rather than as nationals, as the sovereign personal faculty that is superior to all others. In this hypothesis, European democracy would make a decisive advance.

Notes

1. The expression "pluriculturalism" does present the disadvantage of having preceded, between about 1915 and the 1960s the term "multiculturalism" in the United States—moreover with the same meaning. This original confusion does not matter these days, though, having been forgotten.
2. The preceding social pact of the French stipulated that the Republic was "one and indivisible."
3. Rather on the model of educated Jews of Austria-Hungary, whom Emperor Franz-Joseph affirmed to be his best subjects.
4. See the introduction by Riva Kastoryano.

NOTES ON CONTRIBUTORS

Editor

Riva Kastoryano is currently senior researcher at the Center for International Studies and Research (CERI) at Sciences Po/CNRS, Paris, and visiting professor at the New School for Social Research in New York since 2005. Her research in political sociology focuses on Europe, nationalism, identities, communities, territories, and diasporas. She has published, among others, *Negotiating Identities: States and Immigrants in France and Germany*, Princeton University Press, 2002. She has edited several volumes in French and English, among others, *Les Codes de la Différence. Religion Race et Origine en France, Allemagne et Etats-Unis* (Codes of Otherness: Religion Race and Ancestors in France, Germany and the United States) Presses de Sciences Po, Paris 2005; a special issue "Turkey and Europe," *Constellation, An International Journal of Critical Democratic Theory*, May 2006; and many articles, among which "Citizenship, Nationhood and Non-Territoriality: Transnational Participation in Europe," *PS: Political Sciences & Politics*, 38(4), October 2005; "Transnational nationalism. Redefining Nation and Territory," in Seyla Benhabib et Ian Shapiro (eds.) *Identities, Affiliations and Allegiances,* Cambridge University Press, 2007.

Contributors

Marc Abélès is professor of Anthropology at the Ecole des Hautes Etudes en Sciences Sociales (EHESS), Paris. He is Director of the Laboratoire d'Anthropologie des Institutions et des Organisations Sociales (Center for the Anthropology of Social Institutions and Organisations—EHESS-CNRS). He conducted fieldwork in different places such as Ochollo in Southern Ethiopia, the French province of Burgundy, the French National Assembly, European Institutions, and the Silicon Valley. Currently, Marc Abélès's investigations center on globalization and the new transnational forms of governance, and more particularly on the WTO. He published, among others *Anthropologie de l'Etat* (Anthropology of the State) Paris, 1990; *Quiet Days in Burgundy: A Study of Local Politics*, Cambridge, 1991; *La vie quotidienne au*

Parlement européen (Everyday life at the European Parliament) Paris, 1992; *Un ethnologue à l'Assemblée* (An Ethnologist at the French National Assembly) Paris, 2000; *Les Nouveaux riches.* *Un ethnologue dans la Silicon Valley* (The New Rich: An Ethnnologist at the Silicon Valley) Paris, 2002; *Politique de la Survie,* Paris, 2006 (The Politics of Survival, Duke University Press, forthcoming in 2009); *Anthropologie de la globalisation* (Anthropology of Globalization) Paris, 2008.

Emmanuel Decaux graduated from Sciences Po Paris, is Doctor of Law from the University Panthéon-Assas Paris II and "agrégé" of public law (1988). He is professor at the University Panthéon-Assas Paris II since 1999, after a tenure at the University of the Maine (1988–1992) and the University of Nanterre Paris X (1992–1999). He is director of the Center for research on human rights and humanitarian law (CRDH) of the University Paris II and editor of the electronic review www.droits-fondamentaux. org. He has extensively published on issues of human rights, international organizations, and the settlement of disputes. He is coordinating a collective commentary of the International Covenant on Political and Civil Rights. He has coedited *From Human Rights to International Criminal Law, Studies in Honour of an African Lawyer, the Late Judge Laïty Kama,* (Martinus Nijhoff, Leyden, 2007). He has been elected member of the new Consultative Committee of the Human Rights Council for a three year mandate (2008–2010), after being a member (2001–2006) of the UN Sub-Commission on human rights, and of its working group on communications (2004 and 2005, 2007 and 2008), and of the WG on contemporary forms of slavery (2003 and 2004, 2006).

Jean-Marc Ferry is professor of Philosophy and Political science at the Université libre de Bruxelles, Doctor *Honoris Causa* at the University of Lausanne. He is the author of numerous books, among which *Les Puissances de l'expérience* (The Powers of Experience) Paris, Cerf, 1991; *Philosophie de la communication* (Philosophy of Communication) Paris, Cerf, 1994; *L'Allocation universelle* (Universal Allowance) Cerf, 1995, 1996; *L'Ethique reconstructive* (Reconstructive Ethics) Paris, Cerf, 1996; *La Question de l'Etat européen* (The Issue of the European State) Gallimard, 2000; *De la Civilisation* (On Civilization) Paris, Cerf, 2001; *Valeurs et normes* (Values and Norms) Editions universitaires de Bruxelles, 2002; *La Question de l'Histoire* (The Issue of History) Editions universitaires de Bruxelles, 2002; *L'Europe, l'Amérique et le monde* (Europe, America and the World) Pleins-Feux, 2004; *Les Grammaires de l'intelligence* (Grammars of Intelligence) Paris, Cerf, 2004; *Europe, la voie kantienne* (Europe, the Kantian Way) Paris, Cerf, 2005. His work has obtained several prizes by the Institut de France (La Bruyère Prize from the French Academy; Louis Martin Prize from the Academy of Moral and Political Sciences).

Virginie Guiraudon is a permanent research fellow at the National Center for Scientific Research (CNRS) in Lille, France. She holds a Ph.D. in Government from Harvard University where she focused on explaining the evolution of the rights granted to foreigners in France, Germany, and the Netherlands since 1974. She has been a Marie Curie Chair at the European University Institute in Florence, and a visiting fellow at the Center for International Studies at Princeton University. She is a recipient of the Descartes-Huygens prize whose tenure she spent at the university of Nijmegen. She was also awarded the CNRS bronze medal for best young researcher and the European Union Studies Association best paper prize. She is the author of *Les politiques d'immigration en Europe* (European Immigration Policies) Paris 2000 and coeditor of *Immigration Politics in Europe: The Politics of Control,* Taylor and Francis, 2006. Her current research focuses on the Europeanization of migration, asylum, and antidiscrimination policies. Her research on mobilization has also focused on mobilization around migration issues in comparative perspective. She has extensively published in journals including the *Journal of Common Market Studies, International Migration Review, Journal of European Public Policy, West European Politics,* and *Comparative Political Studies.*

Guy Hermet is emeritus senior researcher at CERI-Sciences Po and Doctor *Honoris Causa* of Madrid University. He taught in Sciences Po-Paris, Brussels as well as in Geneva, Lausanne, and Montréal universities. He is a political scientist and historian whose main subjects of interest deal with the theory of democracy, comparative politics, populist movements, and nation-building. His most recent book is entitled *L'Hiver de la démocratie ou le Nouveau Régime* (The Winter of Democracy or the New Régime) Paris, 2007.

Yves Hersant has worked more than fifteen years in the French cultural services (as cultural attaché or cultural councellor of the foreign affairs' ministry). He was elected in 1981 at the EHESS. He is currently senior researcher at EHESS and works on the cultural history of Europe and more particularly during *Renaissance.* He is also translator and member of the editorial board of the French journal *Critique.* He recently published *Mélancolies. De l'Antiquité au XXe siècle* (Melancholies. From Antiquity to the XXth Century) Paris, 2005.

Didier Lapeyronnie is Professor of Sociology at the Sorbonne (University Paris IV) and researcher at the Centre d'analyse et d'intervention sociologiques (Center for Sociological Analysis and Intervention) of the EHESS. His most recent publications include "La banlieue comme théâtre colonial. La fracture coloniale dans les quartiers" (The Suburb, a Colonial Scene. The Colonial Break in the Community Life) in Nicolas Bancel, Pascal Blanchard et Sandrine Lemaire, (eds.) *La fracture coloniale* (The Colonial Break), Paris, 2005; *Quand les jeunes s'engagent. Entre expérimentations et constructions identitaires* (Youth Mobilization. Between Experimentations and Construction of the Identity), with Valérie Becquet, Chantal de Linares and Jacques Ion, L'Harmattan, 2006; "Racisme, espaces urbains et ghetto" (Racism, Urban Spaces and Ghettos) in Manuel Boucher (ed.), *Discriminations et ethnicisation, combattre le racisme en Europe* (Discriminations and Ethnitizations. Fighting Racism in Europe), La Tour d'Aigues, 2006.

Rémy Leveau (†) was doctor in Law and professor of Political Science. He was lecturer at the law school in Rabat between 1958 and 1965, cultural adviser to the French Embassies in Tripoli and Cairo, professor at the Law Faculty of University St Joseph

Beyrouth, and deputy director for cultural affairs at the French Foreign affairs ministry. When he returned to Sciences Po in Paris (1983), he established a doctoral programme on the contemporary arabo-muslim world and set up a research team on similar issues. He collaborated regularly with the EHESS, was professor at John Hopkins university in Bologne, and professor at Sciences Po Paris. He authored many books and articles, among which *La beurgeoisie: les trois âges de la vie associative issue de l'immigration* (with Catherine Wihtol de Wenden) (The beurgeoisie: Three ages of Immigration Community Life) Paris, 2001; *La deuxième génération* (The Second Generation) with Catherine Wihtol de Wenden, Paris, 1988; *L'Algérie dans la guerre* (Algeria and the War) Brussels, 1995, as well as many peer reviewed articles. Rémy Leveau passed away in March 2005.

Joseph H. H. Weiler is University Professor at New York University and serves as the Joseph Straus Professor of Law and European Union Jean Monnet Chair at NYU School of Law. He is also Professor at the College of Europe in Bruges, Belgium and Natolin, Poland; Honorary Professor at University College, London; Honorary Professor at the Department of Political Science, University of Copenhagen and Co-Director of the Academy of International Trade Law in Macao, China. He holds degrees from Sussex (B.A.); Cambridge (LL.B. and LL.M.), and The Hague Academy of International Law (Diploma of International Law); he earned his Ph.D. in European Law at the EUI, Florence. He is recipient of Doctorates *Honoris Causa* from London University and from Sussex University and is Honorary Senator of the University of Ljubljana. He is author of articles and books in the fields of International, Comparative, and European law among which are *European Constitutionalism beyond the State,* edited with Marlene Wind (Cambridge University Press, 2003); *Integration in an Expanding European Union: Reassessing the Fundamentals,* edited with Ian Begg and John Peterson (Blackwell, 2003).

Dominique Wolton is senior researcher and director of the Institute for Communication Sciences of the CNRS. He is the director of the journal *Hermès* that he founded in 1988. He is also the editor since 1998 a book series on Communication at CNRS Edition. His research focuses on the analysis of the links between culture, communication, society, and politics—information and communication being considered as major political stakes for the twenty first century, and cultural cohabitation as an imperative condition for the third globalization. After *L'Autre Mondialisation* (The Other Globalization) Paris, Flammarion, 2003, and *Il faut sauver la communication* (Communication Must be Defended) Paris, Flammarion, 2005, he published *Demain la francophonie* (Tomorrow, the French Speaking World) Flammarion, 2006.

GENERAL INDEX